GUIDE TO COUNTRY RISK

OTHER ECONOMIST BOOKS

Guide to Analysing Companies
Guide to Business Modelling
Guide to Business Planning
Guide to Cash Management
Guide to Commodities
Guide to Decision Making
Guide to Economic Indicators
Guide to Emerging Markets
Guide to the European Union
Guide to Financial Management
Guide to Financial Markets
Guide to Hedge Funds
Guide to Investment Strategy
Guide to Management Ideas and Gurus
Guide to Managing Growth
Guide to Organisation Design
Guide to Project Management
Guide to Supply Chain Management
Numbers Guide
Style Guide

Book of Business Quotations
Book of Isms
Brands and Branding
Business Consulting
Business Strategy
Buying Professional Services
The Chief Financial Officer
Economics
Managing Talent
Managing Uncertainty
Marketing
Marketing for Growth
Megachange – the world in 2050
Modern Warfare, Intelligence and Deterrence
Organisation Culture
Successful Strategy Execution
Unhappy Union

Directors: an A–Z Guide
Economics: an A–Z Guide
Investment: an A–Z Guide
Negotiation: an A–Z Guide

Pocket World in Figures

The
Economist

GUIDE TO COUNTRY RISK

How to identify, manage and mitigate the
risks of doing business across borders

Mina Toksöz

PUBLICAFFAIRS
New York

The Economist in Association with Profile Books Ltd. and PublicAffairs

Typeset in EcoType by MacGuru Ltd
info@macguru.org.uk

Library of Congress Control Number: 2014949753
ISBN 978-1-61039-486-4 (HC)
ISBN 978-1-61039-487-1 (EB)

First Edition

10 9 8 7 6 5 4 3 2 1

Contents

Acknowledgements   xi

1 Introduction: a brief history of country risk   1
   What is country risk?   1
   Thinking about risk came with the Enlightenment   2
   From science of probability theory to management of risk   4
   The rise of international portfolio flows   6
   The principle of national sovereignty   7
   Multinationals, expropriation and loan risk   9
   New financial instruments   10
   Recent booms and busts   12
   Lessons from the 2008–09 financial crisis   14
   About this book   15

PART 1 IDENTIFYING COUNTRY RISK
2 Definitions of country risk   23
   Components of country risk   24
   Difficulties of defining country risk   29
   Three frequently asked questions   31

3 Causes of country risk at global level: excessive lending   33
   Global waves of capital exports and risk of excessive lending   34
   Transition periods: the rise of geopolitical risks   37
   Financial crises: then and now   38
   Contagion risks, spillovers and transmission channels   43
   The real economy, cycles and demographics: the long-term view   47
   Conclusion and country risk pointers   52

4 Payments crises: country vulnerabilities   57
   Learning from different crises   57
   Macroeconomic imbalances   65

5 **Payments crises: in-country causes** 78
Home-grown causes of country risk 79
Financial-sector risks 89
Economic policy risks 95

6 **Political and geopolitical risks** 103
Geopolitical risk and military conflict 104
Tracking social and political trends 111
Political risk and institutions 115
Institutions lagging social and economic development 118
Avoiding implicit value judgments in political risk analysis 123

7 **Identifying country risk at transaction level** 125
Transfer and convertibility risks 126
Exchange-rate, interest-rate and rollover risks 128
Macroeconomic volatility 130
Regulatory and policy uncertainties 131
Sector-specific risks 133
Jurisdiction risks 134
Political risks 138
Conclusion 143

**PART 2 MODELLING, MANAGING AND MITIGATING
COUNTRY RISK**
8 **Country risk models and ratings** 147
Country risk assessment methodologies 148
Country risk indicators 151
Rating model structure 155
How to build a model 157
Other technical issues 160
The time horizon, responsiveness of the model, pro-cyclicality 162
Implicit judgments and prevailing misconceptions 163
What next? 165

9 **Country risk mitigation: global level** 166
Crisis prevention, reregulation and risks of international
fragmentation 167
Evolving role of the IMF: multilateralism versus regionalism 171
Debt restructuring: voluntary versus market-based
burden sharing 174
Conclusion: whither sovereignty? 178

10 Integrating country risk into management structures 181
Regulation and the internal organisation of country risk
   in finance 183
Country risk management in multinationals 187
The tools: basic organisational structures for managing
   country risk 189
Independence of the country risk function 195
Why you cannot outsource country risk management 199

**11 Country risk mitigation at transaction level:
the final defence** 202
The process 203
Commonly used country risk mitigants 206
Structures embedded in transactions for mitigating risks 207
Buy protection: risk transfer instruments 210
Multilateral participation 217
Operational risk mitigants for direct investors 218
Strengths and weaknesses of some mitigation measures 220

12 Conclusion: how to stop being surprised all the time 229
Have a historical perspective 229
Don't fall for the "this time is different" syndrome 230
Understand the new shape of political and geopolitical risks 231
Try to quantify risks, but know the limits of economic and
   political models 231
Identify the drivers of political risks and potential triggers of
   natural catastrophes 232
Know that payments crises and defaults will always be there 232
Countries can move out of the debt-default cycle 234
Policies can cushion against global shocks 235
Follow regulatory requirements but don't box-tick 237
Keep risk management organisational structures flexible 238
No easy formulas 238

Notes and sources 240
Index 256

List of case studies

2.1 Nigeria: country risk vulnerabilities 26
3.1 Turkey: global economic crises and the economy 54
4.1 The European exchange rate mechanism crisis 60
4.2 Mexico 1994: unanticipated crisis in a star performer 61
4.3 Tapering and emerging markets: another repeat of 1994? 68
4.4 The Gulf Cooperation Council: multiple vulnerabilities 73
5.1 Egypt: fiscal and debt crises and policy zigzags 84
5.2 China: financial sector risks 92
5.3 Argentina: fundamental strengths, policy weaknesses 98
6.1 North Korea: known unknowns 105
6.2 Ukraine: worst-case scenario becomes base-case scenario 109
6.3 Emerging middle-class protest and increased policy
uncertainty 113
6.4 The Russian modernisation debate: difficulties of
diversification and institutional reform 119
7.1 Nestlé admits to errors in India expansion push 130
7.2 Russia's state-imposed utility price freeze to hit GDP 132
7.3 Mining hazards of the frontier: companies that flocked to
Mozambique's coal reserves face significant logistical
problems 136
7.4 Rurelec plans to sue Bolivia 138
7.5 Bankia purges 800 external directors 142
9.1 Greece: a historic debt restructuring 175
10.1 Regulating the external rating agencies 186
10.2 Trader versus country risk: Iceland and Hungary 197
11.1 Implats and Zimplats: coping with political risks 219
11.2 Country risks in infrastructure finance: the Dabhol
power project 222
11.3 Mitigating country risks: Roshan in Afghanistan and
Wataniya in Palestine 225

List of figures

1.1 Defaults come in waves: countries in default or
     rescheduling   16
3.1 Gross cross-border capital flows, 1970–2009   31
3.2 Evolution of crises from one type to another   41
3.3 Is the commodity super-cycle over?   49
3.4 Commodity prices and confidence in currency regimes   53
4.1 EU budget and current-account balances and maturing
     sovereign debt: eve of the euro-zone crisis   63
4.2 Country rankings: capital flow and output volatility,
     2000–12   64
4.3 Savings and debt imbalances, 2013   67
4.4 Current-account balance and net FDI, 2013   75
5.1 Change in sovereign ratings: ten biggest downgrades and
     upgrades by Fitch, Moody's and S&P in 2007–13   81
5.2 Middle-income resource economies   86
5.3 Low-income resource economies   87
5.4 Banking and financial sector categories   90
5.5 Private credit as a percentage of GDP   94
6.1 Emerging middle class by region   113
6.2 Institutional strength, 2012–13   116
7.1 Risk factors in breach of contract events   126
7.2 Financial losses due to political risks, 2010–13   140
8.1 Capital bonanzas and busts   154
10.1 Expected and unexpected losses   190
10.2 Main constituents of the country risk management matrix   195
11.1 Historical trends in expropriations, by sector   211
11.2 Breach of contract events by sector   214

List of tables

4.1 Vulnerability factors and indicators   66
5.1 Structural risk indicators   79
7.1 Macroeconomic sensitivity of industrial sectors   134
10.1 Sovereign ratings and risk weights: standardised approach   184
10.2 Controls: tenor (loan maturity) limits, watch listing,
exposure reports, limit breaches   193
11.1 Berne Union claims paid in 2012   213

Acknowledgements

THE IDEA FOR THIS BOOK was hatched following a lecture I gave on country risk at Manchester Business School in 2011, at the height of the euro-zone sovereign debt crisis. I would like to thank Ismail Erturk, director of the MSc Executive Management programme on banking and financial services, who noted that there was not much written on the topic. I took up this suggestion when I left Standard Bank in 2013, having been head of the country risk team for international operations since 2001. The enthusiasm of colleagues and friends then propelled me along. From Standard Bank, I am grateful to Nina Triantis, global head of telecoms, John O'Mulloy, managing director, Jiri Choteborsky, director telecoms and media, and Sophie Papasavva, now a founding member of EFMC Loan Syndicates LLP, for their support and input to the Roshan and Wataniya case studies. I would like especially to thank Laura Rattner, my long-term colleague now heading the western hemisphere country risk team at Macquarie Group, Deborah Bekker at Standard Bank, Alistair Newton, managing director at Nomura International, and Helena Huang at Chatham House for their contributions to excellent case studies on Argentina, Nigeria, North Korea and China respectively.

I began working on country risk early in my professional career as editorial director of the Economist Intelligence Unit's Country Risk Service in the late 1980s. But I would not have been in a position to write a book on this topic without the rich experience gained through working for a unique emerging-markets bank, Standard Bank, which was expanding its reach globally in the remarkable decade of the 2000s. It would not be possible to list everyone, but people who made my work more enjoyable include Neil Holden, a mathematical wizard, and Arnold Gain, with whom we set up the overall framework for country risk, and Santiago Assalini and Annerie Cornelissen, who provided the steely nerves and support during the challenging days of the 2008–09 crisis.

I am also grateful to Daniel Franklin, executive director at *The Economist*, for introducing me to Profile Books where Paul Lewis encouraged me to take up "big themes" and Penny Williams tidied up the material so nicely. The big themes idea led me to the discovery of a wonderful book, *Against the Gods*, by Peter Bernstein, which matched my own thinking on risk: yes, there are many risks out there in this complex world, but humanity has the ability to manage most of them. This is what this book is about. This is the message I would like to give my daughter, Ozan, as well as thanking her for telling me to "stop procrastinating" when my attention was flagging. And last but not least, I want to thank my partner, Bernhard Blauel, for the long years of support that allowed me to focus on my work.

Mina Toksöz
August 2014

1 Introduction: a brief history of country risk

What is country risk?

Country risk – what can go wrong when business is conducted across borders – can affect any company, any time, anywhere. Its importance must be understood not just by bankers, insurers and other corporate risk managers but by anyone with commercial interests abroad. Whether you are running a factory, investing in a pension fund, or just importing or exporting, it can be perilous to ignore what is going on in overseas markets. As the Arab spring political events in 2011 and the global financial crisis in 2008–09 demonstrated, upheaval in one country can send powerful shock waves far beyond its borders.

Major payments crises occur with alarming regularity. A decade before the banking and sovereign (or public) debt crisis of the southern euro-zone economies, there was a debt default in Argentina in 2001; Turkey had a banking and payments crisis in 2000; Russia defaulted in 1998, a year after the Asian financial crisis, which itself followed a series of defaults in Latin America and Africa in the early 1980s. Further back, there were big defaults in the inter-war years and during the first era of globalisation in the 19th century.

There are always economic and political shocks happening somewhere in the world with the potential to spread. In 2013, the focus of concern was emerging markets and how they would fare if the US Federal Reserve tightened monetary policy. In 2014, it seemed that the Fed was not going to tighten much for some time and the focus moved to a potential bubble brewing in the US corporate bond market. In the past few years, risk managers could fret about the consequences of Cyprus's banking collapse, Syria's civil war, the wobbles in the Chinese financial sector, the Ukraine crisis and the global or regional impact of possible international sanctions on Russia. The impact of such faraway events is easily transmitted through financial, banking and trade flows to all corners of the world economy. There are also upside risks to factor in, such as the lessening of sovereign default risks in the euro zone over 2013, which also need managing.

Given this frequency of crises and our vulnerability, why is country risk so difficult to forecast and manage? In part, this is because the nature of risk constantly changes, and because so much depends on the particular perspective of each business and industry. Each wave of defaults seems unique because of the different global economic context of the time, and the varied histories and economic circumstances of the countries where they occur. This is especially true, for instance, when comparing a payments crisis in an emerging market with the banking and sovereign debt crises afflicting developed economies. A lot also depends on the types of investment instruments that are involved: bonds, commercial loans, long-term project finance, resource-based lending, foreign direct investment and trade finance are affected by economic shocks in their own special way.

Thus it seems that every payments crisis is a new crisis, and each one triggers its own wave of academic research that looks to history to explain its causes, and predict and prevent the next one. But, of course, the next crisis is likely to be caused by a different set of factors, triggering yet another wave of retrospection. Some may argue that because today's world is so complex and interrelated, and as we have more information than we can use, the old risk models no longer apply. New methods are being explored using chaos theory and focusing on unmeasurable uncertainty. But to understand better what lies ahead, we need to consider the history and development of our thinking about risk more generally.

Thinking about risk came with the Enlightenment

Country risk is a post-colonial concept, one that has become ever more important in today's global economy. Today we have the analytical tools and the information to analyse and manage the risks facing international business. We also have a philosophical and international framework in which to do so. The ancient Arab and Chinese traders who traversed the Indian Ocean and the English and Dutch colonists shuttling between the Moluccas and Europe faced massive risks at their destinations – that they might not come back alive, for one. But all they had was a few gunboats to deal with local troubles.

There were not the political conditions, the analytical tools or the country data available to think about future uncertainty and risk. Data did not go beyond patchy rudimentary shipping and demographic records.[1] Clay tablets in ancient Mesopotamia show diligent recording of lending activity and some empires such the Roman and Chinese dependent on tax revenues conducted regular censuses. But it was in the city-states in Renaissance Italy that the recording of trade and financial activities reached a new level, including the introduction of double-entry book-keeping.

More analytical interest in foreign lands and thinking about the future came during the Enlightenment when the mathematical tools to measure probabilities of uncertain events were developed. Two Central Asian mathematicians, Al-Khwarizmi and Al-Khayyami (also known as Omar Khayyam), had invented algebra (al-Jabr) several hundred years earlier. But even though the underlying mathematics had been discovered, the prevailing political ideas at the time of the Arab and Seljuk empires were not amenable to developing these tools further into risk analysis. As Peter Bernstein puts it in his book *Against the Gods: The Remarkable Story of Risk*: "The idea of risk management emerges only when people believe that they are to some degree free agents."

What Bernstein calls the first step in making measurement the key factor in the taming of risk was taken by an Italian, Leonardo Pisano, who became acquainted with the Hindu–Arabic numbering system. He then wrote *Liber Abaci* in 1202, which contained the numerical sequences that came to be known as the Fibonacci series – still a favourite of financial whizz-kids today. The next breakthrough came in Italy in the 15th and 16th centuries where men such as Luca Paccioli and Girolamo Cardano began attaching probabilities to measure risk. Then came the great men of mathematics – Thomas Bayes, Jacob Bernoulli, Abraham de Moivre, Pierre-Simon Laplace and Carl Friedrich Gauss – who inched towards the discovery of the bell curve, the normal distribution and the law of large numbers. Eccentrics such as Francis Galton (a cousin of Charles Darwin) put forward the radical idea of regression to the mean, which remains a key notion for investing in stockmarkets.

While the French, the Italians and the Germans developed the mathematics of probability, the British and the Dutch put them into practice and created new institutions. John Graunt and William Petty, working on birth and death records in 17th-century England, introduced statistical sampling and key concepts such as averages. This enabled calculations for life insurance policies, which the Dutch and British governments used to raise public funds. Around this time, with the expansion of international trade, Lloyds of London was established in the famous coffee house in the City of London frequented by traders, ships' captains and marine underwriters to exchange information on remote areas of the world. The ideas of the northern Enlightenment influenced two Scottish clergymen in 18th-century Edinburgh, Robert Wallace and Alexander Webster, to calculate average life expectancy and create the first pension fund in the world. Thus in Britain, risk mitigation with life insurance, pension funds and marine insurance policies had become so widespread that, according to Niall Ferguson in his book *The Ascent of Money*: "By the middle of the 19th century being insured was as much a badge of respectability as going to Church on a Sunday."

From science of probability theory to management of risk

By the end of the 19th century there was a more critical view of science and an emphasis on the limits of human reason. And after the cataclysmic events of the two world wars in the 20th century, Bernstein says:

> [T]he dream vanished that human beings would know everything ... and that certainty would replace uncertainty. Instead, the explosion of knowledge has served to make life more uncertain.

These concerns switched the focus from the laws of probability to the management of uncertainty with the work of Frank Knight and John Maynard Keynes. But even before these thinkers, two late 19th-century mathematicians, Jules Henri Poincaré and Laplace had already recognised that there were situations where there was too little information to apply the laws of probability since mathematical probabilities can only be derived from large numbers of independent (and homogeneous) events, such as the rolling of dice. Knight made the crucial distinction between risk and uncertainty – that risk was measurable uncertainty – in his 1921 book, *Risk, Uncertainty and Profit*.

Knight also highlighted the difficulty of the forecasting process and considered the reliance on the frequency of past occurrences to be extremely hazardous. Working at about the same time, Keynes (whom Knight disliked) agreed. In *A Treatise on Probability*, Keynes emphasised the importance of intuition as opposed to the science of probability theory. These sentiments paved the way for game theory, invented by John von Neumann, who first busied himself discovering quantum mechanics and was a leading member of the team that made the atom bomb. The modern critique of the mathematical, "scientific" treatment of risk was shaped by Kenneth Arrow and Frank Hahn. They focused on the lack of information faced by economic decision-makers and on unmeasurable uncertainty as opposed to measurable risk. This was followed by chaos theory, which tried to make sense of the increasing complexities of a globalised world, and, in the aftermath of the 2008–09 global crisis, focused on tail risks and unmeasurable uncertainty.

The evolution of country risk roughly followed these trends in broader risk analysis. The small number of observations of country defaults, their interrelatedness and lack of homogeneity, and the unreliability of history to forecast future crises were all issues that framed the development of analysis. But despite these problems, efforts to quantify country risk have continued. In this book a country risk-rating model is proposed (see Chapter 8) in the tradition of Robert Solow, an economist, who once characterised economic model builders as "the overeducated in pursuit of the unknowable. But it sure beats the alternatives". However, bearing in mind the limits of this approach, the rating model should be used as only one component of the overall country risk management process.

The rise of international portfolio flows

Thinking about country risk became more systematic in the late 19th century and the early years of the 20th century when a global capital market emerged with international capital flows larger in scale than anything seen before (that is, relative to the global GDP of the time). Its centre was the City of London with UK overseas investment amounting to 150% of UK GDP in 1913. The bulk of this investment – around 80% – was portfolio capital in the form of stocks and bonds, mostly issued in the City of London; foreign direct investment (FDI) was not that significant. Most of the lending was for infrastructure investment with railways alone accounting for about 41% of the total.

British overseas investment was mostly in the colonies. A major risk mitigant for the buyers of these colonial securities was the explicit guarantees by the British government decreed by the Colonial Loans Act of 1899 and the Colonial Stock Act of 1900.[2] Crédit Lyonnais set up a research department called Service d'Etudes Financières in 1871 to monitor overseas risks and Moody's issued its first sovereign credit rating in 1919, though these activities were wound down after the Great Depression in the 1930s.

The 19th-century era of globalisation was one of reckless lending and, not surprisingly, major waves of defaults, including several US states, Austria, the Netherlands, Spain, Greece, Portugal, Australia, Canada, the Ottoman empire, Egypt and almost every country that had recently gained independence in Latin America.[3] However, these series of defaults did not generate the pre-emptive risk management activity that was to come after the second world war and become systematised following the 1980s series of defaults.

This was still the era when colonial powers did as they pleased, as seen in 1840, when the Qing emperor, Daoguang, ruled that British subjects were subject to Chinese law as he confiscated and destroyed the opium shipped to Canton (today's Guangzhou) by two British traders, William Jardine and James Matheson. In response, the British prime minister, Lord Palmerston, sent in gunboats, taking Hong Kong and establishing the principle of extraterritoriality in the treaty (of Nanking) ports. When the Ottomans defaulted in 1875, European creditors established themselves in the heart of Istanbul, overlooking Topkapi Palace, set up the Ottoman debt office – the Duyunu Umumiye – and took over all tax revenues and money printing from the Ottoman authorities. When Spain defaulted in 1847, some MPs in the House of Commons suggested that the UK should take over the Spanish territories of Cuba and Puerto Rico to repay the British bondholders. But there were limits to how much support the UK government was prepared to provide. This time Palmerston demurred; he prophetically warned about moral hazard and that creditors would become reckless if they always expected the government to step in.

The principle of national sovereignty

Just as it took the Enlightenment ideas to deal with risk in the broad sense, it needed the establishment of national sovereignty as the international norm before international business began to take responsibility for their dealings and systematise the management and mitigation of country risk. The shift towards sovereignty in international law began in the aftermath of the first world war and Woodrow Wilson's declaration of "the right of nations to self-determination" in 1918 (though this was mostly meant for European states). This was followed by the Atlantic Charter of 1941, signed between Franklin D. Roosevelt and Winston Churchill, with unclear implications for colonial territories. (Historians trace the first emergence of the concept of the sovereign state to the Treaty of Westphalia in 1648.) Finally, UN Resolution No. 1514, "Declaration on the granting of independence to colonial peoples", passed by the UN General Assembly in 1960, provided the political and legal link between self-determination and decolonisation and enshrined national sovereignty in international law.

The risks for international business in the inter-war years and during the two world wars, and the process of decolonisation that began in the 1920s, were mostly discussed in terms of political risk.[4] International investors faced nationalisation and expropriation of their assets, with resulting losses depending on how smooth or disruptive the process of decolonisation had been.[5] These risks escalated during the two world wars (when German firms operating in the US and almost anywhere else in the Americas were expropriated) and following the second world war as radical regimes in the colonies came to power, gaining independence and pursuing policies of nationalisation of industry and land reforms in agriculture.[6]

The reaction from Europe and the United States to such expropriations was still political. The British response to the nationalisation of the Anglo-Persian Oil Company (precursor of BP) in Iran by Mohammed Mosaddegh, the prime minister, was to engineer a coup in 1953 to bring down the democratically elected government and restore the monarchic rule of Reza Shah. Similarly, gunboats were sent in response to the nationalisation of the Suez Canal in 1956 by Gamal Abdel Nasser, and Egypt paid compensation to the mainly British and French shareholders of Universal Suez Ship Canal Company until 1962. The US government's approach to what was then called the third world remained fixed in cold war terms – as seen in Cuba in 1959.

But public opinion was becoming more critical of political interventions. As far back as the 1920s, following the occupation of the Ruhr by French and Belgian forces in 1923 to obtain reparation payments from Germany, British and American financiers had concluded that force would be of little use in collecting the debt. The corporate landscape was also changing. Multinational firms not associated with colonial rule were approaching risks in international business with new measures. Swiss firms such as Nestlé, Brown Bovery and Sandoz devised strategies to deal with political risks, relying on Switzerland's neutrality to keep their international businesses going, even during the war. These included long-term strategies to sit through the political problems, multiple headquarters, appointing politically influential local figures on their boards and the "cloaking" of the firm to appear local.[7]

Institutions that brought a more pre-emptive approach to manage the risks facing international business were playing a bigger role:

■ In 1919 the Export Credits Guarantee Department (ECGD) was established in the UK, the first in the world to provide exporters with credit insurance.

■ In 1934 the Berne Union, an association of public and private export insurance firms from the UK, France, Italy and Spain, was founded.

■ In 1944 multilateral institutions were founded at the Bretton Woods Conference with the aim of averting the devastating problems of international trade and finance that had emerged in the inter-war years. These included the International Monetary Fund (IMF) and the World Bank.

■ In 1947 the General Agreement on Tariffs and Trade (GATT), a multilateral agreement to regulate international trade and promote reduction of tariffs and trade barriers in a mutually beneficial way, was signed.

■ Not all were for pre-emptive risk management. In 1956 the Paris Club of official creditors to work out defaulted debts was formed.

Multinationals, expropriation and loan risk

The rapid global expansion of US multinational companies following the second world war generated more analysis of the identification and management of overseas risks. (The book value of direct investments by US firms abroad rose from $7.2 billion in 1946 to $70.8 billion in 1969, with $21.6 billion located in Europe.) The Cuban revolution of 1959 and the expropriations that followed further increased the focus on the political risk facing US multinationals. The Multilateral Investment Guarantee Agency (MIGA), the political risk insurance arm of the World Bank, estimated in 2011 that the number of expropriation acts during 1960–79 stood at 560 and that about 15–20% of all US FDI abroad measured in volume terms was nationalised. Hence political risks – expropriation, licence cancellation, nationalisation, currency devaluations and capital controls – were identified as key risks that needed to be managed. One of the earliest risk services, Business Environment Risk Intelligence (BERI), was founded in 1966 by F.T. Haner, based on his experiences as international manager of the American Cement Corporation in Greece and Spain. BERI rated countries on the basis of aggregated scores on political risk, operations risk, and remittance and repatriation risks.

It was not until the 1970s, when the first oil boom generated Gulf oil surpluses that were recycled by international banks as foreign loans, that cross-border risk became more broadly defined as country risk rather than political risk. To capture all the risks facing cross-border loans, the analysis of balance-of-payments problems contributing to payments risks was required in addition to the political risks. Citibank was one of the first to establish a more systematic approach to managing country risk in the early 1970s. Rating agencies began to expand their work, undertaking sovereign ratings as well as credit ratings. In 1975, the US Securities and Exchange Commission (SEC) decided to link ratings and the regulatory capital requirements for banks and broker-dealers, and relied on a select few nationally recognised statistical rating organisations (NRSROs). The Basel Accord adopted in 1988 expanded the influence of rating agencies. The experience of the Latin American debt defaults in the 1980s led the big European banks with international lending exposures, such as Commerzbank, to add country risk to their risk management functions. These defaults also led to the creation of the London Club of commercial creditors.

New financial instruments

The resolution of the 1980s debt overhang through the Brady Plan, agreed in 1988, freed up international banks' balance sheets and set the stage for another round of global international expansion.[8] Periods of globalisation had been dominated in the 19th century by the issue of bonds, after the second world war by multinational companies' FDI, and in the 1970s by commercial bank loans that recycled OPEC oil surpluses. In the 1990s the expansion was characterised by cross-border financial flows and the proliferation of a wide variety of financial instruments. International bonds were back – for the first time since 1913, other portfolio flows included equity into international stockmarkets, commercial bank loans, trade finance, project finance, as well as FDI. Given the strong growth and export performance of the Asian Tigers, such as Taiwan, South Korea, Thailand, Indonesia and Malaysia, most of the financial flows headed for Asia. With the collapse of the Soviet Union in 1989, eastern Europe was the other destination for EU investors as these countries embarked on a deep restructuring and transition to market economies.

The terms of the debate had shifted from protectionism and statist policies towards market liberalism and openness to the global economy. Whereas in previous decades countries had allocated foreign exchange via permits and current and capital accounts were controlled, many began to move towards floating exchange-rate regimes and relaxing capital controls. There was a focus on developing and deepening banking and capital markets and the easing of FDI regulations. Out of 1,097 changes in national FDI laws adopted between 1992 and 2000, 94% created a more favourable climate, according to the MIGA. Its 2009 *World Investment and Political Risk* report notes that the risks of expropriation fell drastically from 423 cases in the 1970s to only 17 in 1980–87 and zero in 1987–92. Political risk was receding but not country risk, as the Asian crisis was to show.

The Asian crisis taught country risk analysts a hard lesson: that every crisis highlights a different set of risks. The payments crises of Mexico in 1994 and the Asian countries in 1997 were different from ones that had happened before and they hit countries that were considered star performers (see case study 4.2). Country risk models had failed to track the big build-up of debt by private corporations in Asia. Nor did they anticipate how the sudden increase in interest rates by the US Federal Reserve in 1994 would translate into liquidity crises and could quickly transform into defaults. Contagion risk had arrived and no one really knew how to deal with it.

But it was possible to see some defaults coming. The 1998 Russian debt default – unusually in both foreign- and local-currency debt – was predictably, given the fiscal crisis and the fall in oil prices. Yet demand for Russian debt was still strong throughout 1997 and into early 1998 as international portfolio flows were being redirected from crisis-struck Asian economies. Similarly, it was inevitable that with the Brazilian economy in downturn and the real depreciating rapidly, Argentina was not going to be able to sustain its currency board and payments by the time it defaulted in 2001. But some lenders were too focused on the high yields to curtail their activity and others failed to exit, believing that things would be all right once the IMF stepped in. The importance of external push factors driving capital flows and the problem of excessive lending leading to waves of defaults are key themes in this book.

Recent booms and busts

The 1990s experience resulted in a shift of focus from a reactive response to crises to a more pre-emptive and preventive approach. A new international financial architecture began to be constructed with greater emphasis on prevention of financial crises, with greater responsibility given to international financial institutions to monitor and direct emerging-market economic policies. Also, on the investor side, there were efforts to prevent moral hazard, with the terms of loans structured to involve the private sector in the resolution of the crises and ensure burden sharing.

There was more emphasis on currency and banking crises as a driver of country risk.[9] It was noted that changes in international investor sentiment could result in a rapid shift in the direction of capital flows and cause what came to be called sudden-stop crises. This triggered another round of adjustments, including more liquidity indicators to country risk models. By 2000, a survey of international banks carried out by the Institute of International Finance (IIF) noted that "robust methods exist for generating country risk ratings and incorporating (them) into the economic capital allocation process". However, the problem – as Keynes warned back in the 1920s – that past data and models that explain previous crises are not a reliable basis for explaining future crises remained.

Moreover, the focus of most country risk work was almost entirely on what came to be called emerging markets, with little attention being paid to the debt build-up in the "risk-free" developed markets. In addition, the emphasis was on the in-country features of emerging markets that were associated with payments crises, with external push factors remaining a neglected component of country risk analysis.

Global financial flows from 2003 onwards were stronger, fed

by the easy monetary policy of the US Federal Reserve, and more complex than they had been before:

- There were convoluted instruments such as CDOs (collateralised debt obligations – loans repackaged into a bond and backed by "risk-free" assets as collateral) that were little understood. The development of local capital markets in emerging markets also attracted foreign investors to take positions in local-currency debt.

- Many more countries were involved as new areas became part of the global destination of finance. Africa was the new big destination with investors expanding their horizons to "frontier markets" such as Angola and Mozambique and West Africa. There were also other resource-rich new destinations such as Mongolia and Kazakhstan in Central Asia.

- Whereas previously the bulk of the flows mostly originated in developed markets, there was a significant increase in financial flows between emerging markets – what has come to be called South-South trade – and investment flows led by China's trade and investment.

- There was the rise of new investing entities – sovereign funds from Russia and China but also small but rich city-states such as Singapore and Qatar. They had been around for a few decades, but their funds had grown to huge proportions with the commodity boom of the 2000s and they had become important international investors, but with low transparency.

For a while, the country risk models that monitored emerging-market risks seemed to be working. International organisations, whose focus in previous decades had been to monitor, direct emerging-market government policies and step in with precautionary emergency lending before defaults occurred, seemed to be doing their job. Economists congratulated themselves that they had learned how to beat devastating economic cycles as both upturns and downturns seemed to be less pronounced. The debt sustainability of most emerging markets had improved: fiscal policies were generally prudent and inflation was mostly tamed. The banking sectors had been restructured in previous crises and currencies were floating, thereby providing a cushion against external shocks. As a result, in the decade after 2001 there were no major defaults in emerging markets. Those that did occur were mostly home-grown crises in smaller economies: Belize (2006), Cameroon (2004) and the Dominican Republic (2005), for example. Data availability had improved beyond recognition from 25 years before, with the widespread use of the internet and online data sources that delivered live data from Bloomberg and Reuters.

There were still major worries, such as the risk of a sharp collapse in international commodity prices. Also, given the vast amount of liquidity in the global economy and the openness of relatively new and shallow capital markets, there was the potential for international investor sentiment to turn suddenly and disruptively away from emerging markets. There were also worries about global imbalances, such as the ever-expanding US current-account deficit financed by Chinese purchases of US bonds. Everyone knew this could not go on forever and some warned about the underlying mortgage and credit bubble in the US economy. But the Bush administration was tied up in wars in Iraq and Afghanistan and seemed unprepared to do much about it. Thus the next big shock was not to be in the troublesome emerging markets with sub-investment-grade ratings, but in those economies with AAA ratings that were considered risk-free.

Lessons from the 2008–09 financial crisis

The 2008–09 financial crash and the global recession that followed have changed much of our thinking about country risk. The terms of the debate have shifted from an almost religious belief in the power of financial markets to regulate the global economy, to pessimism about their true effectiveness. Just as multinational companies had overreached themselves in the 1960s and 1970s, today, in a different way, the role of financial entities is being examined critically.[10]

The role of government has taken centre stage in this debate, and its influence is seen all around. This is resulting in an increase in political risk as political leaders turn to unorthodox economic policies and ad-hoc administrative measures to manage exchange rates, balance budgets and reduce debt. Cyprus, a member of the euro zone, did what once seemed unthinkable: it imposed capital controls.

Although few are calling for far-reaching protectionism, many now doubt the value of globalisation. Cross-border capital flows have fallen by around 60% from their 2007 peak. The independence of central banks has been challenged as quantitative easing policies have blurred the line between fiscal policy and monetary policy. In the crisis-hit euro-zone economies, so-called technocrats, deemed better at understanding economic complexities and free from electoral pressures, have been installed in office. The rating agencies have also come under intense scrutiny as a result of awarding investment grades to subprime mortgage-backed products and failing to warn of the unsustainable build-up of sovereign, or public, debt in the southern euro-zone economies.

In response to the new environment, country risk analysts have had to rethink their assumptions. Some initially scrambled to refocus attention on developed markets, only to find that their models were relevant only to emerging markets. Others began questioning old-style country risk models that focused on fundamentals, and set up early-warning models that use market signals to watch for unusual movements. There are efforts to map linkages between countries, sovereigns and financial entities. A few have incorporated aspects of chaos theory to explain the complexity and contagion in the global economy. Some think data mining is the answer. Popular books such as Nicholas Taleb's *The Black Swan* suggest that we should stop focusing on causality, because humans are not wired to be rational, and instead embrace uncertainty.

About this book

What is needed is the opposite: a return to fundamentals and to an understanding of the underlying causes of payments crises and defaults and how these fit into the big picture. A historical perspective (bearing in mind that old risks can return in new guises and be difficult to see) is also useful given that country defaults have historically come in waves associated with investment cycles of the global economy (see Figure 1.1). Hence country risk analysis needs more focus on the contribution of the external push factors that drive capital flows in addition to the in-country vulnerabilities and weaknesses that are

FIG 1.1 **Defaults come in waves: countries in default or rescheduling**
Proportion of borrowers, %

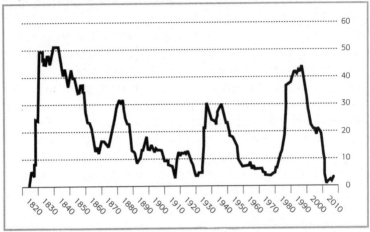

Source: Tomz, M. and Wright, M.L.J., *Empirical Research on Sovereign Debt and Default,* Working Paper, Federal Reserve Bank of Chicago, 2012

associated with payments crises and defaults. These are some of the themes of Part 1, which addresses the question of how to identify country risks at the global, country and transaction level.

Part 2 focuses on how to manage and mitigate country risks. It evaluates crisis-prevention efforts at the global level, regulation and risk management structures at the firm level, and the use of risk mitigants at the transaction level. It also contains practical proposals on how to manage country risk. A country risk-rating model is proposed in Chapter 8. There are suggestions and tools for the organisation of country risk management in enterprises in Chapter 10. Chapter 11 shows how to structure transactions and use transfer techniques to mitigate country risks, presenting three case studies of transactions and the mitigants that were used: two that were successful (Roshan and Wataniya telecom projects, see case study 11.3) and one that was a disaster (Dabhol power project, see case study 11.2).

So what are some of the big-picture factors that might be brewing up the next storm? The following may provide some important clues:

- **A transition period for the global economy.** Chapter 3 highlights some specific features of the global economy, suggesting that there is now evidence of several transitional trends. Transition periods, which can involve a change in the international currency regime, have been extremely unstable. The growth in international capital flows and the integration of the global economy generate new risks, challenging multilateralism and its institutions, which were conceived under very different conditions after the second world war.

- **Follow the capital sloshing around.** Chapter 3 also highlights the features of the financial booms and busts of the past three decades and shows how they are interconnected, with capital flows sloshing around. Since the global financial crisis and the historically low international interest rates, emerging-market consumers and corporations are experiencing the joys of credit. Average credit-to-GDP ratios are not as high as in the developed world, but they are rising fast. Fuelling this has been an estimated $1.5 trillion that flowed into emerging markets in 2012, surpassing the 2007 peak and comprising 32% of total global capital flows compared with only 5% in 2000. But since 2013 and the gradual tightening of monetary policy in the US, this trend has begun to reverse, also reversing the strong commodity price boom and raising worries of a repeat of the emerging-market crises of the 1990s. Chapter 4 highlights the features of the domestic economy that make countries more vulnerable to these sudden-stop crises or other global shocks. Chapter 5 describes some fundamental economic features and banking-sector structures associated with country risks and discusses how, even if the global economy is favourable, the wrong set of policies can cause home-grown payments crises.

- **Rise of geopolitical and other fat-tail risks.** As already evident in Ukraine, geopolitical risk is likely to be a major destabilising factor in the coming decades with the rise of new powers such as China, Russia, Brazil and India, and a number of mid-level emerging markets also aspiring to a greater global role. This is the topic of Chapter 6. Many international investments take place in hazardous regions with limited infrastructure. Climatic and natural hazards are the most difficult risks to manage. But they do not come out of the blue and there are ways of managing and possibly mitigating even these most uncertain of all risks. This is one of the topics addressed in Chapters 7 and 11.

■ **Return of political risk in new forms.** Political developments – including the Arab spring protests, the rise in resource nationalism (such as Argentina's takeover of YPF, a foreign-owned energy company) and the emergence of separatist regions in Europe – are again having an important impact on risk. As the global recession bites into living standards in developed markets, business interruptions through strikes and protest are growing. But because the social pressures that drive political and geopolitical risk develop slowly, they can be difficult to predict and forecast. (Political and geopolitical risks are discussed in Chapter 6.)

■ **Risk of global fragmentation and infringement of sovereignty.** Crisis-prevention at the global level is the topic of Chapter 9, which identifies the principal risks in this process. One is that regulation that makes up the current international rules-based system has become too complex and can give rise to new risks. The regulatory measures that aim to mitigate global crises could fragment the global economy. Sovereignty is being constrained by global integration, and independent national policies are limited by the size and volatility of global capital flows. Sovereignty is also being chipped away by the very international entities that have been tasked with crisis prevention and regulation of the global economy. Hence increasingly it is trends in the global economy and decisions by international and regional entities that are becoming important determinants of country risk.

■ **More contractual disputes.** Chapter 7 identifies country risks at the micro-level – because every transaction is vulnerable to different country risks in different ways. It notes that nationalisation or expropriation may be rare now, but contractual disputes in regulated sectors such as water, power, telecoms and mining are becoming more frequent. Australia, Ghana, South Africa, Indonesia, Zambia and Mongolia have all introduced new mining tax regimes and regulations. The top three investor concerns, according to the 2012 MIGA-Economist Intelligence Unit political risk survey, are adverse regulatory changes, breach of contract, and transfer and convertibility risks.

■ **Risks of regulation-driven risk management.** Chapter 10 presents a review of the interaction between regulation and risk management, examining the Basel process and enterprise risk management (ERM) and how these have affected country risk management. It concludes that some of the regulation is becoming too complex and prescriptive, thus increasing the risks of unforeseen consequences and the process becoming a box-ticking exercise. There are also suggestions on how to structure country risk management to avoid these pitfalls.

PART 1

Identifying country risk

2 Definitions of country risk

THIS BOOK MOSTLY DEALS with the broad definition of country risk – that is, the losses that could arise as a result of the interruption of repayments or the operations of entities engaged in cross-border investments caused by country events as opposed to commercial, technical, or management problems specific to the transaction. This is also referred to as generalised country risk.[1] Country risk can also be defined as what it is not, for example: country risk is everything that is not counterparty credit risk. Corporate risk analysts see it as the potential reduction of expected return on a cross-border transaction over and above an equivalent one internally that is caused by events other than those under the control of a private investor.[2]

Cross-border flows refer to all types of international financial flows. The interruption (the most extreme case being outright default) of payments refers to debt-service payments on loans or trade finance, profit repatriation on an investment, or earnings on portfolio investments.

Generalised country risk analysis is concerned with the risks of a payments crisis arising not just from vulnerabilities in the economic and political structure of a country, but also from external shocks caused by international economic and geopolitical crises. Causes of the interruption of repayments can be difficult to isolate as they are often related. A deep political crisis, such as the one in Ukraine in 2014, increases the risk of sovereign default; this could be combined with capital controls that prevent the exchange of local currency into foreign currency. A sudden stop of capital inflows caused by a crisis in the global financial centres could also cause a currency crisis and a liquidity crisis, interrupting repayments even if solvency risks as indicated by the level of foreign debt in the country were initially low. Both these events are likely to be combined with a major depreciation of the currency, which could cause a banking crisis if the local banks had substantial borrowings in foreign currency, as in the extreme case of Iceland in 2008. Or repayments could be blocked because a balance-of-payments and/or currency crisis has frozen access to foreign currency. These are discussed in Chapters 3 and 4. Because often all the causes are related, it is best to discuss country risk management in its broad context.

Components of country risk

Country risk can also be defined by its different components (see case study 2.1). This definition comes from Investopedia:

> A collection of risks associated with investing in a foreign country. These risks include political risk, exchange rate risk, economic risk, sovereign risk, and transfer risk, which is the risk of capital being locked up or frozen by government action. Country risk varies from one country to the next.

Not only does country risk vary from one country to the next, but the list of country risk components can also vary.

Sovereign risk

Risk of non-payment on a sovereign (or government) bond issued by a public or publicly guaranteed entity is referred to as sovereign risk. Sovereign risk is high in some euro-zone economies that have built up unsustainable public debts. The analysis of sovereign risks considers the sovereign as a distinct counterparty with its own ability to honour its debt obligations. The debt obligations could be in foreign currency or local currency. The most common sovereign rating is the foreign-currency ratings showing the risk of a government defaulting on its foreign-currency debt. History shows that governments default on both local- and foreign-currency debt – as in the Russian default of 1998. However, defaults on local-currency debt are less frequent. This is because the sovereign can always print more money and, depending on the depth of its domestic capital markets, convince local banks, pension funds and other investing entities to buy its treasury bills. Because of this additional room for policy manoeuvre, local-currency ratings are usually a few notches higher than the foreign-currency sovereign ratings.

Of all the components of country risk, sovereign risk (foreign currency) is the most measurable. It is a distinct event with a history of data – though some consider the 250 or so data points in the past 300 years insufficient for rigorously meaningful probability estimations. In contrast, country risk in the broad sense is not amenable to the same treatment. This is because countries do not default: it is economic entities within the country that default. Even in the worst countrywide payments crises not every entity defaults. Some crucial cross-border activity, usually trade finance, tends to continue. Hence the statistical basis of the ratings model proposed in Chapter 8 is strongest in relation to the sovereign risk ratings, which can indeed be mapped to probabilities of default. In addition, the numerical ratings (say, on a scale of 0–100) can be mathematically presented to reflect risk not just in the relative sense (ordinal rankings) but also in the absolute sense – that is, the distances between the ratings have meaning.

Transfer and convertibility risks

Investors have to be cognisant of the risks arising from the possible imposition by governments of capital controls or limits on foreign-exchange availability. These are called transfer and convertibility (T&C) risks. Malaysia imposed capital controls in the context of the 1997 Asian debt crisis. Venezuela is an example of an economy where convertibility has become progressively more difficult. The increased global integration and liberalisation of capital flows in the world economy in the past few decades reduced T&C risks. Monetary unions are also associated with lower T&C risks.

However, in the aftermath of 2008, this may be changing with increased government intervention and corporate and financial regulation. There is also a new recognition that some selective capital controls can be useful when economies are confronted with external shocks and sudden changes in direction of international capital flows.

T&C ratings are often treated as a mark-up (or mark-down, depending on the circumstances) to the sovereign foreign-currency ratings, taking into account the degree of global integration of the economy, the type of currency regime, and the independence of the central bank and other relevant institutions.

Operational or jurisdiction risks

This is another subset of the wider country risk components, referring to country-specific business environment risks such as governance, transparency and red tape, rule of law, infrastructure availability, regulatory risks and banking system fragilities. It is also possible to construct another subset of risks that focus on banking-sector risks. These are the topics of Chapters 5 and 7. Combined with an assessment of the local-currency sovereign risks, these can be useful as inputs into counterparty credit risk analysis. A country's jurisdiction risks can be very different from its sovereign risks. For example, in a country such as Indonesia where the business environment is full of risks, jurisdiction risk is high; but sovereign risk, with low levels of public debt, is low.

CASE STUDY 2.1

Nigeria: country risk vulnerabilities

Nigeria has rebased its GDP statistics to become the biggest economy in sub-Saharan Africa. However, despite its huge potential, the Nigerian economy has several features that increase its vulnerability to external and home-grown shocks and keep country risks high. This was shown in the multiple risks that were revealed during the 2008–09 global crisis.

In the past, Nigeria had benefited from a strong external balance sheet. A low foreign-debt burden and robust oil-export revenues had built up a foreign-exchange reserve buffer that peaked at $53 billion just before the onset of the global financial crisis, lowering the perceived transfer and convertibility risk. This in turn sustained the managed exchange-rate regime, aimed at reducing risks associated with naira volatility. However, a managed exchange-rate regime can also exacerbate exchange-rate risk under stressed conditions. By the end of 2009, Nigerian foreign-exchange reserves had fallen by 20% to $42 billion (and they continued to decline to $34 billion in 2010) as oil revenues fell and the central bank intervened to support the currency. But the monetary authorities had to opt for a 25% devaluation of the naira over a period of less than two months when it became too costly to support the dollar/naira exchange rate at 117 (in late 2008). This implied that the cost of imports, foreign-debt service and other exchange-rate-linked expenses suddenly rose by 25%.

The financial and banking-sector risks also rose. Capital inflows, loose monetary policy and poor regulation allowed rapid credit growth in the run-up to the crisis. Tightened liquidity from international banks in 2008 exposed local banks' vulnerabilities, bursting lending bubbles and causing multiple bank collapses. Rising interest rates, accelerating inflation, sharp currency devaluation and slower GDP growth combined to increase the macroeconomic risks.

The decline in global oil prices to below $40 per barrel increased energy sector risks: oil-price assumptions for cross-border transactions had to be reconsidered, and the borrowing base – an indication of borrowers' debt capacity – plummeted. The economy's excessive reliance on oil as a source of growth, foreign-exchange earnings and fiscal revenues came under scrutiny. Amid the turmoil, the Nigerian authorities introduced the first draft of the Petroleum Industry Bill in 2008, targeting an overhaul of the oil sector. The bill has so far not been passed by the legislature, but there have been various revisions over the past five years – all adding to regulatory risks for investments in the sector.

Fiscal revenues, relying largely on the oil and gas sector, fell by 40% in 2009, pushing the budget into a sharp deficit of almost 10% of GDP, from a 5% surplus the year before. Positively, the previous restructuring and prepayment of external debt meant that Nigeria's sovereign debt burden was at a comfortable level, mitigating immediate sovereign risk concerns. The events, however, highlighted the susceptibility of a decline in government revenues to global commodity cycles, and underlined the need for the establishment of a sovereign wealth fund (SWF – a state-owned investment fund), which would provide at least a temporary cushion against commodity price shocks.

The political risks remain high. In 2010 the incumbent president and PDP leader, Umaru Musa Yar'adua, died. The interim passing of power to a southerner and the re-election of Goodluck Jonathan in the 2011 polls sparked widespread discontent and violent riots in some northern states. Social strife is not yet posing a threat to the stability of the Nigerian state. But operational/jurisdiction risks stem from concerns that ethno-religious violence could destabilise some of the affected states. Additional security risks stem from sporadic attacks by Boko Haram, a militant group, in the north, and sabotage and theft of oil and oil infrastructure in the Niger Delta.

Political and geopolitical risks

Partly overlapping with sovereign and jurisdiction risk is political risk. This subset of country risk is the risk of disruption of operations or repayments as a result of political events in the host country or geostrategic changes in the international environment. A politically motivated change in government policy on taxation or regulation that undermines the revenue stream of a transaction could be defined as political risk. An example is the super-profits tax the Australian government had proposed to levy on mining companies in 2010.

Other government actions defined as political risks include nationalisation and expropriation, and breach of contract. Political risks such as terrorist attacks, civil strife, or ethnic conflict can arise not just from the actions of a government but also from other political actors such as minority groups. These risks can develop slowly over time and can be difficult to predict. Often political strife, as seen in North Africa in 2011, reflects deep social changes, which is why it is important to analyse underlying social and political trends and not just focus on a few indicators. Political risks such as wars are often associated with defaults and payments interruptions on cross-border investments. Geopolitical risks are the most difficult component of country risk to manage (see Chapter 6).

Economic risks

These typically refer to features of an economy that increase vulnerabilities to an external shock, or structural fundamentals and policy that can be the basis of home-grown payments crises. Countries with savings and foreign-payments imbalances are more vulnerable to external shocks. It is these indicators that singled out the "Fragile 5" group of countries – Brazil, India, Indonesia, South Africa and Turkey – as most vulnerable to a withdrawal of capital flows from emerging markets in 2013. Exchange-rate risks, interest-rate risks and macroeconomic volatility, sometimes singled out as subsets of country risk, are part of these risks. Home-grown vulnerabilities of an economy can explain why a country over-borrows. But often there are two sides to a payments crisis. Under some conditions in the global economy, international investors have become more susceptible to over-lending. Until recently, this factor has not received sufficient attention in the analysis of country payments crises. These themes are discussed further in Chapters 3–5.

Difficulties of defining country risk

Over the past few decades, financial and corporate entities have expanded their risk management structures, building models to deal with credit risk, market risk, operations risk, liquidity risk and, more recently, country risks. This has not been easy, partly because the definition of country risk that is right for one enterprise or investment instrument may not be right for another. Some entities define sovereign and T&C risk and put everything else under jurisdiction risk. Others focus mostly on political risks. All these risks are related and overlap and change over time, so it is difficult to draw clear distinctions between them. It is important that each entity agrees on a workable definition of the country risks that need to be managed for its business.

Moreover, these manifold and seemingly labyrinthine aspects of country risk mean that it has been difficult to define it. In his book *Risk, Uncertainty, and Profit*, Frank Knight proposed a theoretically rigorous definition of risk, making a distinction between risk and uncertainty. According to Knight, risk is measureable uncertainty, while uncertainty is not conducive to being measured. It is possible to attach a probability and a specific loss to risk. In this strictly theoretical sense, only the sovereign risk aspect of country risk is (sort of) statistically measurable. The rest, especially those aspects of country risk arising from political risk and government behaviour, it has to be admitted, are in the realm of uncertainty.

But not being able to apply probability theory to country risk to measure it does not mean that it cannot be managed, as discussed further in Part 2. As Peter Bernstein says:

The essence of risk management lies in maximising the areas where we have some control over the outcome while minimising the areas where we have absolutely no control over the outcome and the linkage between cause and effect is hidden from us.

Furthermore, despite the shaky statistical foundation, the country risk-rating model proposed in Chapter 8 tries to quantify country risk to be used as one of several components of the overall country risk management process set out here.

It is also impossible to draw a consistent hierarchy among the subsets of country risk defined above. There may be a country, such as Russia, where sovereign risk is low because of low public debt and high foreign-currency reserves but jurisdiction risks are high because of the weakness of the rule of law. In this case, an investment decision based on the sovereign ratings on any transaction other than one involving sovereign bonds would be severely understating the risks. Another example is Slovenia, where banking-sector and sovereign risk are high but jurisdiction risks are low. It would be just as erroneous to use the sovereign rating for Slovenia for a direct investment, as this would overstate the country risks. In the case of Greece, T&C risk is low (unless you think that it might exit the euro), but sovereign risk – foreign and local currency – is high.

Lastly, the aim of most country risk analysis is to avoid risk, but it can be equally useful for risk-assertive approaches. Country risk analysis is used not just to warn of payments crises and defaults but also where risk is declining: for example, in the southern euro zone from 2013; or Ethiopia, which is slowly beginning to reform its economy; or Colombia and the Philippines in the past few years where the governments are finally reaching agreements with their long-running insurgency movements, the FARC and the Moro National Liberation Front respectively. Thus this exercise can be used to direct investment decisions. Sometimes also called smart risk, country risk analysis, mitigation and management can identify opportunities as well as risks. Chapter 11 presents two case studies of successful transactions in high-risk areas that would be beyond most investors' radar.

Three frequently asked questions
1 Why should country risk refer only to cross-border risks?

This is a good question. After all, financial and corporate entities face macroeconomic and political risks in their home country. These range from regulatory risks, taxation changes, interest-rate risks and monetary-policy adjustments to macroeconomic risks due to volatility in domestic demand growth. They are also vulnerable to political risks, such as nationalisation, expropriation and social and political unrest, and even exchange-rate risks if their products have a high import content. Hence the suggestions in Chapter 11 on mitigating country risk also apply to home-country investments.

Traditionally, there have been two reasons for country risk to refer only to cross-border risks. One is to identify the risks in cross-border transactions. Investing in another jurisdiction requires the gathering of extra information and knowledge. There are risks in geographical, institutional and cultural distance, as well as in dealing with local politicians. This is the case even if the recipient country has a better sovereign rating than the country of origin of the investment. Many international banks investing in the US financial markets, for example, found themselves the target of heavy fines.

The second is that investors have a choice of countries to go to, and this book helps make that choice an informed one. It is assumed that there will be several target countries. The approach here helps them decide how much to invest in the chosen countries and how to diversify risks to optimise risk/return for the overall portfolio. It is also assumed that a decision has already been made on the location of the headquarters of a financial institution or the home-production centre of a multinational company.

2 Are the local-currency exposures of a subsidiary bank or investment entity a country risk?

Given the definition of country risk as cross-border, this would not be counted as country risk. The original equity injection into a country to set up a subsidiary is counted as country risk exposure. It would be double counting if the lending on of that equity was also counted as country risk exposure. But whether it is counted as country risk or not, the local-currency exposure of subsidiaries needs to be managed. This task is sometimes assigned to local asset-liability committees (ALCOs).

This decision also depends on whether a bank's headquarters is prepared to back up its subsidiary if it fails. Most international banks will support their subsidiaries, but some make exceptions if they fail because of political risk. It can be tricky to decide whether it is political factors or just bad management that cause a bank to close its doors.

3 How do you decide the country risk in the case of "brass-plate" incorporations?

There is an increasing tendency for the country of incorporation of an enterprise to be chosen for its favourable tax and legal environment. This is called a brass-plate incorporation if the actual operations of the enterprise are elsewhere. Countries often used in this way include the Cayman Islands, the Bahamas, Jersey, Luxembourg, the Marshall Islands, Mauritius (used by many Indian entities) and Switzerland. A discussion between the credit analyst and the country analyst is required to decide and in most cases to transfer the country of exposure from the brass-plate jurisdiction to the country of operation and domicile of the assets.

3 Causes of country risk at global level: excessive lending

IT IS NOT POSSIBLE to manage country risk by following developments in countries in a timeless, isolated way by tracking a few magical indicators. Organisations operating in the global economy require an understanding of the specific risks that pertain to each country in the context of international trends that have global risk implications.

Much country risk analysis focuses on the domestic factors that drive the demand for and possible interruption of cross-border financial flows in the recipient country. The aim is to identify the indicators of potential payments crises arising from excessive borrowing. The factors determining the supply of cross-border capital – the drivers of excessive lending – have been secondary in country risk analysis. Yet the financialisation of the global economy over the past few decades has meant that the size of financial flows has become greater than the size of most national economies, with the result that control exercised by national governments over domestic economic policy is becoming increasingly restricted.[1]

This chapter examines the association between the historical clusters of defaults and the movements of international capital flows, the contagion risks, and the possible cyclical patterns of the global economy. The aim is to manage country risk better by having a big-picture and historical perspective of global economic crises. This can help to highlight the specific features of current global trends and to identify possible historical breaks and turning points that can lead to crises. The analysis of the vulnerability of national economic and political structures to global pressures and of home-grown country risks that cause excessive borrowing is discussed in Chapters 4, 5 and 6.

Global waves of capital exports and risk of excessive lending

Sustained periods of excessive lending and clusters of defaults in modern history are associated with the two major waves of cross-border capital exports in the early 19th century and the late 20th century, mostly referred to as the first and second eras of globalisation. The UK was the dominant financial power at the beginning of the first era when the international monetary system was the classical gold standard. Capital mostly flowed from Europe to the New World to fund investments in infrastructure, tap raw materials, and establish economic and political spheres of influence and control. There were several lending booms and busts, with some 70% of the defaults in Latin America clustering around crises in the international centres of finance: the 1825 crisis in London; the 1873 crisis in Vienna, Amsterdam and Frankfurt; the 1890s Baring crisis in London; the start of the first world war in 1914; and the 1929 stockmarket crash in New York and London. The 1825 London crisis was triggered by the Bank of England raising its discount rate to defend its foreign-currency reserves. It was followed by the default of Argentina, Brazil, Chile, Colombia, Costa Rica, Ecuador, El Salvador, Guatemala, Honduras, Mexico, Nicaragua, Peru and Venezuela during 1825–29. *The Economist* called it "the first emerging-markets crisis". The direction of capital flows from Europe reversed sharply after the first world war, with the US emerging as a major international creditor to Latin American and war-worn European governments. The first wave of globalisation ended with the 1930s depression triggering defaults in a dozen Latin American countries and leaving nine European countries with debt-servicing difficulties by 1933.

In the 1920s investment boom, bankers in New York and London were competing to lend to Latin American countries. In a *New York Times* article, one commentator says of the 1920s lending spree:[2]

> *Many of the Latin American nations have doubtless over-borrowed or, what would seem to be more accurate, we have over-lent ... to create booms in Latin America and the result was ... boomerangs.*

But the problem was not just over-lending. The protectionist policies adopted by creditor countries once the 1929 crisis struck severely eroded the debtors' ability to pay. The crisis brought a sharp reversal and decline in the flow of international credit, blocking the rollover of loans. The main creditor countries – the UK, the US and France – abandoned the gold standard, hoarding their gold stocks and limiting the supply of gold in the rest of the world. Tariffs were raised which, along with the collapse in commodity prices, reduced borrowing countries' export earnings, further undermining their ability to pay.

The next big acceleration of international capital flows – the second era of globalisation – began in the 1970s following the end of the Bretton Woods system (the system of fixed exchange rates pegged to the US dollar that was linked to gold at a fixed rate). The US dollar, no longer linked to gold, became the global reserve currency, ushering in flexible exchange rates. Financialisation and the extension of supply chains across countries by global system-integrator firms became the defining features of this era. The result was the integration of developing countries into the global financial system, the opening up of post-communist economies to foreign investment and the rise of new emerging economic powers.

Competition to lend and the search for yield remained, as ever, fierce. Charles Kindleberger, an economist, lists the structural reasons for excessive lending as the oligopolistic nature of international loan markets; competitors' goal of increasing their market share; lenders' tendency to under-assess risks (credit markets "learn nothing"); and a tendency for loans to be clustered among a few favoured borrowers leading to high concentrations of risk. There is also the role of the IMF and bilateral creditors in bailing out countries in payments crises, which came to be seen as a moral hazard that allowed indiscriminate excessive lending to continue.

Total global cross-border capital inflows rose from around 2% of global GDP in the 1980s to 15% by the mid-2000s. Gross cross-border capital flows (inflows from foreign investors and outflows from domestic investors) were even larger (see Figure 3.1). The growth in capital flows was predominantly among developed markets, though during the past decade there was also an increase in flows to emerging markets. The IMF argues that this rate of increase in cross-border capital flows is well beyond the scope attributable to cyclical behaviour and suggests a number of structural push factors

FIG 3.1 **Gross cross-border capital flows**
% of trend GDP of high, middle, and low income countries, 1970–2009

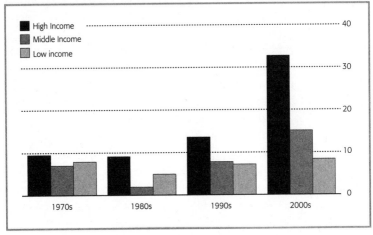

Source: Bruner, F., Didier, T., Erce, A. and Schmukler, S., *Gross Capital Flows: Dynamics and Crises*, Discussion Paper No. 8591, Centre for Economic Policy Research, October 2011

including demographic changes, financial deregulation, and advances in transport and communication; and new financial instruments including derivatives, which promised to mitigate the cross-border risks. Changes in the international investor base, such as the growth of assets under management of institutional investors, a decline in home bias and the rise of sovereign wealth funds in emerging markets, also contributed to the growth of cross-border capital flows.

Between their mid-2007 peak and 2009 collapse there were deep gyrations in capital flows; by mid-2013, they had recovered to only about 70% of previous peak levels. Most of the decline is a result of the financial fragmentation of euro-zone economies following the banking-sector crisis, and there should be a gradual recovery as the euro zone strengthens. Since 2013, the main emerging markets have had to contend with the outflow of capital back to the US due to tapering, or the tightening of the US Federal Reserve's monetary policies. However, net capital inflows still accounted for about 5% of the GDP of the major emerging markets, also lower than the peak but double the level a decade ago.

Transition periods: the rise of geopolitical risks

Globalisation eras do not evolve smoothly from one to another. The period between the end of one international monetary regime and investment cycle and the start of the next remains full of risks. The transition period between the first wave of globalisation and the second witnessed the rise of protectionism, the fragmentation of the global economy, two world wars, a deep global depression, systemic social revolutions that resulted in autarchy in large swathes of the world economy, and the coming and going of international monetary systems. The Bretton Woods system established in 1944 during the second world war was a transitional monetary system based on the US dollar with a fixed link to gold which fell apart in 1971. Financial markets remained highly regulated and capital controls were still predominant, while policies prioritised multilateral trade expansion. Capital exports moved in tandem with the trade and supply chains of mostly US multinationals in the form of FDI or trade finance.

Some argue that we are now at the beginning of another transitional era, possibly paving the way to a new age of international finance and changes in the global balance of power. The debate over the role of the US dollar as a reserve currency, the rise of gold, global imbalances and the 2008–09 crisis, volatility in capital flows, and the emergence of new powers such as China and India could all be expressions of this transition.

The past decade has been marked by the catch-up growth of many emerging markets. The rate of catch-up with the US of the main emerging markets doubled from 1.5% per head per year in the 1990s to around 3% over the past decade. As evident since 2012, the heady rates of growth seen in the past decade are unlikely to be repeated. It may be that, with the reversal of the loose monetary policies of the EU, Japan and the US, and increasing political risks, there will be further capital outflows from emerging markets, triggering the next wave of crises and defaults.

But long-term growth driven by positive demographics, urbanisation and the emergence of middle classes supports the notion of continued catch-up by emerging markets. It is possible that the long-term growth differential with slower-growing developed markets and the search for yield could continue to direct capital flows to emerging markets. The World Bank forecasts that capital flows to developing countries could triple from their 2010 levels to $6.2 trillion by 2030, with the share of total gross capital inflows rising from 23% of the global total to 47% over the same period.[3] This could be the defining feature of the third globalisation era.

The rules-based international structure that emerged after the second world war has many strengths compared with the earlier globalisation era dominated by colonial powers (see Chapter 9). But the risks of the rise of protectionism, fragmentation of the global economy, major economic conflicts, wars and defaults involved in such transitions remain high.

Financial crises: then and now

Each era of globalisation of trade and finance has its own patterns of crisis. During the gold standard era, the world economy revolved around the production and trade of commodities and manufactured goods. Finance and services that did exist were closely related to the production and trade of goods. Cross-border movements in capital were mostly limited to direct investment flows and bond and commercial bank finance of infrastructure, with governments being the main borrowers. The panic of 1857 triggered by the collapse of speculative railway investments is often cited as the first worldwide crisis engulfing US, UK and European banks. Other crises were caused when the bubble around speculative investments in commodities (such as cotton) burst.

In contrast to the 19th-century globalisation, finance and services have come to dominate most developed economies. There has also been rapid growth in the household sector – consumer credit, mortgage lending and private pensions – which widened the reach of the financial sector. The IMF's April 2007 *Global Financial Stability Report* highlights the features and potential risks (in a somewhat understated manner) of the past decade:

> *The diversity of assets, source countries, and investor types now involved in cross-border asset accumulation suggests that this form of globalisation should, on balance, support financial stability.*

However, the sheer size of flows raises concerns about the increasing exposures of both source countries and recipients. Furthermore, investors have been encouraged by the generally benign economic environment to venture into markets previously regarded as excessively risky. A deterioration in the economic environment may lead to unpleasant surprises.

Features of this phase of globalisation included:

- **Floating exchange rates and monetary policy changes by independent central banks.** The move to floating exchange rates from the mid-1970s gave central banks more independence to alter monetary policies. Abrupt changes in monetary policy, or the anticipation of such changes, have induced sudden, large cross-border financial flows. The increase in the number of countries moving to floating exchange rates has made this more difficult to monitor. The sharp reversal of US monetary policy has been the trigger for at least two of the crisis waves in 1979 and 1994. Recognition of this risk has heightened anxiety about the ending of quantitative easing (QE) by major central banks today.

- **The IT revolution and the liberalisation of global markets.** The liberalisation of global financial markets, which has increased the interconnectedness of the global economy, and the communications and information revolution brought by the internet have allowed the rapid movement of information and financial flows around the world in search of often seemingly marginal differences in returns.

- **The volume of global financial flows.** International financial flows now dwarf many national economies. Assets managed by the top 500 asset-management firms stood at $63 trillion at the end of 2011. The biggest asset manager, Blackrock, has $3.5 trillion under management – similar to China's foreign-currency reserves.[4] The size asymmetry between financial institutions (which are becoming more concentrated) and the countries they are lending to (which have become more numerous, and sometimes smaller) creates additional risks.

■ **The rapid growth of financial instruments.** New financial instruments enable banks to manage their credit risks better. The wider dispersion of risks through transfer, outsourcing and warehousing instruments was designed to "de-risk" the banking system and create more resilience to shocks. Moreover, the active trading of risk, such as through the credit derivative markets, increased price transparency. But these new products and the growth of off-balance-sheet accounting made it more difficult to track who held what amounts of risk, reducing the level of information in the market. Back in 1985, Alexandre Lamfalussy, an economist and banker, warned about new financial instruments that "the world needs experience in learning to handle".

■ **Heightened sensitivity to liquidity conditions.** These new financial instruments and the new market-based risk management environment had become highly sensitive to liquidity conditions, with any interruptions in liquidity potentially leading to amplified market corrections.

These new developments in the way the global economy operated contributed to a series of crises and their increased amplification. In the four decades since the end of the Bretton Woods system there have been four capital export cycles, involving in every decade various combinations of types of crises: in the 1980s, 1990s, early 2000s and 2008–09.

Stijn Claessens and Ayhan Kose, in their paper *Financial Crises: Explanations, Types, and Implications*, classify financial crises in four groups: currency crises, sudden stop (or capital account crises), debt crises and banking crises. From a country risk perspective, several types of crises – currency, sudden-stop, debt and banking – overlap and are connected. A currency crisis is frequently caused by a sudden stop or reversal of capital inflows, which then leads to a currency and payments crisis and, depending on how highly leveraged the banks and corporations are, causes a banking crisis, which forces the government to bail out the banks resulting in a public debt crisis (see Figure 3.2). The most severe banking crises are also associated with currency imbalances and sustained large current-account deficits

FIG 3.2 **Evolution of crises from one type to another**

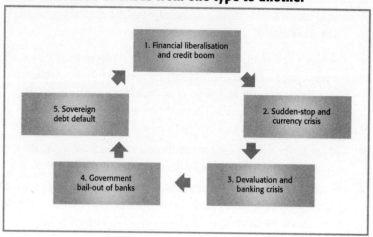

– including in many developed countries: Iceland, Ireland, Spain, UK, US, Greece.

Carmen and Vincent Reinhart's study of capital flow bonanzas (which they identify by abrupt V-shaped shifts in current-account balances) with data going back to the 1960s shows that bonanzas have become more frequent with the liberalisation of capital flows since the 1980s. These periods are also associated with a higher occurrence of banking and currency crises, and "capital flow bonanzas systematically precede sovereign default episodes". A common feature of all these crises is that they have been preceded by asset-price and credit bubbles. According to research by the Bank of International Settlements in 2013, the total-credit-to-GDP ratio seems to have some historical explanatory power in tracking credit cycles and identifying the build-up of credit bubbles.

Kindleberger and Robert Aliber in their much cited study, *Manias, Panics, and Crashes: A History of Financial Crises*, going back to the 17th century, observe that in the past 30 years more national banking systems have collapsed than in any other previous comparable period and that the range of movement in currencies has been much larger than in previous periods. Moreover, they argue that these crises are all connected, driven by the liberalisation of cross-border financial flows and involving increasing amounts of money "sloshing around" the globe in search of yield:

■ The 1980s emerging-markets debt crisis built up in the 1970s with the recycling of OPEC petrodollars by international commercial banks. Debt defaults followed in Latin America, Africa, eastern Europe and Asia once the US raised interest rates in 1979 (also triggering the US savings and loan crisis).

■ Capital flows then shifted to Japan, contributing to the Japanese equity and property bubble in the second half of the 1980s.

■ The implosion of the Japanese bubble in the early 1990s resulted in money flowing out of Japan and into the rest of Asia, building up an Asian credit bubble that burst as US monetary policy tightened from 1994, triggering debt crises from Mexico to Asia.

■ With the collapse of the Asian markets in 1997, money headed for the US (supporting the US dotcom bubble), eastern Europe and Russia. Still in the midst of its economic transition, Russia was in no state to absorb the capital flows and defaulted in 1998, followed by Argentina in 2001. At the end of this investment wave, Turkey and Brazil suffered currency and banking crises and needed IMF support to cope with capital outflows.

■ From 2003 onwards, the bigger emerging markets had a period of respite from financial crises. Meanwhile, the biggest of all credit bubbles was building up in the US and the euro zone. It ended with a crisis of historic proportions in 2008, when problems in the US subprime property market led to the collapse of several big financial entities in the US and UK.

■ Following the 2008 crisis in the developed world, capital flows relocated to emerging markets and commodities. We are now seeing the beginning of the reversal of this process.

To sum up, during the second era of globalisation, notable financial developments contributing to the nature and scale of financial crises include the growth of global financial assets relative to national GDP; the increased global interconnectedness of financial markets; changes in the role of central banks and the growing number of independent countries; the impact of floating currencies; the growth of consumer finance; and the mushrooming of new, often opaque financial instruments. Also associated with the 2008 global financial crisis is the growth of off-balance-sheet accounting and the high degree of leverage of financial institutions.

Contagion risks, spillovers and transmission channels

Once a crisis strikes, contagion is the mechanism by which the crisis spreads. This highlights any related imbalances in countries around the world, which in the absence of corrective policies are "solved" through crisis. The contagion-generating ability of the global trade and financial system has been amply demonstrated in all crises. But contagion effects have become more extensive in recent decades because of the faster speed at which information travels since the IT revolution and the deepening interdependence between geographical, sector and various segments of finance. At the same time, the widespread use of derivatives and other transfer instruments has compounded the layers of linkages.

Until the 2008–09 financial crisis and the euro-zone sovereign debt crisis, risk management mainly sought to prevent crises in emerging markets spreading and triggering systemic risks in the centres of global finance. International co-ordination contained the regional crises in Latin America in the 1980s, the huge bail-out of Mexico in 1994 and the Asian crisis in the 1990s.

Following the 2008 crisis, there has been more focus on the shocks emanating in the reverse direction, from the centres of global finance to the rest of the world. The Gulf Cooperation Council economies typify the multiple vulnerabilities to external shocks (see case study 4.4), even though there was little direct exposure to the toxic US mortgage securities in the region. The G20 (a group comprising the finance ministers and central-bank governors of 20 major countries) and the IMF have identified five systemically important economies (the S5) – the US, the UK, the euro zone, Japan and China – where fiscal and monetary policy shifts and any domestic shocks have global implications. There is also the added complication when a crisis strikes of the policy reaction of one country to another country's measures – which is impossible to foresee.

Transmission channels of contagion risks include finance (capital flows, banking sector, payments systems), trade and international supply chains, and political ideas, which are discussed below.

Financial transmission mechanisms and international risk appetite

The most powerful transmitter of financial contagion is the sharp reversal of international risk appetite, or what is known as ro-ro (risk-on, risk-off) volatility, driven by global events. The liberalisation and large size of cross-border financial flows, and their proclivity to move swiftly among countries, sectors and investment instruments, put this at the top of the external risks.

The changes in US Federal Reserve monetary policy, the collapse of the euro and the risk of a slowdown in China have been major drivers of risk appetite in recent years. Other contributors to global risk sentiment are geopolitical events with global risk implications, such as political instability in the Gulf and its contribution to a political risk premium on oil prices, conflicts in the East and South China Seas over seabed rights, and the threat of a new cold war following the Ukraine crisis. Market sentiment can change daily, overshoot, or signal the wrong risks. Hence it can be difficult to know when to act. Sometimes markets panic about risks that turn out to be manageable. This was the case with the overly hyped Y2K problem, or Millennium bug, which simply required a fix in computer software to deal with the congruence of many zeros as calendars moved from 1999 to 2000 – not beyond the creative capacity of humanity.

When risk is on, global investors diversify and are prepared to ignore spotty creditworthiness and extend their investment scope to frontier markets. The good thing about this is that countries thirsting for investment finally receive an injection of capital into vital projects. But often at these later stages of an investment cycle, these are the countries with the greatest vulnerabilities. For example, in 2012 Mongolia issued sovereign or "Ghengis" bonds, but when sentiment turned in mid-2013 with US Fed talk of tapering, there was a sharp sell-off. The yield on these bonds jumped from 5.125% to 7% and they were trading at 87.245 cents to the dollar by August 2013.

Financial sector integration and close regional linkages become a liability when there is a shock in the partner country. This is illustrated in the euro zone: the crisis in Greece spread to Cyprus owing to the high exposure of the Cypriot banking sector to Greek banks and sovereign debt, which led to a €10 billion bail-out of Cyprus in early 2013. A banking-sector crisis in Sweden, which has close regional links, resulted in the Nordic banking and financial crisis in the 1990s. And the Souk al Manakh stockmarket collapse in Kuwait in 1982 shook the Gulf economies.

Sometimes contagion takes place even though direct links may be tenuous. Carmen Reinhart and Kenneth Rogoff, in their book *This Time is Different: Eight Centuries of Financial Folly*, distinguish between contagion and common fundamentals in the spread of a crisis across borders. The latter was the case with the bursting of the Dubai property bubble at the end of 2009. With the exception of a few banks in Bahrain, the Gulf banks held no significant amounts of toxic derivatives nor had major exposures to the US housing crisis. Yet the 2008 crisis focused attention on the property bubble in the Gulf region and revealed the vulnerability of Dubai banks to the property sector and hence to refinancing risks.

There is now a body of literature that examines the financial transmission mechanisms of crises globally and maps networks. Recent network maps have focused on interbank exposures within countries and across borders. The aim is to study how the network of investing agencies – from banks to fund managers and from hedge funds to corporations with supply chains – operates at many levels, including trade finance, commercial loans, and portfolio and direct investment flows.

Trade transmission mechanism

Outside the financial sector trade is the main channel of transmission of shocks across borders. These too have become more intensified with the extensive linkages of the supply chains in manufacturing sectors through giant system-integrator firms such as those in the telecoms, IT, aerospace, automotive and energy sectors.[5] Highly integrated regions such as South-East Asia or Mercosur (a free-trade area comprising Argentina, Brazil, Paraguay, Uruguay and Venezuela) are more vulnerable to contagion effects. The growth and expansion of global platforms for commodity trading in the past decade has made speculative demand another unpredictable factor in transmitting shocks in international commodity prices.

Economic history is replete with terms-of-trade shocks when sharp fluctuations in the price of strategic exports or imports have a severe effect on the national economy. Ukraine's crisis in 2009 was preceded by a collapse in the price of metals, a major export, as the global economy slowed and demand for metals fell. The dramatic increase in oil prices by the OPEC cartel in the 1970s contributed to recessions in the US and Europe, and caused debt crises in energy importers. Food prices are a key indicator of political stability in Egypt, which imports 40% of its food. It is no coincidence that the protest movement against the Mubarak regime in 2011 followed a period of high international food prices. These vulnerabilities are discussed further in Chapter 4.

Political contagion

There is also the contagion of political protest, which would fit in the common fundamentals category. Examples include the series of revolutions that engulfed Europe in 1848; the wave of Arab nationalist revolutions in the 1950s; the domino collapse of communist regimes in 1989; the Orange revolutions against autocratic post-Stalinist elites in the early 2000s in Georgia, Kyrgyzstan and Ukraine; and the Arab spring protests in 2011. More recently there have been waves of middle-class protest in emerging markets such as Brazil, India, Thailand, Turkey and Ukraine. Although these protests are all driven by home-grown factors, there are similarities; for example, the initial participants are mostly urban middle class, there is hatred of corruption, and there are demands for greater political and personal freedoms (see Chapter 5).

The real economy, cycles and demographics: the long-term view

The discussion of global capital flows and financial and payments crises is not complete without reference to the real economy. Payments crises and defaults are triggered by shocks that arise from imbalances in the financial sector, the real economy, demographics, institutions and political conditions – and their interactions. All are important for country risk analysis. To understand these underlying issues it helps to track not just financial and credit cycles but the real-economy cycles of investment, commodity, technology, construction and demographic trends.

Even though the 2008–09 crisis reflected mostly the bursting of a financial bubble, worries about a Japanese-style secular stagnation in the EU and US economies suggest that more has happened to high-income economies than just a financial crisis. Financial crises ultimately reflect weakening underlying conditions in the real economy.[6] And a credit boom is not just a monetary phenomenon. The underlying causality could be a complex mix of economic and political trends. For example, it could begin with a period of strong productivity-driven GDP growth, which is amplified by an increase in capital inflows in the context of liberalised capital markets. If monetary policy remains accommodative, credit growth boosts housing and other asset prices. If continued over a long period, this could result in growing debt burdens and marginal loans with potential for systemic risks. This could correspond to an election cycle preventing a tightening of policy that could have contained the incipient bubble if the central bank or the regulators lack expertise or independence. Or, there is what happened in the US. The demand for US Treasury bonds by Asian countries to build up foreign-currency reserves after the Asian crisis and their export-led growth suppressed domestic consumption and created what Ben Bernanke, a former chairman of the Federal Reserve, calls a "savings glut". This contributed to keeping US interest rates lower than they should have been, building up a credit bubble, even though the underlying economy was slowing and building up overcapacity.

Business cycles

Business cycles have been tracked back to the 1790s in the US and UK economies where data goes back the farthest. A focus on cycles should be useful for country risk management – given the ebb and flow of capital flows as highlighted in the previous section and as debt crises come in waves (see Figure 1.1). Throughout history dozens of cycles have been identified, including "psychological" and "chaos" cycles. The agricultural cycle is the shortest, then comes the inventory cycle (which has become shorter with the advance in inventory management).[7] The fixed investment cycle was estimated to be 7–11 years and was studied by Joseph Schumpeter, an Austrian-American economist, who came up with the theory of "creative destruction". Tracking the fixed investment cycle has become more difficult with Keynesian fiscal policy interfering with investment and growth trends. The building cycle has a dual long and short duration, with the latter tied to the credit cycle and the former to demographics. The longer cycle is also referred to as the Kuznets cycle after Simon Kuznets, a Belarusian-American economist. The longest cycle – the long-wave cycle – with a duration of 45–60 years is associated with Nikolai Kondratieff, a Russian economist who worked at the Conjuncture Institute in Moscow in the 1920s. It had earlier been noted by Schumpeter in 1911 and by Jacob van Gelderen, a Dutch economist, in 1913, who along with Walt Rostow, an American economist, thought the long-wave cycle could correspond to the innovation cycle.

The current obsession with empirical "scientific" testing of economic ideas has somewhat discredited the long-wave theory. Deindustrialisation and the lower share of heavy, cyclical industries are also thought to have reduced the cyclical impetus of the developed economies. And some studies suggest that there are no economic cycles, just a series of shocks. Yet interest in the longer-term cycles of the global economy has continued and has increased in the aftermath of the 2008 crisis. The recent debate on crises has revived interest in Hyman Minsky's financial instability hypothesis (that financial markets are inherently unstable) and his theory of credit cycles. Minsky, an American economist, believed that during times of stability, economic agents become complacent. He identified

FIG 3.3 **Is the commodity super-cycle over?**
Commodity price index, 2005=100

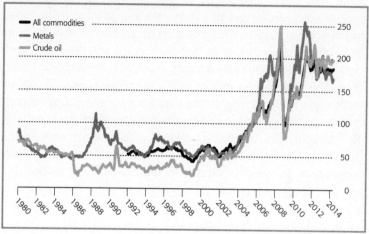

Source: IMF, World Economic Outlook (WEO) database

three distinct stages to his lending cycle: the hedge (when economic agents are cautious and risk averse); the speculative; and the Ponzi stage. Following from this analysis, economists refer to the "Minsky moment" that occurs when creditors and debtors all realise the underlying asset prices are heading down.

The strength of commodity prices over the past decade has also reignited interest in the commodity super-cycle (see Figure 3.3). An understanding of the dynamics of this cycle could help assess country risk in economies dependent on commodity exports. The swings in commodity prices cycles compared with manufacturing price cycles have been debated for many decades. Despite some lingering disputes, historical data collected by the World Bank in the 1980s and recently updated seems to point to a possible long-term inverse relationship between commodity prices and manufactures over the past couple of centuries.[8]

Besides sine-cosine shaped cycles in the global economy, economists have also noticed other long-term patterns. Commodity price movements seem to have a possible inverse relationship to the strength or weakness of global currency regimes. When the global currency regime weakens and uncertainty and risk increase, commodity prices tend to rise as investors turn to physical assets such as gold. Strong commodity prices since 2003, initially driven by the rapid growth in emerging markets, continued after the 2008 crisis, reflecting the travails of the US economy and the dollar. With signs of recovery in the US economy in 2013, commodity prices have fallen. This pattern appears historically in the pre-first-world-war era to the 1930s, when the international guarantor of the global currency system, the UK, seemed to be faltering. It reappears in the 1970s with the breakdown of the Bretton Woods system. Conversely, strong global economy and credibility in the international monetary system corresponds to weaker commodity prices, boosting profitability and investment in manufacturing. Although other factors such as increased supply could also have contributed, in the dynamic first era of globalisation there was a 49% drop in commodity prices in UK pounds in 1864–97, according to *The Economist* commodity index. Increased confidence in the US dollar, following the Volcke-inspired reforms at the US Federal Reserve from 1979 to the mid-1990s, also brought one of the largest falls in commodity prices in history (see Figure 3.4).

Investment booms

An investment boom that turns into a bubble in sectors accounting for a large share of GDP and employment can often trigger financial crises and defaults in the wider economy. When the textile industry was the motor of the first phase of the industrial revolution, the gyrations of cotton prices caused periodic financial crises in the US, Europe, the Middle East and India in the 18th and 19th centuries. The 19th-century railway-investment boom and its prolonged bust caused a series of financial crises that engulfed the US and European financial centres and their colonies. A more recent example is the spectacular dotcom crisis in 1997–2000, where euphoria over the "new economy" drove stockmarket valuations of internet and IT firms to unsustainable levels. In this case the Fed pricked the NASDAQ bubble, raising interest rates six times during 1999 and early 2000. As commodity prices soften, the next critical sector could be mining and linked suppliers with negative consequences for commodity exporting countries and regions.[9]

Housing booms

There has been more interest in housing-sector cycles since the 2008 crisis. Housing booms and busts have a long history.[10] In recent decades, some big financial crises relating to the housing and property sector occurred in the US in the 1980s (the savings and loan crisis), Spain in 1977, Norway, Finland, Sweden in 1987–91 and Japan in 1992. The UK had a massive property bubble in the early 1990s but managed to deflate it without significant financial fallout. The Asian crisis of the 1990s included a housing price boom and bust, with the magnitude of decline in real house prices ranging from a low of around 20% in South Korea and Thailand to over 50% in Hong Kong and the Philippines, with a period of downturn stretching from four to seven years.

High rates of urbanisation and housing construction are major drivers of growth in emerging markets. Most of these housing cycles should be seen as belonging to the demographically driven, longer, Kuznets-cycle variety where there is strong demand for housing by rural migrants into cities and upgrading of the housing stock for the aspiring urban middle classes. Nevertheless, the financing of housing purchases in emerging markets – usually with shorter-term credit and at higher interest rates than in developed markets – is risky.

Housing bubbles often reflect the absence of other attractive investment products, either because returns are not as high, or because financial markets are not that developed. Both these factors are evident in China, where the government has been trying to contain the housing bubble, allowing periodic failures of property developers and finance entities to reduce the perception that bail-outs will always be provided. With the slowdown in growth, a lacklustre stockmarket and a narrow bond market, investment in property has been the best option for Chinese investors. Finance from the shadow banking sector that many property projects seem to rely on only amplifies the risks.

Demographic trends

Demographic trends are critical to the analysis of political risk as well as longer-term trends in employment, productivity and public finance. The impact of ageing populations on social welfare, pension burdens and the youth bulge are important drivers of political and fiscal instability, as is the demographic dividend that can create self-reinforcing positive growth effects. The long-term consequences of ageing populations in developed markets have been extensively analysed. Less discussed are demographic studies linking political and subsequent economic crises to specific demographic patterns. Their main thesis is that countries that have entered a youth-bulge phase seem to be more prone to political violence. There seems to be some historical evidence for this, with both the English and French revolutions apparently having occurred during periods of youth bulges in Britain and France.[11] This became one of the themes in trying to explain the simultaneous occurrence of the youth protests in the Middle East in 2011.

There can also be a positive shock to the economy from demographic trends, which is called the demographic gift. This happens when the economy accelerates as population growth peaks. With more people entering the labour market, the dependency ratio falls. This combination of trends increases productivity per head as well as income and savings. It generates a demographic dividend by allowing the benefits of economic growth to be spread more evenly around the population, providing a self-reinforcing multiplier effect to growth. This is what happened in Asia in the 1980s.

Conclusion and country risk pointers

- Push factors that drive excessive lending have become more important for country risk analysis as the size of international financial assets relative to world GDP has risen to unprecedented levels. The rapid reallocation of asset portfolios can destabilise national economies, limiting the room for national policies. International co-ordination to contain global risks in turn encroaches on sovereignty.

- There have been two globalisation eras with major capital export waves in modern times. We could now be in a transition

FIG 3.4 **Commodity prices and confidence in currency regimes**

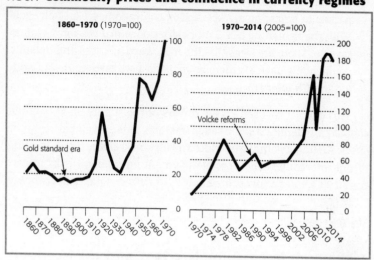

Sources: *World Business Cycles*, The Economist Newspaper, 1982; IMF, WEO database

period before another one. With changes in global international monetary systems transition periods can be tricky, making the management of cross-border risks more important than ever.

- History shows that debt crises come in waves. Hence it is useful to track business, financial, commodity, sector and demographic cycles. But it is also the case that history does not repeat itself, making it difficult to identify inflection points, when a particular trend will turn or a bubble will burst.

- Commodity price cycles seem to be inversely correlated with manufacturing prices, and strength of the international reserve currency providing valuable pointers to country risk analysis (see Figure 3.4). Though not all housing cycles lead to financial crisis, they are associated with banking crises and defaults – so far, mostly in developed economies. The current credit and construction trends suggest this may become a feature of emerging-market crises too.

- These features of recent crises potentially point to where and how future crises could arise. Since the bursting of the credit bubble in 2008–09, money sloshing around had mostly been parked in emerging markets and in commodities, especially gold. With the tightening of US monetary policy in 2013, this began to reverse. There are signs that the next wave of crises and defaults could swing back to emerging markets. (See case studies 3.1 and 4.3 and Chapter 11.)

This chapter focused on the drivers of the supply of cross-border capital and identified some salient features of recent global economic crises. An understanding of wider and historical global trends is crucial to put into context the possible payment and default risks in each country. Chapter 4 covers the analysis of risks in a national economy.

CASE STUDY 3.1

Turkey: global economic crises and the economy

World crises	Impact on Turkey
1873–77 crisis	1881 Ottoman debt default
1929 stockmarket crash	Banking and liquidity crisis
1958 Korean war recession	1958 economic crisis IMF standby loan 1961 military coup
Early and mid-1970s recession	1970 devaluation IMF agreement 1971 military coup
Early 1980s recession	1977–81 debt crisis IMF and rescheduling 1980s coup
2000–01 dotcom crisis	2000–01 banking and payments crisis IMF standby loan
2008–09 global recession	2009 sharp GDP contraction Strong recovery but high current-account deficit

Crises in the Turkish economy have been highly correlated with global trends. In the 19th century, global shocks came through commodity prices and trade.

In the 20th century the economy developed and industrialised, becoming the 15th biggest in the world. But low domestic savings and energy-import dependence have kept it vulnerable to global shocks. In the 19th century the Ottoman economy was integrated into the global economy as a raw material producer. The mid-century global economic boom, the stimulus from the Crimean war in 1853–56 and debt-funded railway investments boosted growth. But this became unsustainable with the decline in commodity prices in the 1870s and the 1873 crisis in Austria and Germany. By 1881, Ottoman budget and foreign-payments deficits resulted in debt default. Defeat in the first world war caused the demise of the Ottoman empire.

Founded in 1923, the Republic of Turkey inherited a rural economy and a depopulated country, with its physical stock in ruins from decades of war and the violent collapse of the multi-ethnic empire. It was not a good time to build a new country. In 1926, the fragile economy was hit by a sharp recession and the collapse of several local banks when commodity prices fell. Then came the 1929 global crisis that halted capital inflows and accelerated the exodus of foreign investors. This propelled policy towards state-led industrialisation and protectionist measures. The establishment of the Central Bank in 1930 and an import quota regime in 1931 brought some control over the currency and international trade, cushioning the infant industries from the global storms.

Despite the Turkey's neutrality, its economy contracted by around 6.4% per year during the second world war. An ill-thought-out liberalisation programme initiated by the Democratic Party in the 1950s ended with a stifling array of price controls, import restrictions, multi-tier exchange rates, and budget and foreign-payments deficits. The fall in commodity prices after the Korean war and political unrest led to a payments crisis, an IMF bail-out in 1958 and a short-lived military coup in 1960. Turkey had been ill-prepared for the 1950s liberalisation with underdeveloped financial markets and little enthusiasm for privatisation of the public-sector enterprises, as they were a critical source of employment and political patronage. The consequences of the missed opportunity of the 1950s policy turn became apparent with the onset of the 1970s global recession. Turkey's foreign balances suffered a double blow from the OPEC oil price hikes and the collapse of export revenues, resulting in the 1977 payments crisis.

An IMF standby loan, and in the midst of civil unrest a military coup in 1980, paved the way for tough reforms as the global economy entered recession in the early 1980s. A radical policy shift towards export-led growth to boost foreign-currency earnings tripled exports by the end of the 1980s. But the

1980s reforms left deep political scars, weakening institutions. Liberalisation of the banking sector had come before stronger regulation. Double-digit inflation and rising budget and current-account deficits led to another IMF standby loan in 1999. Before the economy could stabilise, a poorly designed currency peg and the bursting of the US dotcom bubble resulted in sharp capital outflows, causing a liquidity crunch. This, combined with a political crisis in November 2000 and devaluation, triggered a massive banking crisis. The banking-sector restructuring that followed more than doubled public debt to 80% of GDP.

A restructured financial sector and large-scale privatisation attracted foreign direct investment and enabled the Turkish economy to benefit from favourable global economic conditions in the 2000s. Export markets were diversified from the EU to the booming Gulf, Russian and Central Asian economies. The export drive to these regions was led by newly emerged Anatolian businesses, represented by the Justice and Development Party (AKP), which came to power in the 2003 elections.

Turkey's performance during the 2008–09 global crisis showed its strengths and weaknesses. After a sharp 5% GDP contraction in 2009, growth of 8–9% was restored 2010–11 as capital flows recovered. A better-regulated banking sector, a low public debt ratio and the diversification of exports to emerging markets gave the economy resilience. Although growth has moderated, policy was slow to rein in retail credits and the current-account deficit remains high: combined with debt repayments it amounts to around 25% of GDP, leaving the economy vulnerable to international shocks. Moreover, high inflation undermines competitiveness. Over the coming years, the economy will have to cope with rising international interest rates and the potential shock of a sudden stop of capital flows. Furthermore, social and political changes have increased domestic political risks. The government must tread a fine line between these domestic and global pressures, Middle Eastern conflicts and structural impediments such as high energy-import dependence.

4 Payments crises: country vulnerabilities

THE PREVIOUS CHAPTER focused on the external, global drivers of cross-border capital flows and the risk of excessive lending that leads to payments crises. It highlighted the specific features of recent crises and the importance of tracking cycles of the global economy to manage country risks. Here the focus shifts to the risks at country level – at the receiving end of cross-border capital flows. This requires an analysis of economic, institutional and political features of a country that increase its vulnerability to global shocks and the risks of over-borrowing that could impair its ability to meet foreign financial obligations.

This chapter shows how the analysis of country risk has evolved and identifies features that increase a country's vulnerability to external shocks. Chapter 5 considers the structural fundamentals of an economy and underlying home-grown country risks, and Chapter 6 deals with political and geopolitical risks.

Learning from different crises

The analysis – and understanding – of a country's vulnerability or resilience to payments crises has changed over the years. It has followed the evolution of the size and composition of international capital flows, features of global crises (see Chapter 3) and the understanding of the economic development process. Each lending and borrowing spree also had its typical misconceptions and blind spots.

Late 19th century

Early country risk analysis by Crédit Lyonnais in the late 19th century focused on the revenue-generating capacity of an investment and the debt-service ability of the sovereign using a balance-sheet approach. There was also focus on whether the borrowing was for productive investments, such as infrastructure, or to fund current spending, such as wars, which was seen to lead to defaults. This analysis failed to dampen repeated waves of lending to Latin America and subsequent defaults or the surge of lending to Russia in the lead-up to the Bolshevik revolution.

Inter-war and after second world war: fundamentals and development

Decolonisation from the 1930s onwards and, after the second world war, the growth of multilateral credit and official aid flows led to a widening of the analysis to include the fundamentals of the economy and the drivers of growth and development. A 1960s introduction to country risk suggests:[1]

> For this analysis, there is no formula ... it depends on the analyst's perception of the country's development process. A debt service crisis ... is in essence a balance of payments crisis, which in turn, is a development crisis.

More specifically, the domestic resource gap between savings and investment was linked to the persistence of balance-of-payments imbalances: a foreign-exchange gap. External finance was seen as the missing link in development, which was to be covered by public bilateral aid and multilateral development assistance. Private financial flows took the form of trade finance or foreign direct investment (FDI) mostly by US and UK multinationals. Their major cross-border concern was political risk, in the form of nationalisation and expropriation in the 1950s such as in Cuba. The focus was on industrialisation and developing countries, rather than developed economies, although several European countries were still using IMF emergency funds in the 1950s. This was a blind spot in country risk analysis that was to persist for several decades.

In the 1960s, persistent global inequalities generated radical critiques of the neoclassical growth theories. Some, such as "dependency theory" and "unequal exchange", regarded low commodity versus manufactured prices as the main culprit. This seemed to explain the situation in Latin America in particular, where state-led industrialisation took off but seemed only able to survive behind high tariff walls. These economies became highly import-dependent and exports were limited mainly to primary commodities vulnerable to the fluctuations of commodity prices. The growing external gap was covered by foreign credits, building up foreign debts. From the 1970s onwards creditors also included commercial banks, essentially recycling the OPEC oil surpluses. This lending boom was accompanied by misconceptions such as lending to "oil-producing countries was as good as gold", and $21 billion of loans were made to Mexico in 1981 alone, the year preceding the 1980s debt crisis. The unsustainability of this approach by both borrowers and lenders was revealed when international oil prices and interest rates rose at the end of the 1970s, triggering a series of defaults, called the third world debt crisis.

1980s and 1990s: currency regimes in the spotlight

The 1980s debt crisis took almost a decade to resolve. With little access to international financial markets, many indebted countries undertook deep restructuring, privatising the inefficient state sector and strengthening their foreign-payments position. In the 1980s there was liberalisation of global financial markets and in the 1990s the resurgence of commercial bank lending. Country risk analysis began to focus more on economic policies, especially the mismatch between domestic fiscal policy and – at that time mostly pegged – currency regimes. The currency crises of the 1990s, not just in emerging markets but also in Europe (see case study 4.1) revealed the susceptibility of currency pegs to speculative attack.

CASE STUDY 4.1

The European exchange rate mechanism crisis

During the European exchange rate mechanism (ERM) crises of 1992–93, the UK, Italy and Spain abandoned their pegs to the D-mark and exited the European Monetary System (ESM). This is a good example of a currency crisis caused by discrepancies between an economy's fundamentals and economic policy, and a mismatch with major trade partners.

■ At the time, these countries had no major problems with their fiscal policies or a too rapid growth of credit, and they had full access to international capital markets.

■ But currency investors, led by George Soros, a business magnate, increasingly saw these pegs as unsustainable. This was not so much because of problems with policy in the countries themselves, but rather the regional context and the incompatibility with German monetary policy.

■ The tight monetary policy pursued by the Bundesbank to offset the German government's expansionary fiscal policies in the aftermath of the fall of the Berlin Wall was not appropriate for other countries in the ERM.

■ This was the case in the UK, which needed an easier monetary policy to encourage growth and reduce high levels of unemployment.

This cyclical and structural disjuncture among European economies was to re-emerge with the euro crisis 20 years later.

Capital flows as crisis triggers

The 1990s crises showed that looking at the underlying fundamentals was not enough to see a crisis coming (see case study 4.2). Sudden changes in international risk appetite by investors could trigger one that came to be called a sudden-stop crisis. This initially appeared as a liquidity crisis, but if not halted quickly transformed into a solvency crisis. The capital account of the balance of payments received more attention. The notion of a liquidity crisis expanded the role of the IMF, which began to provide large emergency liquidity-lending facilities and started the process of generating moral hazard (that is, commercial banks and bondholders take more risks on the expectation of bail-outs by multilaterals).

These crises exposed another problem. During the 20th century the role of central banks as lender of last resort had reduced the frequency of domestic financial crises. But with international capital-market liberalisation, central banks struggled with externally generated crises. Policy became trapped between defending the currency (by raising interest rates) or domestic financial stability and supporting the banks. This inability of policy to achieve simultaneously all three goals of open capital markets, monetary independence and exchange-rate stability came to be called the impossible trinity or "trilemma".

It was also noticed that many banking or financial crises followed a period of liberalisation and financial deregulation. Examples in developed markets include the US savings and loan crisis of the 1980s and the Nordic countries' banking crisis in the 1990s. The Mexican crisis in 1994 and the Asian crisis in 1997 illustrated the dangers of capital-account liberalisation before strengthening banking regulation and other market institutions. These experiences brought institutional development and the sequencing of market reforms fully into country risk analysis and came to be seen as the risk of liberalisation running ahead of institution strengthening.

CASE STUDY 4.2

Mexico 1994: unanticipated crisis in a star performer

Referring to the Mexican and the Asian crises of the 1990s, Guillermo Ortiz, governor of the Bank of Mexico, admitted in a lecture in 2002 that these countries were considered "star performers", and these crises "were not anticipated". But the raising of interest rates by the US Federal Reserve in February 1994 (continuing relentlessly with seven jumps until February 1995) triggered capital outflows from emerging markets. This exposed the vulnerabilities of Mexico, including the persistent current-account deficit, largely funded by capital inflows. This had resulted in the appreciation of the peso, straining the currency peg. But this had been ignored, given Mexico's oil reserves and the prevailing misconception that "current-account deficits mattered only if they reflected public sector deficits". Markets also ignored the furious issuing of *tesebonos*, US dollar-indexed short-term Mexican government paper. It was the combination of these vulnerabilities and the hike in US interest rates, the assassination of the Mexican presidential candidate and the Chiapas uprising that triggered the sudden-stop crisis in Mexico.

Furthermore, while the focus was on the public-sector balance sheet, private-sector external borrowing was found to be a problem that was compounded by global financial-market liberalisation. This was the case in the Asian crisis, where private-sector foreign-currency borrowing and an associated real estate bubble exposed these economies to sharp currency devaluations, as seen in Thailand in July 1997. Thus the analysis of a country's debt sustainability now needed to include the structure of the debt.

Sovereign risk in developed economies after 2008

The crisis of 2008 turned the focus back onto developed markets' vulnerability to default risks. Most lost their risk-free AAA status on sovereign debt and some in the euro zone also lost their investment-grade status. Once more, prevailing misconceptions were exposed, such as the idea of the great moderation in US and UK financial centres. In the euro zone, the belief that the current-account deficit does not matter in a currency union was overturned by the fact that the one common factor distinguishing the troubled euro-zone economies from the rest was their high and entrenched current-account deficits. The EU Commission now produces a regular Alert Mechanism Report as part of the annual Macroeconomic Imbalance Procedure which tracks five indicators for external imbalances and competitiveness and another six for internal imbalances.

The crisis highlighted another risk factor: the ownership of the debt. Countries with large foreign ownership of their public debt, such as Greece, were more exposed to changes in international risk appetite, while those with high domestic ownership had more cushion against volatility, as in the UK, Italy and Japan (see Figure 4.1). Furthermore, the behaviour of central banks after the 2008 crisis

FIG 4.1 **EU budget and current-account balances and maturing sovereign debt: eve of the euro-zone crisis**
% of 2011 GDP

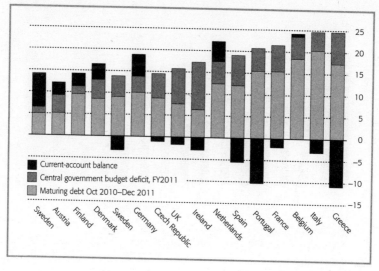

Source: IMF, WEO database

has raised new questions about economic policy, including possible inflationary risks from quantitative easing (an unconventional monetary policy where central banks buy financial assets from commercial banks to boost the price of the assets and increase the monetary base to stimulate the economy). And the extensive bond-purchase programmes of the Fed, the European Central Bank (ECB) and the Bank of England have blurred the line between fiscal and monetary policy. Between 2007 and January 2012, the balance sheets of the Fed and the Bank of England increased from around 5% of GDP to 20%, and that of the ECB from 12% to 32%.

Another misconception was the notion that the EU umbrella would mitigate country risks on the mistaken expectation of policy discipline and the foreign-payments cushion provided by EU budget transfers. This led rating agencies to upgrade eastern and central European countries to investment grade when they became EU members, ignoring their institutional fragility. Yet this was one of the worst-affected regions during the 2008 crisis, with several countries

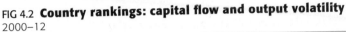

FIG 4.2 **Country rankings: capital flow and output volatility**
2000–12

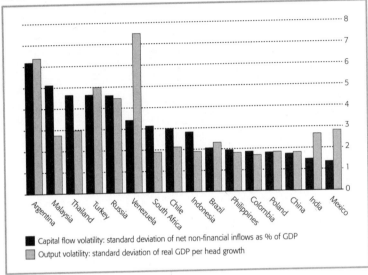

Source: IMF, *World Economic Outlook*, 2014

requiring IMF and EU emergency loans. The build-up of consumer credit in foreign currencies was also a symptom of this complacency. Mortgage and other consumer credits denominated in Swiss francs and euros were a critical risk factor in Hungary when its payment crisis broke in 2009.

The importance of external factors

Six years after the 2008 crisis, as the recovery in the developed economies took hold and there was a prospect of monetary-policy tightening, focus shifted somewhat back to emerging markets. There was concern about the impact of capital that had been parked in emerging markets while growth stagnated in the developed world, and worries that this could undermine growth or even trigger a new emerging-markets crisis.[2] As the IMF noted in its 2014 *World Economic Outlook*: "external factors induce significant fluctuations in emerging-market economies' growth, explaining about half the variance in their growth rates." (See Figure 4.2.)

This strong direct emphasis on external factors is different from earlier approaches, despite studies from the late 1990s (by, for example, Guillermo Calvo and Paul Krugman) showing their importance (see Chapter 8). The general thrust of mainstream thinking on development and payments crises has tended to be on in-country weaknesses and fragilities. This has been the central feature of the perennial debate on the success of Asian economies versus Latin America, which focuses on the importance of national characteristics such as the legacy of Confucian versus Catholic counter-reformation cultures. It might have been possible to brush off the impact of external factors in payments crises in the past. But, given the growth in the size of international capital flows, as described in Chapter 3, and the depth of developing-country capital markets today, the elephant in the room could no longer be ignored.

The analysis of country risk too has mostly been structured around in-country features, although since the 1990s crises there has been more emphasis on contagion effects, with indicators showing the vulnerability of the domestic economy to external shocks incorporated into the analysis. The discussion about the tapering of the Fed's bond-purchase programme and the resulting volatility of capital flows as well as the spillover of the economic policies of globally important economies to the rest of the world has now become mainstream and a central element of the country risk debate (see case study 4.3). This recognition enables a more balanced country risk analysis to be conducted and is the basis of incorporating more external/push factors and cyclical factors in the country rating model proposed in Chapter 8.

Macroeconomic imbalances

Thus, over time, and learning from each crisis, a framework has emerged for thinking about country risk, balancing the global factors that drive excessive lending with the features of an economy that increase its vulnerability to global shocks. External economic shocks to national economies can never be completely offset, but it is possible to cushion against them – at least temporarily. It is also possible for countries to learn how to manage their economies better and come off the fragility list for extended periods of time. (These points are discussed further in Chapter 12.) In contrast, countries that sustain structurally entrenched imbalances – whether in savings, foreign payments or the financial sector – remain vulnerable to external shocks. (Savings and foreign-payments imbalances are covered in this chapter and the financial sector in Chapter 6.)

TABLE 4.1 **Vulnerability factors and indicators**

Vulnerability factors	Indicators
Savings imbalances	Low national savings
	Endemic fiscal and/or current-account deficits
	High public and external debt/GDP ratio
	Composition of foreign debt such as maturity and ownership
Foreign-payments imbalances	Concentrations in exports and imports
	Current-account balance/GDP ratio
	Exchange-rate trends
	Low share of FDI inflows
	External payments requirements/foreign-exchange reserves and other liquidity ratios
	Terms of trade
Financial sector imbalances	Credit/GDP ratio, credit growth, loans/deposits ratio, non-performing loans
	Asset concentrations
	Size of shadow banking sector
	Interest-rate spreads

Savings imbalances

Whenever a country enters a payments crisis or defaults, the first suspects are the persistent fiscal and/or current-account deficits. Correction of these imbalances is also the first target of economic policies for coming out of the crisis. But underlying these imbalances and harder to tackle with quick policy measures is the savings imbalance. A country with structurally low levels of national savings becomes dependent on external capital inflows to drive investment and growth. This is a critical structural factor that increases the vulnerability of an economy to sudden-stop external shocks.

FIG 4.3 **Savings and debt imbalances**
%, 2013

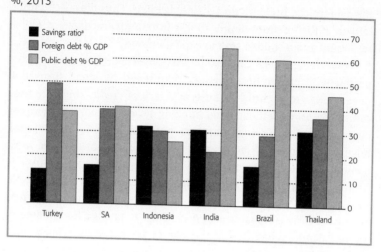

a 2009–13 average.
Source: Institute of International Finance

A savings imbalance not only increases a country's vulnerability but, as long as capital inflows continue, also has a reinforcing effect, which increases dependence on external funding. An entrenched decline in savings over time is often a reflection of a period of capital inflows that has fuelled domestic demand, increasing consumption and thus driving a decline in savings.[3] An example is the secular decline in the national savings ratio in Turkey and Brazil over the past decade.

The savings deficit could be in the private sector, the public sector, or both. If it is in both, this is likely to be reflected in a persistent double deficit in the fiscal and current-account balances. The fiscal deficits become funded by growing public debt, part of which could be in foreign currency depending on the depth of the local capital markets. This deficit spending can in turn fuel domestic demand (which again reduces savings), which can combine with private-sector borrowing to boost imports and further widen the current-account deficit. The demand for credit encourages banks to seek funds in international markets, rather than rely on the slow accumulation of local deposits. Depending on the starting level, just half a decade of this pattern can build up unsustainable debts. Thus these economies remain at the forefront of any shocks from a major change in global sentiment and a sudden stop to capital inflows.

Low savings ratios can also be associated with low-income, low-productivity economies, possibly dominated by small firms that never quite grow, partly because of a lack of credit. Therefore they can reflect an underdeveloped banking sector. In many developing countries, where savings data are not that reliable, institutional, religious and cultural factors also seem to be important. The most commonly referred to thesis on the determinants of savings is Milton Friedman's permanent income hypothesis: that people save to smooth out consumption over a life cycle, spending when young but increasing savings in middle age to prepare for retirement. There is some evidence that the rate of savings is associated with demographic and urban structures: younger populations save less; rural households save more. This would imply that as a country with a younger demographic profile becomes urbanised, the rate of savings declines. This ties in with the suggestion made in Chapter 3 that it is important to understand the demographic cycles in a country and its urbanisation trends.

CASE STUDY 4.3

Tapering and emerging markets: another repeat of 1994?

Since 2009, currencies in developing countries with relatively deep and liberalised capital markets have been on a roller-coaster ride:

- **First they appreciated.** As the dollar depreciated with the start of the Fed's quantitative easing policies, competitiveness in emerging markets weakened and current-account deficits widened. Brazil was first to react in 2010. Guido Mantega, the finance minister, grumbled about "currency wars" and imposed capital controls on short-term inflows. Facing a record current-account deficit in 2011, the Turkish Central Bank cut interest rates to weaken the lira and boost exports, and used macro-prudential policies to slow credit growth. By 2013, east European politicians, from Poland's

Janusz Piechocinski to Hungary's György Matolcsy, were on the case too. As the Japanese central bank initiated its quantitative easing, Russia's central bank governor, Alexei Ulyukayev, declared the world was "on the brink of currency wars".

- **Then they depreciated.** These pressures had sharply reversed by mid-2013 as the Fed signalled that it might start tapering its bond purchases. Emerging-market currencies immediately dived 10–20%. Brazil's central bank governor, Alexandre Tombini, warned about the "vacuum cleaner of rising interest rates" and lifted most capital controls. Indonesia and India raised rates to slow the outflow of capital. Turkey's prime minister, Recep Tayyip Erdogan, lambasted the "interest rate lobby" as the lira plummeted. Indian policymakers called for "co-ordinated intervention" by 12 big emerging economies. The IMF president, Christine Lagarde, said the world economy needed to "bolster its defences" as markets began to debate the risk of another emerging-market crisis similar to that of 1994, when the hike in US interest rates had triggered the Mexican and Asian crises.

- **And then recovered – sort of.** The decision by the Fed in October 2013 to postpone its tapering once again reversed capital flows and some emerging-market currencies recovered. Many emerging-market central banks also raised interest rates and lifted capital controls on inflows. As precautionary measures, swap facilities were discussed.

It is not over yet

Various emerging markets have been singled out as being the most vulnerable and a "Fragile 5" identified – Brazil, India, Indonesia, South Africa and Turkey – with worries that any defaults among these would have a significant global impact. Yet the 1994–97 crises are unlikely to be repeated in the same way. The tightening of monetary policy in the US will not be unexpected or sudden, giving time for proactive policies that could bolster defences and provide more resilience. The next global crisis will be different, possibly emanating from China or the euro zone. But this episode has for the first time focused minds on the risks to the global economy of capital flow volatility and the contribution of external factors as drivers of these movements that have the potential to trigger financial and payments crises.

Foreign-payments imbalances

Current-account imbalances

Current-account imbalances mirror the underlying strengths and weaknesses of the economy. Entrenched current-account deficits and surpluses are expressions of underlying structural imbalances. The current-account surpluses in China and Germany, for example, are a reflection of highly competitive economies but also the low share of consumption. The latter creates problems for trade partners as seen in the euro-zone imbalances and the fraught debate over global imbalances between China and the US. However, for this discussion of external vulnerabilities, the focus is current-account deficits.

The importance of current-account deficits as an indicator of vulnerability has frequently been contested. If temporary, they may simply reflect a growth spurt, which as long as foreign-debt levels are low, may be totally sustainable. However, entrenched current-account deficits as seen in the southern euro zone, reflecting a long period of declining international competitiveness, may have appeared sustainable but when capital inflows dried up they suddenly were not. There can also be persistent current-account deficits without fiscal deficits, as was seen in Asia in the lead-up to the 1997 crisis. The budget finances may even be in balance. In this case a high and rising current-account deficit signals a loss of competitiveness and that the fiscal stance needs to be tighter, with a sufficiently high primary surplus (the budget balance excluding interest payments on the public debt) to dampen domestic demand. Many governments and investors fail to understand this. Or governments fail to act on it, especially if an election is due.

Current-account imbalances can arise in trade, services, or other financial transactions (invisibles and transfers). Trade deficits can reflect a lack of competitiveness of exports, because of either declining productivity or an overvalued currency. Or the current-account deficit can reflect an unsustainably high import bill due to high domestic demand. There could be a structural imbalance such as a dependence on high food or energy imports. The services balance could cause current-account imbalances if the economy has a high reliance on external demand-driven services sectors such as tourism. These tend to be volatile and relatively sensitive to domestic political and global shocks, as Tunisia found with the collapse of tourism revenues following the 2011 protests that ousted President Ben Ali.

Imbalances in the current account could also be caused by heavy financial outflows of profit remittances abroad, interest payments on foreign debt, or workers remittances or other transfers. A disruption in these flows, depending on how big they are or how dependent the economy is on them, can increase payments risks – as in struggling Central American and Caribbean economies as remittances from immigrant workers in the US and revenues from American tourists declined with the US economic crisis.

Persistent currency overvaluation (in real terms) is a precursor of currency and payments crises. Sometimes it is difficult to judge whether a currency is overvalued. Different methods – some deflated by trade-partner inflation (real effective exchange rate) and others by labour cost, or consumer or wholesale price indexes – can give different results. Depending on the starting point, these exercises can also reach different conclusions. Debates can continue for a long time. However, when the current-account deficit persistently widens in conjunction with the deterioration of other economic conditions, an adjustment to the exchange rate becomes inevitable if the currency is to be spared a speculative attack. Partly to avoid having to risk this, and partly to boost export growth, many emerging-market governments, especially in Asia, have had a bias towards undervalued currencies. Hence the appreciation of many major emerging-market currencies on the back of capital inflows as the dollar weakened in 2009 alarmed many governments, undermining a long-established growth model (see case study 4.3).

Trade structure vulnerabilities

A foreign-payments imbalance can also reflect underlying problems in the structure of trade. Concentration by trade partner is a major source of vulnerability. Statistical studies show the vulnerability of growth to major trading-partner growth is one of the most important external factors: medium-term growth shows a correlation close to one. Economies with a small domestic market dependent on export-led growth are more sensitive in this respect. Not just growth but also changes in the trade partner's exchange rate are transmitted. For example:

- About a third of Argentina's exports go to Mercosur, the South American customs union, the bulk of them to Brazil. The crisis in the Brazilian economy and the massive depreciation of the real in the late 1990s contributed to undermining Argentina's currency peg.

- Turkey is reliant on the EU for about half of its exports. The euro-zone crisis and the weakening of the euro versus the dollar was a major blow for Turkey's exports. It not only affected the demand for its goods but also undermined its competitiveness: Turkey imports energy and raw materials priced in dollars and exports manufactures and services to the EU.

- Mexico had a double hit when the US economy weakened in the early 2000s. Not only did exports to the US weaken, but Mexico lost market share to more competitive Chinese and South-East Asian imports.

There are also terms-of-trade shocks, which can be positive or negative. These refer to sudden changes in the prices of key exports or imports. Price shocks can be triggered by changes in the global supply of commodities because of new discoveries, the exhaustion of resources, or climatic conditions – a bad coffee harvest in Brazil will affect coffee prices globally. New technologies can affect the supply and global price of commodities, such as the recent expansion of shale gas, which is positive for the US, reducing its reliance on oil imports (and supporting the correction of its current-account deficit), but has mixed strategic implications for the global energy market. Terms-of-trade shocks can also be a reflection of changes in global demand for a key export.

A heavy concentration on primary commodities exports amplifies this vulnerability. The softening of oil prices was one of the underlying factors in the collapse of the Soviet Union in 1989 and, a decade later, the 1998 Russian default. With the exception of Australia, Canada or Norway, which have high-tech and high-productivity primary sectors, this economic structure tends to perpetuate this overreliance and make economic diversification difficult.

The Gulf Cooperation Council: multiple vulnerabilities

The Gulf Cooperation Council (GCC) economies proved relatively resilient to the 2008 global financial crisis. Foreign-currency reserves built up during the oil boom of the 2000s enabled most governments in the Gulf to pursue expansionary fiscal policies, thus providing a cushion to growth in the global economy. But the crisis also highlighted their multiple external dependencies and vulnerabilities to global shocks. The 2008–09 global recession underlined the need for further regional integration to develop an internal market as a cushion against fluctuations in external demand.

- Several Gulf economies, especially Dubai, were caught in a property bubble, which had begun to deflate from early 2008 with the outflow of capital.

- Oil export revenues fell as oil prices collapsed from $140 per barrel to under $40 per barrel in just three months to December 2008.

- Despite large oil surpluses, there had been a rapid rise in foreign borrowing by corporations and banks, the latter with short-term tenors (or maturities of the loans). Several overleveraged investment banks in Kuwait defaulted and financial entities in Bahrain, Kuwait and Dubai had to be bailed out.

- There were risks to the sustainability of the dollar pegs in view of the falling value of the dollar and high inflation in the region.

- The small size of the national markets (all less than 5m, apart from Saudi Arabia with 25m) and low levels of regional integration left the GCC producers dependent on external demand. As non-oil exports also fell with the recession in export markets, problems in the real economy led to negative feedback effects on the financial sector.

- The capital-intensive diversification projects provided few jobs for the national workforce, resulting in high youth unemployment and brewing political problems for the future.

- Despite the fiscal stimulus real GDP in the GCC stagnated in 2009, with the combined nominal GDP shrinking back to 2007 levels of around $825 billion from just over $1 trillion in 2008.

Financial sector in the front line

The rapid (and debt-driven) growth of the financial sector over the past decade put this sector in the front line of the global crisis. Credit had grown at a high 30–40% per year in 2007–08 in the UAE, Oman and Bahrain, and by 50% in Qatar, with concentrations of banking assets on the construction and real estate sectors signalling looming problems.[4]

- The worst hit was the UAE, where Dubai financial and government-related entities were highly leveraged. Dubai's debt-to-GDP ratio was around 120%, with debt service due in 2009 at 29% of GDP. Property prices fell 50% when the property bubble burst. Dubai had to rely on Abu Dhabi to provide emergency financial support.
- In Kuwait the regulators had missed the explosive growth of investment companies. Dabbling in complex products was another problem. Losses suffered by Gulf Bank (the fourth biggest in Kuwait) in October 2008 on currency derivatives created a panic, prompting the Kuwaiti government to guarantee all deposits and inject $1.4 billion of capital to stop a run on deposits.
- With banking-sector assets four times the size of GDP, a limited fiscal cushion and a concentration of toxic assets, Bahrain was one of the most vulnerable economies in the global credit crisis. Two of the biggest offshore banks, Gulf International Bank (GIB) and Arab Banking Corporation (ABC), had to be recapitalised to cover losses of up to $1 billion.

Structure of capital flows, debt and liquidity

A current-account deficit must ultimately be funded either by net capital inflows to the capital account or by a drawdown of the central bank's foreign-currency reserves. Vulnerability to external shocks differs according to the composition of capital inflows. Of the non-debt-creating capital inflows, a higher share of FDI inflows to fund a current-account deficit provides a bigger cushion against

FIG 4.4 **Current-account balance and net FDI**
$m, 2013

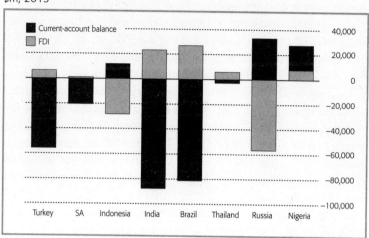

Source: IMF, WEO database

global shocks (see Figure 4.4). This is because unlike portfolio investment flows, which can suddenly leave the country, FDI is not as mobile. Of the portfolio flows, fixed-income or bond investors seem to be the more trigger happy, leaving at the first sign of trouble, while equity investors seems less so, possibly because they are more associated with institutional investors with a longer-term view. Speculative currency traders, seeking higher interest rates and betting on the appreciation of the currency – carry traders – are the most skittish and often the target of capital controls by national governments.

Vulnerability is further increased if savings and/or budget and current-account deficits have been met with foreign-currency borrowing. The size of foreign debt relative to GDP and debt-service payments relative to export receipts are two classic indicators in country risk analysis. But determining the sustainability of a given debt or debt-service level is never easy. Zaire, the first country to default in the wave of defaults in the late 1970s to early 1980s, suspended its interest payments when its debt-service ratio was only 17%. It was also noted that Latin American countries were defaulting at unexpectedly low levels of debt and debt service, leading to the concept of some countries having low levels of debt tolerance.

In contrast, developed countries carry public and external debt loads of well over 100% of GDP for extended periods of time. The structure of the debt, the depth of the domestic capital markets, global liquidity and international risk appetite are the main factors that have to be considered to judge whether a country has over-borrowed. But given the volatility of global markets and currencies over the past few decades, lower is definitely better – or at least a declining trend. This seems to have been well understood by most of the older emerging markets – those that have emerged. Over the past decade, emerging-market governments have almost halved their foreign-currency borrowing from just under 30% of GDP in 2002, thus reducing their vulnerability to external shocks. This partly reflects a more prudent fiscal stance, but also the development of local-currency debt markets. But governments in sub-Saharan Africa, having just benefited from debt relief under the World Bank's heavily indebted poor countries initiative (HIPC – see Chapter 8), seem to be rapidly re-accumulating foreign-currency debt.

While sovereign foreign debt has declined in many emerged markets, the low international interest rates since the 2008 crisis seem to have encouraged foreign-currency borrowing by the private sector, particularly by corporations and banks in developing countries. An additional new risk has been the foreign borrowing of emerging-market multinationals by their subsidiaries abroad, which is not part of the usual definition of foreign debt. A significant part of this debt is short term, further increasing exposure to a sudden-stop crisis. Or, if international interest rates rise, credits are rolled over at higher interest rates, increasing the debt-service bill. Liquidity becomes critical at these times and the size of (liquid) foreign-currency reserves relative to short-term foreign financing needs (the current-account deficit, principal repayments on long-term debt, plus short-term debt) becomes a key parameter, as seen in Mexico in 1994 and South Korea in 1997.

Liquidity crises not only affect economies with savings and current-account deficits; as the GCC case study above shows, liquidity and payments crises can also affect economies with budget and current-account surpluses even where the sovereign is a net international creditor. In the case of the UAE, this was caused by a combination of the heightened risk aversion and contagion brought by the 2008 global crisis, the bursting of the Dubai property bubble, the highly indebted semi-sovereign entities and the short-term repayments structure of their debt.

Then there are financial vulnerabilities. As discussed in Chapter 3, a prime transmission channel of contagion is the financial sector. Financial sector integration and close regional financial linkages transmit external financial shocks. This is amplified with a depreciating currency if the domestic banking sector has built up foreign-currency debts that may, in turn, have fed domestic credit and property bubbles. These are discussed further in the next chapter.

5 Payments crises: in-country causes

THE PREVIOUS CHAPTER highlighted the features of an economy that increase its vulnerability to external shocks. But even if the global environment is benign, the fundamental structural weaknesses of an economy at a particular stage of development or just bad policy can generate risks of home-grown debt crises. Egypt and Argentina are examples of countries where policies have a tendency to do just that.

John Calverley, who wrote about country risk in the 1980s, stressed the importance of fundamental analysis as opposed to simply tracking the symptoms of country risk such as declining reserves or rising debt. This is particularly important in understanding the origins of current problems, and can also be effective for early warning. In his book *Country Risk Analysis*, he categorised countries in "country risk types": advanced industrial, newly industrialising, primary commodity exporting, heavily indebted (referring to the group of countries in the Brady debt rescheduling programme in the 1980s) – and in the 1990 edition he added east European transition economies.

This chapter takes the same approach but with updated, more generic typologies based on a heterodox view of country risks in economies at different levels of development. It draws on a neostructuralist view of development with an emphasis on structural changes and the role of institutions (see also Chapter 6). Given the close link between financial crises and country defaults, there is also a section on financial sector risks including a case study of the difficult reforms facing China (case study 5.2). The chapter ends with a "rogue's list" of policies that undermine the ability to pay. No matter how well endowed with resources a country is or how favourable the global economy, ultimately it is economic policies and how the country responds to changing domestic and global conditions that determine its prospects. Institutional structure and political and geopolitical risks are discussed in Chapter 7.

Home-grown causes of country risk

Structural risk typologies:

- **Advanced economies** – return of default risk, weak growth and deflation stalk outlook.

- **Diversified developing economies** – middle-income trap, growth volatility.

- **Resource-based economies** – elusive quest for diversified economy.

- **Frontier markets** – on the margins of the global economy.

- **Small-island economies and offshore financial centres** – not so balmy.

TABLE 5.1 **Structural risk indicators**

	GDP growth %		Current account % of GDP		Public debt % of GDP		Savings % of GDP	
	1994–2003	2004–13	1994–2003	2004–13	2003	2013	1994–2003	2004–13
Advanced	2.9	1.6	–0.3	–0.5	74	106	22.1	20.3
Diversified	5.3	6.2	–0.9	–1.2	48	39	25.9	29.7
– Asia	7.2	8.6	0.9	3.3	41	35	33.3	43.2
– Europe	3.3	3.9	–2.7	–5.6	55	45	18.5	16.3
Resource	1.1	4.6	1.6	5.2	51	31	23.8	29.3
– MENA[a]	4.0	5.0	2.7	11.6	59	32	27.4	39.6
– CIS[b]	0.8	4.7	4.3	4.7	38	14	25.6	27.8
Frontier	3.9	5.6	–2.3	–0.8	59	34	15.2	21.0

a Middle East and North Africa.   b Commonwealth of Independent States.
Source: IMF

Advanced economies

These include the mature economies in Europe, North America, Japan and Australasia and others such as South Korea and Singapore. They are characterised by high-value-added industry (even though the share of the manufacturing sector has shrunk over the past few decades), knowledge industries, high-productivity agriculture and a dominance of services in the economy.[1] Their political and economic institutions have been honed over hundreds of years and they are relatively stable democracies. Until recently, many of these countries were AAA rated or risk-free. Despite being buffeted by a series of financial, currency or banking crises, since the 1950s these economies had managed to avoid debt-default crises and had not needed multilateral bail-outs (apart from the UK). The prevailing view has been that there was sufficient flexibility in political and market institutions and policymaking to deal with problems pre-emptively.

However, country risks in these economies have been rising since the end of the post-second-world-war boom in the 1970s. Over the past decade, increased country risks in the form of the build-up of credit bubbles, rising private-sector debt, the costs of military intervention and high government spending relative to GDP were not reflected in their ratings. They have deep financial markets but these have grown too big; and they carry the fiscal weight of ageing populations. There was also the problem in the US of stagnant real wages and the wide current-account deficit. Belated downgrades of sovereign ratings followed the 2008 global financial crisis, and the government bail-outs of strategically important banks raised public-sector debt to unsustainable levels (see Table 5.1).

In the euro zone, Cyprus, Greece, Ireland, Portugal and Spain (for the banking sector) needed bail-outs. The crisis reflected the imbalances in the euro zone and a combination of home-grown factors, including bursting property bubbles and banking crises (Spain and Ireland), unsustainable government borrowing, loss of competitiveness and large current-account deficits. In mid-2013, five years after the crisis, rating agencies were still reporting that developed- and emerging-market ratings continued to converge, mostly because of the downward movement of developed markets (see Figure

FIG 5.1 **Change in sovereign ratings**
Ten biggest downgrades and upgrades by Fitch, Moody's and S&P in 2007–13

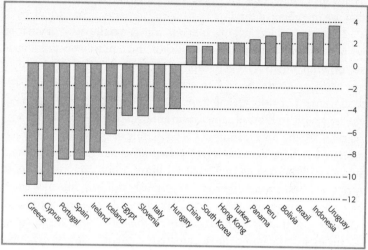

Source: *Financial Times*, March 27th 2013

5.1). Although risks seem to have receded in the euro zone, growth remains fragile, and deflation and high rates of unemployment could become entrenched.

Elsewhere, there are concerns that technological progress and innovation have stalled compared with previous decades. There is also political deadlock over US fiscal policies, preventing an infrastructure-led investment spurt. And, until the recent monetary easing by the Bank of Japan, the Japanese government has found it difficult to reignite growth. All this keeps the major world economies overly reliant on monetary policy, so an extended period of low growth is a major risk.

Diversified developing economies

This category is full of acronyms: BRIC, CIVETS, the Next-11, 3G, the 5% and 7% Club. These all refer to emerging markets with fast growth potential but also high growth volatility, reflecting country risks. They include the biggest emerging markets – Brazil, Russia, India and China – as well as a broader group including Mexico, Indonesia,

Thailand, Turkey and South Africa, which are increasingly referred to as advanced emerging. There are also some east European countries that are members of the EU.

The advanced emerging markets are generally well-diversified economies with a dynamic export sector and a mostly open financial sector with relatively deep capital markets. Because of this they are a major destination of international capital flows. Hence the management of risks arising from their global integration is a major challenge. The outflow of capital from emerging markets since mid-2013 triggered by the anticipation of US tightening of monetary policy has brought a notable deceleration in growth. This has generated another subcategory known as the Fragile 5: Brazil, India, Indonesia, South Africa and Turkey. But other more obviously troubled big ones could be added such as Argentina, Egypt, Hungary, Ukraine and Venezuela.

After a period of high instability in the 1980s and 1990s, many countries in this group have pursued prudent policies, defeating hyperinflation and reducing public debts in the past decade (see Table 5.1). This gave them room to pursue counter-cyclical expansionary policies during the global crisis which some, such as the Fragile 5, are struggling to rein back. Particularly noticeable is the high rate of credit growth, though in many countries this is still from a low base. Financial sector structures vary widely from highly developed and competitive to state dominated (see section on financial risks below). In the latter, credit tends to be either absorbed by the public sector or allocated to a narrow elite. It mostly remains short term and expensive. This forces domestic investors to resort to foreign-currency borrowing, thus building up external debts and currency devaluation risks.

Other emerging markets that have integrated into the global economy mostly as commodity exporters are now developing a manufacturing base with potential for further diversification and growth. These include Tunisia, Nigeria, Argentina, Bangladesh, Colombia, Egypt, Ghana, Kenya, Peru, the Philippines and Vietnam (this list is not meant to be exhaustive but to give examples). High growth rates over the past decade have been driven by favourable global trends, positive demographics, high rates of urbanisation, a rising middle class and purchasing power, and being located on a trade corridor or part of a high-growth trade block. Often these economies are locked into global supply chains.[2] Income distribution is not their strong point. This is a key indicator of high country risk, with studies showing that the higher the income inequality, the higher the recurrence of debt and payments crises.

Nigeria is a good example of an economy that has most of these favourable dynamics. Unlike the Gulf economies, it also has a large domestic market that can sustain the establishment of automotive and consumer-goods industries. Non-oil exports make up only 5% of total exports, with a secular appreciation of the naira where the real exchange rate has almost doubled since the early 2000s, eroding competitiveness. Hence future prospects will depend on political and institutional factors and economic policy.

A major country risk with both these groups is that political and economic institutions struggle to keep up with the social change brought by fast growth. Institutional development, including transparency and adherence to the rule of law in judiciary and supervisory institutions, is a weak feature of these countries. This institutional fragility remains the biggest barrier to advanced emerging economies overcoming the middle-income trap, as South Korea has done. Moreover, when growth slows as in 2013, underlying structural weaknesses are revealed such as low national savings rates and low levels of productivity, which lead to persistent and large current-account deficits (see section on savings deficits above). Some of countries, mostly in emerging Europe, have seen their savings rates decline precipitously over the past decade, which is reflected in their high current-account deficits (see Table 5.1).

Economic policy instability is another major risk (see case study 5.3). The historical legacy of mostly state-led development is difficult to shed (see case study 5.1). Structural reforms, such as privatisation and liberalisation, mostly happen under pressures of crises. As the economy develops and becomes more complex, the switch to more appropriate market instruments as policy tools remains difficult, partly due to resistance from the incumbent elite to give up some control. Business regulations tend to be complex, with a tendency to generate corruption. The rewards are among the highest in this group of countries, and pose greatest challenges for country risk management.

CASE STUDY 5.1

Egypt: fiscal and debt crises and policy zigzags

Despite its diversified economy and potential for high growth, Egypt has struggled with periodic fiscal and payments crises. Over the years, the country has had to rely on external injections of funds to meet its domestic and foreign-payments shortages:

- **1960s.** State-led import substituting industrialisation under Gamal Abdel Nasser was accompanied by expulsion and/or nationalisation of private capital. The era ended with a balance-of-payments crisis and the first of several IMF agreements in 1964 which began the retreat from state socialism.

- **1970s.** Anwar Sadat's policy of *Infitah*, opening to private capital, was supported by the first oil boom and remittances from Egyptians working in the Gulf countries. Private capital emerged with links to Gulf and Islamic finance. The era ended with the 1973 war causing high defence spending and foreign debt to build up. In 1976 an IMF programme was agreed. Cuts in food subsidies led to bread riots in 1977, resulting in another policy reversal.

- **1980s.** Hosni Mubarak reverts to Nasserist protectionist policies with an emphasis on state industries. But, with the oil boom over by 1983, this strategy proved unviable. Budget deficits reached 10% of GDP, and total debt peaked at 173% of GDP. In 1986, Egypt defaulted on its foreign debt. In 1987, an IMF programme was agreed, but not implemented.

- **1990–2003.** A return to the private sector driving growth in the "Tiger on the Nile". Egypt received massive debt relief and external assistance for supporting the 1991 Kuwait war and the 2003 US intervention in Iraq. This, along with two devaluations, helped ease fiscal pressures temporarily. But public finances deteriorated again due to expanding security spending and revenues stagnated. Although Mubarak's security apparatus budget rose, allocations to the military declined. The army expanded its economic activities to meet funding needs.

- **2004 onwards.** The Nazif government was established and Mubarak's son, Gamal, was put in charge of policy. Favourable global conditions, the second oil boom and Gulf FDI drove GDP growth. Dynamic sectors such as telecoms, finance, real estate, tourism, media and transport emerged; and with generous fuel subsidies to Mubarak's cronies, so did cement, steel, chemicals, fertilisers. Rapid urbanisation, high youth unemployment, and a growing educated and aspiring middle class increased political pressures. The army was becoming increasingly wary of Mubarak's privatisation programme.

- **Post-Mubarak.** The complex tug of war between the public sector, the army and parts of the private sector continued after the fall of Mubarak and the military overthrow of President Morsi. But now the private sector is fragmented among Mubarak's old cronies, the Muslim Brotherhood's associated Islamic businesses, export-oriented but narrow competitive sectors and the army's economic activities, which are likely to expand further following the July 2013 coup. The country faces severe water, energy and wheat shortages. With the population deeply polarised, the situation remains inherently unstable and only sustainable through Gulf financial support.

Resource-based economies

With export and budget revenues heavily dependent on a few resource sectors, the primary country risk facing these economies is their vulnerability to exhaustion of resources or fluctuations in international commodities prices. These economies generate fiscal and current-account surpluses but can quickly build up debts when prices of their principal export fall. This was the case in Saudi Arabia when the 1980s decline in oil prices swiftly raised public-sector debt to over 100% of GDP (this was partly because Saudi Arabia acted as the swing producer in OPEC – a role it is unlikely to repeat). The economic structure of such economies is state (or royal family) dominated; high energy and other subsidies characterise the fiscal structure. For example, pre-tax energy subsidies in the Middle East and North Africa (MENA) region constituted half of the world's total energy subsidies and were equivalent to 8.5% of the region's GDP. Reliance on tax revenues is usually minimal.

Over the past decade, many resource exporters established national wealth funds to provide a counter-cyclical policy and a temporary cushion for the economy when commodity prices fall, somewhat reducing risks. Country risks can also be reduced with

FIG 5.2 **Middle-income resource economies: resource dependence has risen in the 2000s**
$5,000–12,000, purchasing power parity, 2011

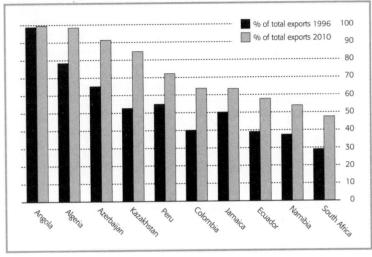

Source: Hagland, D., *Blessing or Curse? The Rise of Mineral Dependence Among Low- and Middle-Income Countries*, Oxford Policy Management, 2011

policies that aim to diversify the economy. But the lower the level of development and the more dominant the resource sector at the early stages of development, the more difficult this becomes. This is the stage that Indonesia is now passing through. Over half of its exports, mostly to China, are primary commodities such as iron ore, coal, coffee and palm oil. Indonesia needs to move up the value-added chain to offset the impact of China's economic slowdown and the softening of commodity prices. But hampering this process are a weak infrastructure and the education and skills required by manufacturing industries.

A 2011 study by Dan Haglund, an economist, concluded that of the 61 low- and middle-income countries identified as mineral dependent (if mineral exports constituted 25% or more of their total exports), a third were seen as especially vulnerable to the resource curse – the risk that sharp fluctuations in commodity prices could affect their development. This dependency has increased in almost all countries

FIG 5.3 **Low-income resource economies: high and rising resource dependence**
Less than $5,000, purchasing power parity, 2011

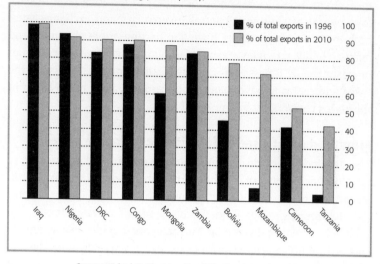

Source: Hagland, D., *Blessing or Curse? The Rise of Mineral Dependence Among Low- and Middle-Income Countries*, Oxford Policy Management, 2011

over the past decade (see Figures 5.2 and 5.3). Even an economy with the skills and technology of Russia remains heavily dominated by the resource sector, finding it difficult to diversify and modernise (see case study 6.4).

Often these resources are located in areas that are difficult to reach or are landlocked, with the disadvantage of high transport costs. For example, Mongolia, with its vast mineral reserves, remained off the radar for international investors until metal prices rose sufficiently to cover the extra costs of transport.[3] This is also the case in a new country, South Sudan, which has oil reserves but is landlocked and dependent on hostile (north) Sudan for its pipeline network. Economic policy can be erratic and unpredictable. In Latin America, in countries such as Bolivia, Ecuador and Venezuela where some democratic structures exist, governments have attempted to address poverty and income inequality, but policies have tended to become incoherent and largely ineffective. As seen in Argentina (see case study 5.3) and

Venezuela, these policies rely on social handouts that relieve political pressures in the short term but by fuelling inflation and undermining investment only increase these problems in the long term. After a long period of stultifying controls over prices and exchange rates, both these governments are having to become more pragmatic and relax exchange-rate rules and other administrative controls. Peru is an interesting case: it passed through this radical populist phase in the 1980s and seems to have managed its resource curse much better in the 2000s commodity boom.

Frontier markets, serial defaulters and fragile states

These include many developing countries that are still on the edge of the global economy, but depending on global financial conditions can still attract cross-border inflows. Though not a major focus for country risk managers, projects funded with a mix of private, charity and multilateral finance do crop up. This category includes new countries created by ethnic fragmentation of existing nation-states. Some, such as Albania, Armenia, Georgia and Rwanda, have sufficient international investment interest to issue sovereign bonds in international markets. Others, such as Angola, Mozambique and Sierra Leone, are endowed with rich resources, but having recently emerged from long-running civil wars present all the dangers of over-rapid external borrowing. The latest additions to the UN are East Timor, Kosovo and South Sudan, with more to follow in the Middle East.

These nations represent high country risks as they learn how to steer their economies without falling into unsustainable debt and default. Some don't manage and become serial defaulters, such as the Democratic Republic of Congo (the Republic of Zaire until 1997), which underwent 20 rounds of sovereign debt restructuring between 1976 and 2010.

Another challenge for country risk management is countries moving into or out of self-imposed autarchy or international sanctions and those sometimes referred to as fragile states – roughly 50.[4] In countries that have recently rejoined the global economy, such as Cambodia, Ethiopia and Myanmar, country risk remains high because of the fragility of economic and political institutions.

Others with once promising economies, such as Cuba, Bolivia, Iran and Zimbabwe, fall into a political crisis and recede to the margins of the global economy. Fragile states are characterised by humanitarian concerns, such as mass migration and a legacy of violent conflict, and often harbour terrorist networks.

Small-island economies and offshore financial centres

The spectacular currency and banking crisis in Iceland – an early precursor of the 2008 global crisis – and the contentious bail-out of Cyprus in 2013 highlighted the high country risks in these otherwise balmy seeming economies. Both illustrate the risks of a weakly regulated, oversized financial sector. To be fair to Cyprus, contagion from Greece added to its troubles, but high vulnerability to the conditions in their economic partners is a feature of small economies. In contrast, and reflecting China's strength during the 2008 crisis, there was the stoic performance of Hong Kong, which is run under the iron discipline of its currency board backed by massive foreign-currency reserves. But even so, Hong Kong has had its share of speculative attacks on the currency and bursting asset and property sector bubbles in the past – a reminder that financial and payments crises can affect all countries. The travails of the Caribbean offshore financial centres, already weakened by a series of damaging hurricanes, have been compounded by the global crisis. For example, Jamaica, which had restructured its debts several times, was bailed out in early 2013. The financial sector risks discussed below apply fully to this category.

Financial sector risks

Differing levels of development of a financial sector based on its size and depth relative to the economy, and its structure such as the role of the state banks present different types of country risk and vulnerabilities to global shocks. The categories of the banking and financial sector shown in Figure 5.4 highlight some salient features and their associated country risks as development progresses. In reality countries cannot be slotted cleanly into these categories and overlap. This also does not take into account the benefits and risks

FIG 5.4 **Banking and financial sector categories**

Source: Author

of the new frontiers in banking that are emerging through mobile banking and the emergence of e-money.

Small/lacks transparency

This is the case in many low-income developing countries with a large subsistence agrarian sector. They are typified by a cash economy where gold and land are the preferred savings instruments. Banking-sector presence is minimal in rural areas, though microfinance and mobile money are helping to change this by channelling funds to tiny enterprises.[5] Private-sector credit is under 30% of GDP (defined throughout this section as private credit to non-financial entities, average, 2008–10). Most of these economies are in sub-Saharan Africa where, for example in Angola, this ratio is 15%. The banking sector is mostly state dominated and relatively insulated against global shocks. The risks are weak transparency, low levels of financial intermediation and, often, high levels of fraud and corruption.

State dominated/inefficient

This typifies a large number of emerging countries where private-credit/GDP ratios range from over 100% in China to 30% in Egypt. The financial structures may seem to have low risks based on standard indicators and can survive for long periods. They may even show considerable resilience, as the underlying banking model is relatively conservative with low credit/deposit ratios and low reliance on wholesale funding from international banks.

The risks are more internally generated in these banking sectors. A 2008 Indian government report on financial sector reforms talked bluntly about India relying too much on force-feeding government debt to its financial institutions and the need to free up their balance sheets. Access to credit is politically directed and tends to be limited to narrow circle of government entities and cronies, which receive subsidised credits. Research by Sergio Lazzarini and colleagues on state-owned banks in Brazil (2002–09) showed that credit was noticeably allocated to firms in regions where government-allied politicians were facing political competition or firms that made financial donations to candidates that had won recent elections.

Many financial institutions may be effectively bankrupt, with high levels of non-performing loans to state entities. But this could remain unrecognised for long periods. If the fiscal position of the sovereign is strong, as in China, the non-performing loans are mopped up periodically and put into an asset-management company, clearing bank balance sheets for another round of subsidised credits.

These systems tend to be self-perpetuating and difficult to reform, with low levels of competition. According to the World Bank, banking sectors in the Middle East and North Africa have the lowest levels of competition relative to other developing regions. The Dubai banking sector is a case in point. Although it has many strengths and depth, and despite the deleveraging process since the 2009 property and banking crisis, Dubai banks' exposure to local and other government institutions is at its highest since the 1970s (see case study 4.4).

Control of interest rates is usually central to this model, with a high spread between deposit and lending interest rates, allowing banks to make generous profits. This encourages the growth of a shadow banking sector, attracting savings with higher returns. Shadow banking institutions are often highly leveraged and concentrated in rapidly growing sectors, such as the property sector, sometimes involving commodities as collateral. But as the situation in China shows (see case study 5.2), the liberalisation and sequencing of financial reforms are difficult to manage.

CASE STUDY 5.2

China: financial sector risks

On June 20th 2013, overnight borrowing rates in China's interbank market hit a record high of 30%. This shocked the markets and raised fears of default risks in China's banking sector. It also represented the tipping point of China's unsustainable credit boom and focused attention on the broader issues, particularly the shadow banking sector. Similar episodes followed in December 2013 and January 2014, this time coupled with the first default of wealth management products in China's shadow banking sector – the "Credit Equals Gold: No. 1 Collective Trust Product" issued by China Credit Trust and distributed by the Industrial and Commercial Bank of China. The first default of China's onshore corporate bond was on March 7th 2014 – a failure of coupon payment on a Rmb1 billion five-year bond issued by Shanghai Chaori Solar Energy Science & Technology Co. Then on 24th March came the first run on a small regional bank, Jiangsu Sheyang Rural Commercial Bank, which required the central bank, the People's Bank of China (PBoC), to step in.

The June 2013 credit crunch was widely believed to have been deliberately orchestrated by the PBoC as part of China's deleveraging policies to slow the growth of shadow banking activities. The episode is seen as a major policy shift by the PBoC, imposing greater use of market instruments and discipline. The same motive was behind the widening of the yuan's trading band in mid-March – a warning that the currency was not a one-way bet. Indeed, the PBoC's traditional administrative policy tools are increasingly ineffective in curbing excessive credit expansion to achieve economic rebalancing. But the transition is unlikely to be smooth.

China's credit market has become harder to navigate since the Rmb4 trillion ($586 billion) stimulus in November 2008. Subsequently, total social financing (the overall credit level in China, including bank loans, entrusted loans, trust loans, bank acceptance, net corporate bond financing and non-financial enterprise equity) rose from 129% of GDP in 2008 to 195% at the end of the first quarter of 2013, with shadow banking accounting for around 30% of all regulated bank loans, according the IMF. Although shadow banking activities in China comprise less complex products, the concentration on the overheated property sector and the use of commodities such as copper as collateral, under the guise of wealth management products, holds many risks, not least that of moral hazard. Commercial banks, as the conduit distributing these products, are not immune; nor are commodity traders worldwide worrying about the amount of off-exchange commodity stocks in China.

The root of the problem is the market distortions caused by China's limited flexibility and the drawn-out reform and liberalisation of interest rates. The expansion of the shadow banking sector is, to a great extent, a by-product of the financial suppression of China's fixed interest rates. The PBoC took the critical step of removing controls on the lending rate in August 2013, and but the freeing of deposit rates has been put off until a deposit-insurance system is in place. A structural rise in deposit rates, which could affect the profitability of large banks and state-owned enterprises and hurt local-government finances, is opposed by many powerful figures. This puts the PBoC, traditionally the most reformist of institutions, at loggerheads with those who are not prepared to sacrifice China's fast GDP growth for financial reform.

Mid-size/high vulnerabilities

This stage characterises many of the bigger emerging markets that privatised their banking sectors in the 1980s and 1990s, though some of the biggest banks may still be state owned. The depth of the banking sector is also extensive, with private-credit/GDP ratios ranging from 50–80% in Brazil, South Africa and Turkey to over 100% in Malaysia, South Korea and Thailand. Such economies generally have comprehensive deposit-insurance cover and reasonably good regulation, which has been honed during various banking crises.

These financial sectors also include some deeper capital markets, such as large money and corporate bond markets, and a growing financial services industry. However, deeper financial markets can increase volatility and risk, as they become targets of global capital flows. Studies show that while deeper stock and money markets can increase resilience, deeper debt markets are associated with higher volatility.

Currency and maturity mismatches, concentrations and off-balance-sheet accounting remain major risks in these markets. The banking sector is often the conduit of the external capital inflows that feed a domestic credit boom. Thus these systems are the most vulnerable to a sudden stop of capital inflows and currency

FIG 5.5 **Private credit as a percentage of GDP**

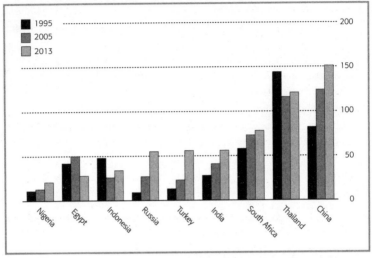

Source: IMF, WEO database

devaluations (which in turn increases non-performing loans), weakening bank balance sheets and potentially entering a negative cycle of banking crisis, sovereign crisis and default.

During the 2008–09 global financial crisis, credit growth of 36% at banks such as the Brazilian Development Bank and China Development Bank supported growth with a counter-cyclical lending spurt. This reversed the trend in the developing economies of a declining state share (of total assets) in the financial sector from 67% in 1970 to 22% in 2007, raising concerns about asset quality given the fast pace of credit creation over a few years.

Developed/complex

This group comprises banking sectors where the private-sector credit/GDP ratio is in a range of 100–200%. Some of the troubled banking sectors in Cyprus, Ireland and Spain have ratios of above 200%. Many of the risks above also apply to developed-market financial sectors, even though the more diversified and deeper bond, foreign exchange and commodity markets, stockmarkets, insurance firms, pension funds and extensive fund-management expertise enable more risk diversification.

The complexity and size of the financial sector and the concentration of assets, with some institutions being too big to fail, have become a major risk factor. The too-big-to-fail banks are now bigger, and banking in the US is more concentrated than before the crisis. There is also the self-generating functioning of financial markets, which are increasingly divorced from the real economy. These concerns are expressed in comments by a former UK regulator, Lord Turner, that in the UK a mere 15% of total financial flows actually go to investment projects; the rest support existing corporate assets, real estate or unsecured private consumer finance. The size and monitoring of shadow banking activities is another major concern. A report by the European Securities and Markets Authority in 2014 noted that shadow banking liabilities in the US stood at 92% of total US bank liabilities at mid-2013, down from a peak of 169% in the first quarter of 2008.

Financial-market vulnerabilities in developed markets have been amply exposed by the 2008 crisis, resulting in a wave of new regulation that brings its own risks (see Chapters 9 and 10). Another issue is the unprecedented expansion of central banks' balance sheets as a result of quantitative easing, which is blurring the line between fiscal and monetary policies. Before 2008, the role of central banks was defined around the objectives of central-bank independence and inflation targeting. The former is now at risk and the latter has been shown to be inadequate as it failed to deal with asset bubbles.

Economic policy risks

The previous section highlighted some structural weaknesses in an economy that could be the basis of payments crises and defaults. Ultimately, however, it is policies that cause payments crises, even when a country is well endowed with human and natural resources. When economic and political pressures increase (see Chapter 6), short of war or debt default, governments opt for a range of responses with different levels of risk. These could include policies such as capital controls that increase transfer and convertibility risks, or expropriation and nationalisation of assets, or licence cancellation. (These classic political risks and their possible mitigation are discussed in Chapters 7 and 11.) Short of these political risks are policy choices – or "rogue policies" – which also increase policy uncertainties and payments risks. In the past decade Argentina has experienced a range of these (see case study 5.3).

Protectionism

There is a universal tendency for national politicians to put the blame for a country's problems on external factors or foreigners. In countries undertaking politically difficult reforms it is the IMF; in EU countries it is the Brussels bureaucracy; in Africa it is Chinese neocolonialism. This deflection of responsibility onto a foreign entity becomes increasingly dominant as economic conditions deteriorate and the political legitimacy and domestic support of national governments weakens. What starts as mere political rhetoric can rapidly lead to bad policies, such as the repeated attempts by the US Congress to label China a "currency manipulator", which would trigger a series of protectionist tariffs and other actions.

As discussed previously, it has indeed become more difficult to manage national policies in a globally integrated world with large capital flows sloshing around. Contagion effects from external shocks and the persistent spillover effects of big-economy monetary and fiscal policies increase external risks. There are also difficult policy dilemmas, such as external competitiveness versus inflation targeting or the impossible trinity: simultaneously achieving the three goals of open capital markets, monetary independence and exchange rate stability. An easy option in the face of these pressures is to opt for some form of protectionism, whether against immigration, trade, or capital flows. This has become more evident since the 2008–09 crisis and may have brought about a pause in globalisation. But there is a risk that this may lead to further fragmentation of the global economy and international conflicts (see Chapters 8 and 11).

Resource nationalism

Governments are resorting less to expropriation or nationalisation of assets and opting more for demanding more onerous terms from foreign investors, sometimes called creeping expropriation. It can make sense for governments to renegotiate terms with foreign investors. Increased budget revenues, if used productively, strengthen a sovereign's ability to pay, and hence are potentially positive for the country and its investors in the longer term (see Chapter 7). Given the high commodity prices, many governments – including Australia, Kazakhstan, Mongolia, the UK and some in Africa – have sought to impose higher taxes or renegotiate agreements in order to tap into the profits of the mining companies operating in their country. The problem is that if this policy becomes a dominant political trend, it will eventually discourage foreign investment.

Government policy reversals and regulatory risk

A policy reversal can spook the markets. This in itself may not be important enough to bring about a crisis, but in conjunction with a wider weakening trend it can trigger an outflow of foreign capital, causing payments problems. It could be a hefty fine or tax, or nationalisation in a sector with a large foreign presence, or the decision to reverse a recently completed privatisation. For example, in Turkey in the 1990s privatisations by the government were challenged by left-wing politicians and reversed by the constitutional court.

Regulatory uncertainty is a major policy risk in all countries. For example, in the UK the promise by the leader of the Labour Party, the main opposition party, to freeze utility prices increased risks for foreign investors in the water and energy sectors. Regulatory risks are compounded by the complexity of most regulatory frameworks, which have usually evolved over time with a patchwork of legislation. Many sectors vulnerable to regulatory risk are state dominated. Even if they are privatised and have some form of independent regulator, the regulators may not be completely independent of the government. Hence it is important to understand the political pressures and agendas of governments to be able to identify the source of regulatory risks.

CASE STUDY 5.3

Argentina: fundamental strengths, policy weaknesses

Argentina has a long history of economic boom-and-bust cycles assisted by a succession of misshaped policies. The country's rich natural resources combined with its human capital present a strong lure for investors, but its ever-changing policies and unstable political, and sometimes social, environment keep country risks high. In the past decade alone under the successive Kirchner administrations there are plenty of examples of failed economic policies, guided by ideological rhetoric and short-term political objectives.

Nestor Kirchner came to power in 2003 when the country was emerging from one of its worst crises. Following its exit from the currency-peg regime and default on its $82 billion sovereign debt, which caused the economy to contract by 10.2% year on year, the country was presented with a golden opportunity. External conditions had turned extremely supportive, with rising commodity prices, booming demand for Argentine exports and low international interest rates. A strong growth cycle began, supported by current-account and fiscal surpluses. International reserves rose as exports regained competitiveness from the depreciated peso, allowing the country to thrive despite not having reached an agreement with its defaulted debt creditors.

However, government policies progressively weakened the investment environment. Kirchner refused to unwind the utility tariff freeze that was temporarily introduced during the crisis. As international energy prices continued to climb, domestic tariffs remained frozen. The most immediate impact was the deterioration of the business environment, as the government's actions constituted a violation of previously signed contracts and concessions. Eventually, this policy became the root of the energy crisis the country is facing now. On the supply side, it eliminated incentives to invest and increase production, in terms of both generation and distribution capacity. In the case of gas, demand grew even faster than the economy as its share in the energy mix grew. The implications were felt as early as the winter of 2004, when cold temperatures resulted in peak demand for gas that had to be met via imports.

Maintenance of the tariff freeze remains a populist measure that serves the government's electoral agenda while starving the energy sector of much needed investment. Across the sector, proven reserves and production fell, leading Argentina to cancel its long-term gas export contract to Chile, damaging its relationship with the neighbouring country, and eventually to rely on gas imports from Bolivia. Electricity generation often has to use more expensive, and also imported, fuel oil or LNG, and energy shortages plague industry. In oil and gas, the privatisation and investment incentives of the 1990s were unwound. Repsol, a Spanish energy company, which had bought YPF, an Argentine energy company, was initially pushed into selling a stake in YPF to a local partner. It eventually lost its majority stake in 2012, as Cristina Kirchner's administration blamed Repsol for lack of investment in the sector. The growing gap between energy supply and demand led the country to become a net importer, with a negative impact on the external balance of payments and fiscal accounts. The rocketing energy bill, as external conditions began turning against Argentina, eliminated the once strong current-account surplus. The fiscal accounts are struggling under the weight of growing energy subsidies and the spiralling cost of welfare handouts.

Over the years, the government has turned to increasingly heterodox sources of financing instead of adjusting spending. In early 2009, an attempt to raise export taxes on agricultural exports sent producers on strike and brought the country close to a political crisis. Later that year, the authorities found a new source of financing through the nationalisation of private pension funds. Now the public pension system provides the government with automatic debt rollovers and fresh funds. But this policy choice damaged and weakened the domestic capital markets. The authorities' next step in augmenting fiscal revenues was to create a deleveraging fund, which allowed the government to use the excess reserves of the central bank to pay down external debt. A further change to the central bank's charter increased the financing available from the monetary authority, in effect monetising the fiscal deficit. With these extremely lax monetary and fiscal conditions, inflation ran out of control, reaching an estimated 20% per year in 2007 to over 40% in 2014.

Externally, the narrowing of the current-account surplus and an increase in capital flight are eroding international reserves and weakening the peso. To slow import growth, the government raised non-tariff import barriers, mandated exporters to repatriate their dollar receipts, created a cumbersome bureaucratic system of import approvals, and eventually implemented strict currency and capital controls. These generated a parallel market, where the peso has at times traded at a gap of over 100% to the official rate. Having severed ties with the IMF and other multilateral sources of finance, and with international capital markets closed because of the bond holdouts, the government is left with few options.

In the first few months of 2014 there was an orthodox policy turn, though still under a guise of populist rhetoric, as the authorities resorted to an unexpected devaluation of the peso and attempted a rapprochement with the Paris Club. Dollar purchase restrictions were marginally eased and the banking system was forced to reduce dollar positions, thus increasing hard-currency supply and stabilising the official foreign-exchange rate. Peso interest rates were allowed to rise, though they remain negative in real terms. The authorities reached a compensation agreement with Repsol over its nationalised YPF shares in an attempt to encourage new investment flows to develop the Vaca Muerta shale gas and oil reserves, believed to be the second largest in the world. On the fiscal front, subsidies on utility tariffs were cut and bus fares raised. Annual wage negotiations present difficulties for a government that can ill-afford to grant wage increases to cover runaway inflation. Threats of strikes by former allied unions are increasing. The political and social climate during Kirchner's remaining months in power was expected to be highly charged, especially given the increased external pressure from the country's second default on its sovereign bonds at the end of July 2014.

There was a nascent wave of optimism about Argentina's prospects in early 2014 generated by the government's marginally orthodox policy adjustments, the May rescheduling agreement with the Paris Club of bilateral creditors and the expectation of a regime change in December 2015. However, until there is cross-party common ground regarding a strategic vision for the future, the prospect of changes in policy direction with every new administration will continue to be a major constraint on investment.

Pre-election expansionary policies and short-termism

Election-related easing of fiscal and monetary policies is seen in varying degrees in all democracies. The 2012 French presidential election was an example of this policy risk in an advanced economy with mature institutions. A budget spending spree when the budget deficit and public debt are already high may win an election, but it increases long-term risks. Electoral spending becomes particularly dangerous if it is financed by central or state bank advances, which amount to money printing. If also combined with low interest rates, this fuels inflation, which is often suppressed with price controls. Recent examples are in Argentina, Ghana and Venezuela. Some governments follow pre-election overspending with an abrupt tightening of fiscal policy, which puts a brake on growth. This then gives the economy a stop-go growth pattern, creating volatility and added uncertainty.

Election spending funded by savings in resource-based wealth funds is more benign. But it can cause an increase in inflationary pressures and, by eroding the fiscal cushion, weakens the economy's resilience to external shocks. This policy pattern was followed in Russia in response to the protests that occurred in 2011, following what was seen as election rigging in the parliamentary elections; it is also being deployed by the Gulf monarchies to stave off public protests similar to the ones in North Africa in 2011.

Policy short-termism in response to political pressures is just as evident in developed economies. The various short-term fixes the UK government has employed to solve the housing problem in London is a good example. It either has to build up into tower blocks, which attract mostly wealthy Asian buyers, or build out into the green belt, which the Conservative Party's constituency opposes. So a number of ineffective measures to make it easier to borrow have been implemented which make the situation worse by further boosting house prices.

One of the most creative governments in inventing short-term fixes has been Argentina's, where every possible policy mistake in this section can be found: utility tariff freezes that were temporary turned into permanent ones; blaming neighbouring countries for economic problems; contract renegotiation creating uncertainties and disincentives to foreign investors; nationalisation of crucial investments; raising export taxes; sequestering private pension funds into the public fund and government accounts; price controls; interest-rate controls; manipulating inflation statistics; central bank money printing; raising import tariffs; creating bureaucratic barriers for foreign-currency convertibility and a black market in foreign currency; not to mention the bad relationship with multilateral lenders and international creditors; and so on (see case study 5.3).

Policy off kilter with global/regional conditions

Another economic policy risk that can arise is the lack of fit between domestic policies and those of major trade partners. This is not a rogue policy like the ones above, but the failure of government policy to adjust to changing global conditions either through lack of understanding or because of political and institutional constraints. This was seen in the European exchange-rate mechanism crises in the early 1990s when the tight monetary policies followed by Germany after unification clashed with the needs of Italy, Spain and the UK, which needed easier monetary policies (see case study 4.1). Similarly, in the 1950s and 1960s when global growth was high and energy prices and interest rates were low, many developing countries pursued industrialisation behind protective tariffs. The lack of competitiveness of these industries was not evident until the 1970s crisis and the rise in energy prices. Only countries that had already prioritised export-led growth, mostly in Asia, came through the 1970s unscathed. Others, such as Turkey, lacking policy flexibility to respond to changes in global conditions ended the decade with a payments crisis. Similarly, the emerging-market model of export-led growth may have run its course. A competitive export sector is still crucial, but slower growth in developed economies suggests a new growth model is needed for emerging markets with more reliance on domestic demand growth.

6 Political and geopolitical risks

AFTER SEVERAL DECADES of liberalisation and countries competing to attract foreign investors, it seemed as if political risk had receded. But, following the global financial crisis, it is back. Cross-border investors now face a broader range of risks than seen in the 1960s and 1970s. The classical political risks of CEND – confiscation, expropriation, nationalisation, and deprivation – are still there (see Chapters 7 and 11). But political risk is now a more complex, multidimensional phenomenon, which requires broader analysis of the political, policy and institutional risks that weaken a country's payments performance and undermine the viability of investments. Furthermore, as discussed in Chapter 3, geopolitical risk has increased because of the current international global conditions.

Political risk is difficult to predict. Daron Acemoglu and James Robinson in their study of institutional development, *Why Nations Fail*, speak of "critical junctures" in history when the social, political and institutional trajectory of a country is interrupted and shifts. Geopolitical and strategic risks are even more difficult to predict because they build up gradually over a long period. Thus geopolitical risk tends to be underpriced by financial markets. Although in most cases it is only possible to identify a critical juncture after it has happened, country risk analysis can help identify the political pressures that are building up to a sharp political break and their associated risks.

This chapter focuses on political and institutional structures and social trends that increase the risks of political instability. Many political risk services provide data on political-instability indicators, such as number of terrorist attacks, which try to quantify complex social trends. This is useful for modelling political risk (see Chapter 8). But in this chapter the aim is to show how to identify the underlying causes of political instability at the global and country level. Political risks in transactions at the micro-level are covered in Chapter 7 and their mitigants are discussed in Chapter 10.

Geopolitical risk and military conflict

Geopolitical risk is the most difficult political risk to forecast and manage because its drivers are mostly long-term trends, spanning many decades, if not centuries. There are also frozen conflicts that rumble on for decades, defying diplomatic solutions, like the Israeli/Palestinian conflict or the status of Nagorno Karabagh or Kashmir, but carry risks that could erupt into bigger ones. North Korea and its attempts to establish a nuclear capability is an example of long-running risks. But as the example of North Korea suggests (see case study 6.1), even if it is impossible to predict what will happen in this most untransparent of regimes, it is possible to identify some patterns and analyse underlying trends at least to eliminate wrong scenarios.

Rising powers, collapsing empires

As some news headlines between March and June 2014 suggest, geopolitical risk is alive and well:

- "Nato's military decline", Wall Street Journal, March 25th 2014
- "Saudi Arabia: a kingdom on guard – the House of Saud is increasingly hardline at home and aggressive abroad", Financial Times, March 26th 2014
- "Philippines files case against China", Wall Street Journal, March 31st 2014
- "Playing Russian Roulette on Sanctions, Oil prices", Wall Street Journal, April 5th 2014
- "Conflict in Iraq adds new angle to US-Iran nuclear talks", New York Times, June 18th 2014

As discussed in Chapter 3, geopolitical risks have increased in the current international environment where older powers, preoccupied with recovery from the deep economic crisis, lack the appetite for a military confrontation. Meanwhile, emerging powers are testing their strength: not just the BRICs (Brazil, Russia, India and China), but also the second layer of middle-income countries that are trying to assert regional authority, including Nigeria, Saudi Arabia, South Africa and Turkey. It is also the case – apparent from the Iraq and Afghanistan interventions – that the increasingly complex, interrelated global and regional threats require a different range of policy instruments. The increasing use of economic sanctions, however, creates its own risks, as evident in the deliberations over how and which sanctions to impose on Russia after its annexation of Crimea without destabilising the global economy.

One of the most dangerous geopolitical risks today is the increasing tension between Japan, an established economic power with a military shackled by history, and China, as a rising power, and its neighbours over seabed rights in the East and South China Seas. How these countries, in particular China and Japan, conduct themselves will reveal their commitment to the rules-based international system. The spectacular growth of Asia is also rapidly increasing the demand for natural resources: oil, gas, water and food. This is creating a vicious cycle of resource stress, potentially increasing the risk of natural catastrophes.

CASE STUDY 6.1

North Korea: known unknowns

In May 2010, *The Economist* opined: "The only predictable thing about the Kim regime is its unpredictability" – a view just as valid today. However, while it is hard to foresee the exact nature and timing of North Korea's bad behaviour, there appears to be a framework of predictability consistent with Donald Rumsfeld's "known unknowns":

■ *The Economist* article appeared after the sinking of a South Korean corvette by North Korea, unpredictable in itself but taking place at a classic time for malfeasance – coinciding with the annual South Korea/US military exercises and the run-up to the April 15th anniversary of the birth of Kim Il-sung.

- In this window in 2012, North Korea carried out a long-range missile test; in 2013, it conducted its third nuclear test. In 2014 North Korea conducted short- and medium-range missile tests; and North and South exchanged artillery fire in disputed waters off the peninsula's west coast.

Clearly, there is a pattern, even if it is surprising that North Korea's show of strength in 2014 suddenly stopped on March 31st, especially after the threat of a new form of nuclear test. It was possibly due to pressure from Beijing, which can – but cannot be guaranteed to – act as a check.

The bigger surprise in the early weeks of 2014 was the optimism in Seoul over gradual and peaceful reunification following a commitment by President Park Geun-hye to lay the ground for it. In a perfect world, one would not rule this out as a long-run scenario. But in today's imperfect circumstances, a less Panglossian view looks more likely. Five factors weigh against the sort of process this would probably involve:

- North Korea shows no sign of relenting in its quest to acquire a nuclear capability. It is not clear that even the combined efforts of China and the US can prevent this, at least by means which do not involve a high risk of disorderly regime collapse. A nuclear North Korea would be even less likely to make – and stick to – necessary concessions.

- Furthermore, as North Korea pursues its nuclear and missile programmes, prospects for serious diplomacy seem bleak when, unless South Korea blinks first, the US remains reluctant to engage directly, and when relations between South Korea and Japan are an additional handicap to the resumption of talks.

- Even if negotiations were relaunched, it is hard to believe that North Korea's leaders would pursue to its conclusion a process which would see them lose power, especially now they face a clear risk of being committed to trial in the International Criminal Court in the wake of the recent UN report on the country's human-rights abuses.

- Domestically, there is clear evidence of a power struggle within the elite as Kim Jong-un looks to consolidate his grip on the country. It is not clear how far he would go to demonstrate strong leadership, but a fatal miscalculation, either domestic or in an act of aggression towards South Korea, cannot be ruled out.

- Reports indicate increasing level of contact with and knowledge of the 'outside world' among 'ordinary' North Koreans. Despite the high degree of repression and the power of the state's propaganda machine, this may, if only slowly, be increasing the risk of a popular uprising.

Thus any moves towards peaceful reunification appear likely to be overtaken by a paradigm-shifting crisis of one sort or another sooner or later. Unfortunately, it is the nature of such known unknowns that their timing is usually unpredictable.

The collapse of empires and long-running autocratic regimes is also associated with heightened geopolitical and political risks. This is evident in the gap between Russia and the new nations carved out of the former Soviet Union. The increased political risk that comes with these changes and regime change can quickly transform into default risk. The collapse of communist regimes in 1989 was accompanied by several rounds of rescheduling in Bulgaria, Poland, Russia and the former Yugoslav republics. Poland underwent 14 rounds of debt rescheduling between 1981 and 1994. The overthrow of the Mubarak regime in Egypt in 2011 would most certainly have led to default – not only on external debt but also on the more onerous domestic debt – if it were not for the financial support of the Gulf regimes.

The long-running conflicts in the Middle East are partly a reflection of the arbitrary carve-up of the mosaic of ethnic and religious groups in the region by France and the UK after the collapse of the Ottoman empire. To these have been added the sectarian division between Sunni and Shia fomented by the Saudi Arabian and Iranian regimes' domestic insecurities and their competition for dominance of the Gulf. These pressures have been amplified by international interference due to the region's strategic position on global trade routes and its oil resources.

Political risk in strategic countries

A country's international strategic position can be a major determinant of political risk. Those situated between big powers or on strategic trade routes are more likely to be involved in military conflicts through an adverse combination of domestic and international factors. A good example is Afghanistan, which over the centuries has been the object of various great games, as are countries from the Balkans to the Baltics sandwiched between western Europe and Russia. Similarly, in Ukraine, which has been an independent country only since 1991 and lacks a functioning army, interventions by the EU and Russia are threatening to split the country (see case study 6.2).

Being a strategically important country is similar to being a resource-rich country. Instead of the resource curse, there is the strategic country curse. The fiscal and foreign-payments position of a strategic country may look decidedly fragile, until the likely prospect of international financial support is factored in because of its strategic importance. Jordan lurches from one fiscal crisis to another, but receives financial assistance from the US and the Gulf states to maintain its position as a frontline state to Israel. Egypt's repeated fiscal crises have been overcome with several rounds of international debt relief to maintain its strategic role in the region (see case study 5.1). These funds provide short-term relief but postpone the resolution of the underlying issues that build up unsustainable debts. They also lock in the incumbent elite and a narrow circle of crony business associates, who survive on state-subsidised inputs and credit, insulated from normal global competitive pressures. It is no surprise that, other than in regard to the export of oil, the Middle East and North Africa has been the least globally integrated region; it is also not particularly regionally integrated, though this has recently begun to change.

Wars and default risks

History shows that military conflict is highly correlated with the build-up of unsustainable debts and default. Wars and military conflict feature repeatedly as one of the combinations of economic and political events associated with defaults. The 19th century is full of defaults that followed wars: the crises following the Napoleonic wars; the crisis of 1857, the first worldwide crisis that came at the end of the Crimean war; the crisis of 1864–66 at the end of the American civil war; and the 1907 panic after the Boer war and the Russo-Japanese war (combined with the impact of the San Francisco earthquake). Many of these wars were accompanied by speculative commodity bubbles that burst when the war ended, causing financial crises and defaults. In the 19th century there were also financial crises and defaults following wars of national liberation in Latin America; and the Bolivarian revolutions in Colombia, Ecuador, Mexico and Venezuela were followed by up to six rounds of default and/ or rescheduling. In the 20th century there was a series of defaults following the two world wars and major regime changes. Future historians are likely to consider whether the financial burden of the military campaigns in Afghanistan and Iraq, which lasted much longer than initially planned, could have contributed to the 2008–09 crisis in the US and UK.

CASE STUDY 6.2

Ukraine: worst-case scenario becomes base-case scenario

"Crimea annexation part of Ukraine worst-case scenario," says Donald Tusk, the Polish prime minister (*Reuters*, March 17th 2014). This quote reveals that even the Russia-sensitive east European flank of the EU did not expect the worst-case scenario that unfolded in Ukraine. But as already discussed, geopolitical risks have increased in an international environment where older powers lack the appetite for a military confrontation while emerging powers are testing their strength. As seen in Afghanistan, Iraq, Syria and now Ukraine, it is likely, though not inevitable, that the worst-case scenarios become base-case scenarios, and country risk analysis must factor this in.

In contrast to the alarming extreme rhetoric from political leaders, the market reaction to the annexation of Crimea was more measured. Ukrainian sovereign bond yields recovered at the end of March 2014 when IMF funding was agreed and the German finance minister, Wolfgang Schäuble, promised EU aid, reflecting the barely concealed enthusiasm of Germany to absorb Ukraine into the EU sphere.

But this is unlikely to be the endgame for Ukraine. Given the state of the Ukrainian economy (no money in the budget to pay pensioners, non-performing loans at 40% of bank assets, periodic cut-offs of gas supplies from Russia), and its fractured politics, not to mention the escalating diplomatic stand-off between Russia and the EU and US, and talk of a new cold war, any longer-term investment in Ukraine (and Russia) would have to consider worst-case scenarios.

Ukraine's independence in 1991 was based on an implicit deal with Russia to allow the old Ukrainian-Soviet elite to remain in power. Since then, despite the 2004 Orange revolution and the disastrous Tymoshenko-Yushchenko regime that followed, Ukrainian independence has remained tenuous. This was starkly illustrated by senior officers of the Ukrainian army defecting to the Russian side at the height of the Maidan protests, and has been underestimated by most Western politicians. Ukraine's link with Russia is not simply the large numbers of ethnic Russians in the country. It reflects deep historical ties, close economic linkages and Ukraine's heavy dependence on subsidised Russian gas. The perennial clashes with Russia over gas-price contracts, the dire state of Naftogaz's finances and the persistent build-up of arrears on gas payments to Gazprom, reveal the weak political authority and fiscal position of Ukrainian governments. Irrespective of who is in power, the energy sector remains a focus of high-level corruption, which boosts the fortunes of politicians and their allied oligarchs.

The Ukrainian economy managed a few years of growth on the back of commodity prices in the 2000s, but failed to recover from the shock of the 2008 global financial crisis. Two IMF standby agreements helped stave off default, but provided only temporary stabilisation. The SDR11 billion IMF loan of November 2008 was cancelled due to weak policy implementation, and the restructuring of the banking sector left incomplete. The SDR10 billion loan of July 2010 agreed with the Yanukovych regime was put on hold. By early 2013 another IMF loan was being discussed, with the government fishing for financial support from Russia and the EU by threatening to tilt further towards the other. But this time, given the intransigence of both the EU and Russia, these tactics were to trigger the series of events that not only caused the loss of Crimea but also left the country exposed to possible further fragmentation. By mid-2014 these risks remained high, despite a SDR10 billion IMF standby agreed in April and a newly elected president in Kiev.

Predicting wars or regime change, or when social strife will transform into civil war, pushes country risk analysis into the realm of uncertainty. One of the biggest defaults in history, by Russia in 1918 following the Bolshevik revolution, was not foreseen. But Ian

Bremmer and Preston Keat, in their study of political risks, *The Fat Tail*, note that "pure bolts from the blue hardly ever occur". They disagree that the 1917 Russian revolution was a black swan event (a rare event with an extreme impact that is not predictable statistically), arguing that the British knew the Germans were funding the Bolsheviks and the Russians knew Lenin would prove a threat. The extreme conditions in Europe at that time, and specifically in Russia under the provisional government, provided many pointers. But it is possible that the complacency that had characterised the European elite, who thought the first world war would never happen, was also extended to thinking that a Bolshevik revolution would never happen. Almost a century later, the Russian default of August 1998 took place. Creditors were lending up to the summer of 1998, underestimating the fragility of Russia's institutions and complacently thinking that superpowers don't default.

This was also the case with the overthrow of long-term autocrats in Tunisia, Egypt and Libya in 2011. Many analysts knew that these regimes were unsustainable. Moreover, it was understood that the overthrow of these leaders was likely to create a power vacuum resulting in civil strife. However, because they had lasted for so long, it was impossible to tell when or how these regimes would fall. It is equally difficult to predict when political risk transforms into default risk. Sometimes it is a long time coming. In the 1980s, during Iraq's decade of war with Iran, given Iraq's ample oil revenues and wide international support, Iraq's creditors could not foresee the combination of political events that eventually led to default and restructuring of $120 billion of Saddam-era debt.

Tracking social and political trends

There are also slow-moving social and political trends which, like geopolitical trends, are often difficult to discern until the critical juncture. For example, the rise of the British working and middle classes and the decline of the aristocracy became all too clear and had dramatic political and policy consequences following the devastating shock of the first world war. A more recent example of the reshuffling of the ruling elite is taking place in Thailand and Turkey. In both these countries urban, educated, bureaucratic elites have established a diversified economy with many strengths. But they neglected the rural population and the new urban migrants and failed to address regional income inequalities. They are now being challenged by these new political forces, with increasing political instability and risks. These types of risks are generated by long-term changes in demography, urbanisation, and economic and human development, and the evolution of political ideas. In this section a few such themes are explored; some, such as the rise of the middle class, are more relevant to emerging markets, but others are global phenomena.

The rise of the middle class in developing countries

One major social change over the past decade of rapid economic growth and urbanisation in emerging markets has been the growing middle class (see Figure 6.1). Historically, the middle class is seen as the source of entrepreneurship and innovation, and its values of education, hard work and thrift as major drivers of economic development. There is still some way to go as the middle classes in India and China make up only around 5% and 11% of the population respectively (based on a $10–100 per day earnings definition). But totalling around 200m this is still a lot of people, and already their consumption habits have established consumer durables and automotive industries as well as a range of fast-growing services sectors, transforming their economies. However, there is a risk that this growth trajectory is not a straight line and could even reverse if growth stalls or income distribution deteriorates. For example, in the mid-1980s South Korea and Brazil both had per-head income of around $6,000, and their respective middle classes accounted for 38% and 29% of the population. But by 2010, with a poorer income distribution trend and the political structure of a resource-based economy, the Brazilian middle class had risen to only 38%, whereas in South Korea it stood at 94%.

The various unmet aspirations and anxieties of this nascent middle class have contributed to an upsurge of protest across the world in Brazil, India, Russia, Thailand, Turkey, Ukraine and Venezuela, and also the Arab spring, and this trend is likely to continue (see case

FIG 6.1 **Emerging middle class by region**
Millions

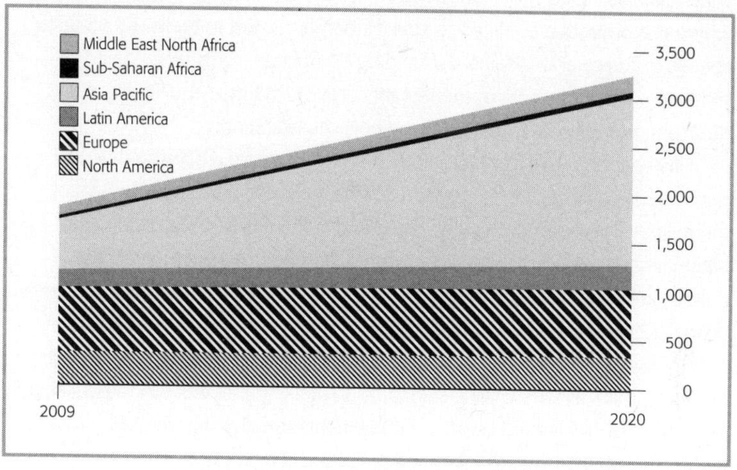

Source: Kharas, H. and Gertz, G., *The New Global Middle Class*, Brookings, 2010

study 6.3). Some of these protests, in Egypt, Libya, Tunisia and Ukraine, succeeded in overthrowing autocratic leaders. As history has shown, however, these wrenching regime collapses leave political vacuums in their wake which hold many risks – as seen in Egypt, Libya and Ukraine.

CASE STUDY 6.3

Emerging middle-class protest and increased policy uncertainty

It would have been impossible to predict the diverse triggers of the wave of middle-class protest in emerging markets in the past few years. These ranged from the self-immolation of a desperate stallholder in Tunis, a rise in public transport fares in Brazil, violence against women in India, to the destruction of a park in Istanbul. The political context of these disparate protests has also varied: some have been in authoritarian regimes of various types, others in long-standing multiparty democracies; some have reflected rural/urban divides, as in Thailand and Turkey, others a strategic/cultural orientation, as in Ukraine.

Political heterogeneity has been another striking aspect of these protests, which has increased policy uncertainty. This is not the case in Brazil and India, where the protests are related to specific demands. But in the wider protests, liberals in Turkey and Ukraine demanding democratic rights were joined by extreme nationalists; and women's rights activists in Egypt and Tunisia stood next to radical Islamists with opposing political aspirations.

Fifty years ago mass protests in these countries would have been led by public-sector unions or the bureaucratic elite, possibly including elements of the military. Their economic policy agenda would have been relatively clear: nationalisation of industry and banking and land reforms. But today, these policies are either discredited or no longer relevant. Some middle-class protesters echo the critical agendas of protest in developed countries: anti-globalisation, anti-consumption and environmentalist. But these have limited mass appeal in emerging markets where living standards are a fraction of those in the developed world. In their place there seem to be few transformative big ideas. In this sense, the decline of ideology has increased political and policy uncertainty.

The risk of national fragmentation

Another long-term political trend is the weakening of secular institutions. Although formulas vary, the separation of politics and religion in a secular state was a founding principle of many countries that became independent in the decolonisation era. However, the weakening of the modernisation model, the collapse of the socialist alternative and the pressures of globalisation have contributed to a resurgence of religious and increasingly localised identity-based politics.

This is a worldwide trend seen from the US to India, but it has been most evident in the Middle East. The Muslim Brotherhood-inspired political movements from Turkey to Tunisia aim for varying degrees of Islamising society and culture. But they seem to have no distinct economic policy angle, besides promoting their people into strategic economic and political positions. This promotion of religiously inspired self-interests in the political arena, combined with a majoritarian view of democracy, seems to be hollowing out secular institutions and the rule of law – already weak from the deep patronage relations – and creating a tendency towards autocratic rule.

The increased consciousness about religious differences easily translates into other ethnic or cultural differences. This deepens political polarisation and weakens national identity, potentially leading to national fragmentation. This has been the fate of Iraq and Syria and, most recently, Ukraine (see case study 6.2). Even if the country remains intact, the social, geographical and political divisions become entrenched, pointing to longer-term problems.

In democratic regimes, this is reflected in political and parliamentary deadlock. Rating agencies refer to political deadlock risk as a factor in sovereign ratings, as in Thailand, where, even after the military coup in May 2014, Fitch had warned that a key long-term issue was the ability of the country to overcome its deep social cleavages and become governable. As seen in Thailand, these pressures can either lead to a military coup or drive the incumbent regime to increase repression. As their domestic support weakens, these more repressive regimes become more belligerent internationally. This increases geopolitical risks, as seen with Russia in Ukraine or Saudi Arabia in the aftermath of the Arab spring.

Mature institutions in developed countries have not prevented these risks of national fragmentation and political deadlock (see below). However, these pressures tend to be managed politically rather than militarily, as seen in many emerging markets.

Political risk and institutions

Institutional strength is a crucial element of political and economic stability, (though it is not clear which comes first). According to Moody's, which has the longest historical database, around a third of past sovereign defaults have been directly related to institutional and political weaknesses, ranging from political instability, to weak budget management, governance problems, and political unwillingness to pay. Examples include the defaults by Mongolia in 1997 and Cameroon in 2004, due to weak budget management institutions and political uncertainty, Venezuela's 1998 default, due mostly to payment delays caused by administrative problems, and Ecuador's 2008 default, which was simply political unwillingness to pay.

These risks are explored in the context of institutional development. This categorisation should not be seen as exclusive. Figure 6.2 shows the relationship between the institutional strength of countries and

FIG 6.2 **Institutional strength improves with economic diversification**

Institutional strength index scores

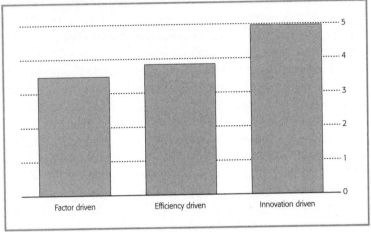

Source: World Economic Forum, Competitiveness Index, 2012–13

their basic economic structure, similar to the fundamental structural categories introduced in Chapter 5: advanced with knowledge industries (innovation driven), diversified (efficiency driven) and resource-based (factor driven). As discussed, resource-based economies have weaker political and market institutional structures; but it is also interesting that the scores of efficiency-driven economies are not hugely improved on the factor-driven ones.[1]

Political risk in countries with mature political institutions

Political risk is not high on the list of country risks in a developed economy with mature political institutions. Keeping political risk low is the flexibility and effectiveness of the political, policy and market institutions to respond to domestic and global pressures. But political risk exists and can rise sharply at times. Political risks include electoral uncertainties, collapse of governments, labour unrest, civil protest, terrorist attacks, and religious and ethnic disputes, as in Northern Ireland and the Basque conflict in Spain.

There has been an increase in political risk in recent years. In the US, political gridlock, gerrymandering, the extensive power of Washington lobbyists and the deterioration in income distribution suggest rising political risks. In the EU, high youth unemployment and the rise of xenophobic and protectionist political currents are increasing political risks.

Growing separatist pressure in Europe, as in Scotland, the northern regions of Italy, or Silesia in Poland, is another element of political risk. Given the maturity of the political institutions, these conflicts are mostly, though not always, mediated through the political sphere. However, depending on the importance of the region – such as Catalonia, known as the factory of Spain – separatist movements can increase uncertainty and reduce investment in the country, causing long-lasting negative effects.

There are also signs of weakness in institutions and loss of flexibility and creativity. In its rating downgrade of US sovereign debt, Standard and Poor's cited congressional paralysis over budget policy that increased risks of sovereign debt default. In the EU, critical decisions seem to be left to technocrats, bypassing the normal democratic political processes – for example, the replacement of elected by technocratic governments in Italy and Greece to pursue the tough reforms required by the troika – the European Commission, IMF and European Central Bank. The ultimate solution to the euro crisis requires further deepening of political, fiscal and banking-sector integration – and new institutions. But the European public mood is heading towards less interference by Brussels in national affairs.

There are also the risks of abrupt policy changes. An example of this was the 40% tax on mining companies' profits operating in Australia. Had it been passed in the form initially proposed in 2010, the policy could have undermined investment in this sector and had a negative impact on the Australian economy, potentially leading to ratings downgrades. (The resource super-profits tax was not passed and led to the resignation of Kevin Rudd. However, after intense public debate, a mineral resource rent tax was passed that was limited to a 30% tax on super profits – that is, above a certain threshold – in the iron-ore and coal sectors only).

There are also times – critical junctures in history – when, preceded by political and economic crises, social change comes abruptly. An example is the UK in the 1980s, under Margaret Thatcher's government, when the relative balance of power shifted dramatically away from nationalised industries and trade unions in favour of private capital and markets. After some conflict, institutions adapted to this with customary flexibility, in line with the country's tradition of managing big changes. Another example is the abrupt split with the Vatican and the establishment of the Church of England in 1534, which allowed the expropriation of church lands by the crown and strengthened the state. This history of management of dramatic changes in the UK may suggest that its EU membership should not be taken for granted. Understanding the history of social and institutional change in a country can reveal future risks.

Institutions lagging social and economic development

Political risk is a major element of country risk in countries that have recently become independent, are growing fast and have undergone rapid changes in their social structure. Institutional development inevitably lags behind the rapid social and political change, adding to the political tensions. Even if some have been a national entity for a hundred years or so, the institutional weaknesses can persist because of repeated political ruptures, such as military coups, social revolutions, or civil wars. The political and business elites are typified by insecurity, as evident in capital flight, and an inability to compromise and give up some control to adapt to change. Hence the only way change comes is through wrenching political shocks. But these in turn interrupt the gradual evolution and maturing of institutions. Thus they are often grafted top-down, rather than allowed to develop gradually, reflecting the local conditions. This means that by definition, institutions are rigid and are not good at adapting to change. Examples of these are too numerous to list here, but the economic and political institutional weakness of southern European countries from Portugal to Turkey with their long periods under military rule comes to mind.

CASE STUDY 6.4

The Russian modernisation debate: difficulties of diversification and institutional reform

The Russian modernisation debate that took place in 2008–10 highlighted the difficulties of diversification of a resource-based economy as well as the political and institutional challenges faced by Russia's transition from the Soviet era. Russian real GDP declined by 7.9% year on year in 2009, in sharp contrast to the performance of the other BRICs. That GDP fell so sharply, despite the drawdown of $221 billion of foreign-exchange reserves to defend the rouble and fund a massive fiscal stimulus of around 10% of GDP, exposed the weakness of the Russian economy. The reaction in the Kremlin was to blame irresponsible US policies. But, behind the rhetoric, Russia's dire performance triggered an intense national debate on modernisation and diversification of the Russian economy.

Everyone for modernisation

Two years after the 2008 crisis, the Russian government seemed to have finally recognised that the expansion of state enterprises had reached its limits and there was urgent need for institutional reforms to improve the business environment. The state's role in the economy had expanded to an estimated 50% of GDP as the government stepped in to rescue banks and automotive firms during the 2008–09 crisis. A priority agenda of reforms was announced to clean up the judiciary and law enforcement agencies, the tax regime and the visa regime. Everyone seemed to agree on the need for modernisation and diversification. But there was much disagreement on how. Should it be state led and top down? Or should it be bottom up, breaking up monopolies and accompanied by economic and political liberalisation?

"Authoritarian modernisation" by the state and the oligarchs ...

A long-term development plan, *Russia 2020*, published in February 2008, had already signalled that this process was to be mostly state led. Vladislav Surkov, first deputy chief of staff to the then president, Dmitry Medvedev, and the author, according to the *Moscow Times*, of the concept of authoritarian modernisation, was charged with leading the reforms, proposing a "Russian Silicon Valley" and an "Innovation City" (bringing back unfortunate memories of the closed Soviet science cities in Siberia). This top-down strategy also relied on the oligarchs. The Modernisation Forum organised in February 2010 in Tomsk was attended by the usual suspects: Viktor Vekselberg (Rusal), Mikhail Prokhorov (Onexim), Anatoly Chubais (Rusnano), Vagit Alekperov (Lukoil) *et al.*

... but without the people

There was a widespread reaction to this top-down approach. Mikhail Gorbachev criticised the Putin government for wanting to "carry out its programme of modernisation practically without the people". A small-enterprise manager from Nevsky Industrial Corporation in St Petersburg suggested at the forum that what was needed was "modernisation of certain big government policies", highlighting the conflict between the interests of the oligarchs and the Kremlin elite and those of small innovating enterprises. Institutional reforms were needed to break up the monopolies, bring a change of culture to support private enterprise, and create a level playing field through adherence to the rule of law that prevents *reidertsvo*, or asset grabbing. This was echoed by 200 or so signatories, mostly from the IT sector, to a petition in support of Aleksei Navalny, a candidate for mayor of Moscow in 2013: "We are entrepreneurs of the knowledge economy ... The rule of law, independent courts, and free elections are for us not abstract values but the most important mechanisms ensuring honest competition and protecting us from the arbitrary behaviour of the authorities."

Could Russia do a China?

China's success in managing a top-down, state-led modernisation and innovation process is unlikely to be replicated in Russia, as there are many crucial differences. One is that Russia's experience with communism lasted 70 years; China's was shorter and the entrepreneurial skills of the older generation had not been completely lost. With market reforms initiated first in agriculture in the 1980s, vast numbers of small and medium-sized enterprises could emerge in China in rural and urban areas. Some scholars (such as Mark Hanson of the University of Warwick and Debin Ma of the London School of Economics) argue that China's regionally decentralised authoritarianism is a crucial element of its success. Moreover, China's low wage costs and strategic policies (pro-US, signed up early to the World Trade Organisation) attracted huge amounts of foreign investment. China also has been able to tap the extensive Chinese diaspora in its innovation drive and in attracting foreign direct investment – a factor that has sadly worked in reverse in Russia.

The "Brezhnevisation" of the Russian economy

Russia lost its capacity to innovate in the 1970s when the Soviet economy ossified. Little progress was made in the 20 years following the end of the Soviet era when there was a huge brain drain of R&D skills abroad. Today there are signs that Russia's political and economic structure may have once again ossified, losing the flexibility to innovate and returning to the "Brezhnevisation" of Russia. The Russian economy bottomed out in mid-2009, but growth has remained fragile and capital outflows relentlessly high. With a weak private sector, the main domestic driver of growth remains the public sector.

Conclusion

The state can be a catalyst for innovation as seen in the Soviet Union (in the early decades), the US, the EU, China and many other countries. But for Russia today, unless it is combined with a bottom-up reform process that widens these efforts, these innovation plans in the Russian economy were always likely to have remained patchy.

Attracting increased FDI could support growth if the Russian investment environment could be improved. But in 2014, in the aftermath of the Ukraine crisis, given the direction of Vladimir Putin's foreign policy and the potential economic sanctions facing the Russian economy, it seemed as if the moment had passed. Policies aimed at improving the business environment, liberalising the economy and attracting FDI, and increasing innovation and modernisation are likely to be put on hold, leaving the Russian economy even more dependent on oil prices and the resource sector.

Political structures vary. But even countries that are nominal democracies tend to carry features of the old regime such as extensive patronage networks and crony capitalists. Sometimes the only element of democracy is periodic – mostly rigged elections, with otherwise highly restricted personal and political freedoms. Often the institutions to mediate change, such as a pluralist political system with a relatively independent judiciary that could provide an element of flexibility, are fragile or non-existent. Policy effectiveness can be strong, however, if there is a highly qualified and motivated civil service and bureaucracy as seen in many Asian countries. But even then, it tends to be hampered by the lack of independence of key institutions.

Institutional risks and large state sectors

Large state sectors tend to be associated with weak governance and market institutions. There are many good reasons for the state's role in an economy, including in developed countries where state funds in fundamental research have been the source of major technological innovations. The state can also be an important catalyst of development and growth in the early stages of development. This is often because an indigenous bourgeoisie with sufficient capital and skills may not exist. Or if they do exist they are in agriculture. Or they may have been driven out, as in the Baathist revolutions in Egypt and Syria in the 1950s. Or as with the countries of the Former Soviet Union, China and Vietnam, there may have been long periods of socialist transformation where private property was banned. Because of these conditions, the concept of the developmental state was strongly supported from the end of the second world war to the 1980s, when its negative features became more dominant. These included poor governance, extensive rent-seeking on the part of the newly emerged private sector, inefficient state industries which were not sustainable and politicians who held onto office through bribery and patronage.

In resource-rich developing countries, the political structures that emerge are often oligarchic and authoritarian. State authority is based on control of crucial resource sectors or their capture by a narrow elite, as with Vladimir Putin's regime in Russia or the royal families of the Gulf states. This perpetuates state dominance of the economy and fosters corruption and lack of transparency, increasing country risks. High levels of corruption and weak rule of law can limit investment in a country. The early enthusiasm of foreign investors for Uzbekistan, a country rich in cultural and natural resources, cooled rapidly because of the corruption and arbitrary policy measures of Islam Karimov's regime.

Corruption can be difficult to stop. In China, corruption cases crop up regularly in the media, and the authorities have pursued several high-profile investigations in recent years. But it is everyday low-level corruption affecting social welfare provision or education that risks eroding the legitimacy of the party–state apparatus. To tackle corruption at all levels, a major reform of the judiciary would be needed to establish the rule of law. This in turn would challenge the authority of the ruling party and require deeper political reform.

Furthermore, political risk remains high. Political unrest is often met with a combination of repression and state handouts. Budget reliance on tax revenues is usually minimal. Hence governments are under little public pressure to move towards a more transparent or representative form of rule. It is no surprise that Turkmenistan, which holds some of the world's largest gas reserves, is one of the most opaque regimes. These regimes also represent high risks associated with leadership succession – a process that becomes more unpredictable and disruptive the longer the regime lasts.

Once a large state sector (combined with private monopolies or oligopolies in key sectors owned by government allies) becomes entrenched, moving towards a more competitive and dynamic economy becomes difficult. (This is not to say that public ownership or a state role in the economy is always a bad thing. The points here concern the overall weight of the state in the economy.) The policy zigzags in Egypt's tortuous path to privatisation attest to this difficulty (see case study 5.1). Even if it is affordable, for example in the oil-rich Gulf economies, long-term productivity and employment issues arise in these public-sector dominated economies. The narrow elite structures that form around the control of public resources also have a tendency towards infighting and can suddenly collapse, as in Libya.

Avoiding implicit value judgments in political risk analysis

The analysis of political risk is often tainted by implicit value judgments. There is also now a well-documented home bias, whereby rating agencies from the US to China rate countries where they are based higher than others. Yet country risk methodology must make these selection criteria explicit. The analysis of political risk should avoid becoming an exercise that takes the political features of developed countries and scores the rest of the world on the basis of how each country approaches them. To be effective, it has to be based on an understanding that, depending on the starting point and specific features of a country and the global environment, there can be many different paths to political and economic development.

It is true that political risk is lower in high-income democracies. But as argued above, there is still political risk and at times this becomes the defining risk in generating a payments crisis, as seen in the euro-zone sovereign debt crisis. At the other end of the spectrum, political risk is high in autocratic regimes, especially if income inequalities are high. Such regimes have weak political institutions that lock in existing elites and reinforce nepotism and crony capitalism. Policy is unpredictable and prone to sharp reversals if the autocrat is overthrown. When this happens there may be no clear successor, resulting in political instability, a power vacuum and possibly civil war.

However, under some conditions, autocratic regimes can temporarily boost growth; and if they bring a measure of centralised authority over a fractious and disparate political structure, they can reduce political and policy risk. Examples include the early years of the regimes of Nursultan Nazarbayev in Kazakhstan and Heidar Aliyev in Azerbaijan. After the traumatic transition from Soviet rule, both provided sufficient centralisation of state power and political stability for investment to take off in the oil sector and growth to recover. In Egypt, Gamal Abdel Nasser managed to strengthen the state and enacted a series of land reforms that provided a growth spurt in the 1960s. There can also be growth spurts when autocratic regimes are loosening their hold and liberalising, as seen with the performance of China under Deng Xiaoping or the rapid growth in South Korea in the 1980s under the single-party rule of Park Chung Hee. Hence country risk analysis needs to be based on not just a static picture of the political structure of a regime but also what risks arise at what stage.

7 Identifying country risk at transaction level

PREVIOUS CHAPTERS SOUGHT TO IDENTIFY causes of country risk at the global and national level, taking a top-down approach. This chapter shows how these high-level country risks translate into risks affecting cross-border transactions. The focus is not on the payments risks caused by the internal technical viability of the investment or financial transaction: that is the job of the credit analyst. The aim here is to highlight country risks that may negatively or positively affect transactions. This is needed because the analysis of country risk is then used to structure a transaction that can avoid those identified risks.

What are the country risks embedded in transactions, when considered at a micro-level? Not surprisingly, they are the mirror image of the top-down risks. However, each transaction will be vulnerable to economic and political risks in a different way, depending on its specific features, such as the sector, the commodity, the ownership, the geographical location and the type of financial product. Broadly, the risks are: transfer and convertibility; exchange rate and interest rate; macroeconomic and growth volatility; economic policy; regulatory uncertainty; sector specific; political; jurisdiction.

Cross-border transactions can take many forms, from the purely financial, such as derivatives or portfolio investments, to trade finance and direct investment, where physical assets are involved. Purely financial or portfolio investments are mostly affected by macroeconomic instability, policy, and transfer and convertibility risks. This holds for even derivative transactions, which have counterparty risks and, depending on the country of that counterparty, country risks. Most other cross-border funding and investments in the form

FIG 7.1 **Risk factors in breach of contract events**
%

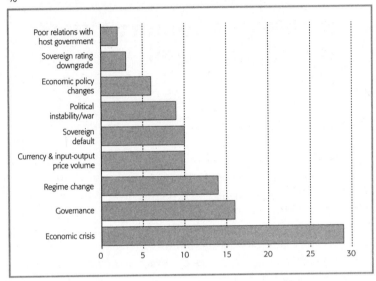

Source: MIGA-EIU, *Political Risk Survey*, 2013

of loans, trade finance, project finance and direct investment are vulnerable to all the risks listed above. This is because they could all affect the revenues and costs of a project, undermining the ability to pay at firm level. Even if an entity's ability to pay is not impaired, it may not be able to remit profits or debt repayments as planned due to country events. Lastly, the project may be expropriated or nationalised.

Transfer and convertibility risks

These are risks that arise when foreign-currency transfers are blocked either by a government order or because of a scarcity of foreign exchange arising from a generalised foreign-payments crisis. The blocked transfers could be remittances such as profits, or debt repayments abroad related to a specific transaction. The local entity, for example a mobile phone company, may be perfectly profitable, earning ample revenues to fulfil its profit-remittance or debt-service obligations, but it cannot convert its local-currency revenues into foreign exchange to send abroad.

This is a risk affecting all cross-border transactions, although trade-finance lines for vital imports often escape even the most draconian controls. Hence an analysis of the vulnerability of the economy to payments crises and an understanding of a sovereign's willingness to adopt protectionist economic measures such as the imposition of capital controls are essential for any cross-border investor.

Like sovereign defaults, wholesale capital controls on the outflow of capital are rare and happen only under conditions of severe economic and political stress. Short of an all-out transfer and convertibility freeze, there can be grades of control over the allocation and transfer of foreign currency. There are heavily managed currency regimes, such as in Venezuela, where foreign currency is administratively allocated, or selective capital controls in countries such as China, which have not fully liberalised their capital account. It is important to have knowledge of the currency market and the currency regime that governs payments, clearance, custody and transfer of foreign-currency payments, which are a major aspect of the operational component of country risk.

Before the 2008–09 global financial crisis, several rating agencies declared that this risk had receded. It was argued that globalisation and financial-market integration had made it too costly for governments to impose freezes on the transfer and convertibility of foreign exchange. However, the instability resulting from the crisis and the sudden stops and reversals of financial flows have reignited governments' interest in some selective capital controls – at least on the inflow of certain types of short-term portfolio flows. Brazil resorted to a wide range of controls, mostly in the currency markets, to slow hot-money flows to curb the appreciation of the real in 2011–12. This, and the tendency for more government intervention in the economy since the crisis, may signal that the risk of governments resorting to more significant capital controls may be back.

Exchange-rate, interest-rate and rollover risks

Unexpected changes in exchange rates and global interest rates can disrupt the repayment profile of a foreign-currency cross-border transaction. This can take two forms: transactional exchange-rate risk and operational risk.

Transactional exchange-rate risk refers to the risk that the value of a capital inflow into a country may be negatively affected by exchange-rate movements. For example, a depreciation of the currency will reduce the value of portfolio investment in a local stockmarket if it was to be repatriated at the new exchange rate. Since a currency crisis is also likely to coincide with a sharp fall in the stockmarket, this could be a big loss. If the currency remains weaker than at the time of entry, exchange-rate losses will persist even if the stockmarket recovers to pre-crisis levels in local-currency terms. Even derivative transactions are vulnerable. In 2008, with the sudden weakening of the Indonesian rupiah, disputes arose regarding currency derivatives sold by international banks to Indonesian firms, with the firms claiming that the derivatives were mis-sold and were too complex to understand; several were annulled by Indonesian courts in 2009, which led to high closing-out losses for the banks.

Operational exchange-rate and interest-rate risks arise in direct investments when the operational revenues of a firm are exposed to unexpected changes in exchange rates and interest rates. The impact of these changes depends on several variables, such as the elasticity of demand for the product, inflation and the currency of inputs. For example, the repayment of a foreign-currency loan from an international bank to a telecoms operator whose revenues are in local currency is at risk of a depreciation of the local currency.

Operational exchange-rate risks are critical to a foreign investor producing for the local market. In this case, the risk of currency devaluation or a rise in domestic interest rates depends on the elasticity of demand for the product. If the investor is Renault, producing medium-range cars for the local market that are purchased using consumer credit, price and interest-rate elasticity will be high and the risk is high. The *Financial Times* reported a €242m currency loss by Renault in the first half of 2013 partly because of movements in the Argentine peso. But if the investor is Procter & Gamble or Walmart, in the food and primary household goods industries, the risk may be low because price elasticity is low for basic consumer goods, giving more flexibility with which to offset higher imported input costs.

In contrast, devaluation of the currency is an advantage for exporters and outsourcing investors not producing for the local market. For example, foreign clothing manufacturers in Bangladesh benefit from a weaker currency because it reduces local costs and boosts the competitiveness of the exported product. In this case the problem would be an unexpected appreciation of the local currency. However, a chronically depreciating currency is often combined with chronic inflation and therefore an assessment of the costs and benefits of currency depreciation will need to take into account real exchange-rate movements. Cross-exchange rates are also critical for manufacturers: they benefit if the local currency appreciates against their imported inputs, say oil in dollars, but depreciates against currencies in their export markets, say the euro.

Exchange rate-depreciation risks are also largely mitigated on cross-border commercial loans to local companies resorting to foreign borrowing as long as they have sufficient foreign-currency-based export earnings. But these companies will still have interest-rate risks, as currency devaluation will heighten risk aversion to the country and raise interest rates at which loans will be rolled over. If the situation deteriorates, or there is a sudden stop of international financial inflows, this increases rollover risk – the risk that short-term trade finance lines and so on are not rolled over, as they would be in normal circumstances. To avoid this many domestic companies and banks maintain funds abroad that can be tapped to stop disruptions in foreign-currency requirements.

As highlighted in previous chapters, given the increased volatility of currencies and the regular appearance of currency and sudden-stop crises, all cross-border transactions should automatically be subject to an exchange-rate risk management process. Fortunately, currency and interest-rate risks are among the most developed aspects of risk management, and there are many hedging products and production and marketing strategies available to mitigate them (see Chapter 11).

Macroeconomic volatility

Strong and sustainable growth and a stable policy environment are among the most important factors influencing investment location decisions. But this is not easily achieved – many international firms and financial creditors invested heavily after the 2008–09 crisis in rapidly growing emerging markets, but since 2012 there has been a sharp slowdown in these economies. Investments dependent on domestic demand and producing for the local market, say consumer goods, are the most exposed to macroeconomic and policy risks (see case study 7.1).

CASE STUDY 7.1

Nestlé admits to errors in India expansion push

This story of Nestlé's experience in India reveals a catalogue of errors, which is unusual for the world's biggest food company with long experience of cross-border investments. Reporting from New Delhi, Amy Kazmin quotes Nandu Nandkishore, head of Nestlé's Asia business, who said that the company "made a mistake … focusing on driving the mass market, and we really ignored the emerging affluent segment". This exposed Nestlé's operational performance to three major macroeconomic headwinds in the Indian economy since 2012: the depreciating rupee, slowing growth and inflation. The rupee has depreciated as India's current-account deficit has increased, which in turn has fuelled inflation, making imported inputs more expensive and increasing costs.

The slowdown in economic growth has also affected the consumption of low-income families – the "large numbers of new, cost-sensitive consumers deep in the countryside" that Nestlé had targeted. In 2009–11, Nestlé's sales growth slowed sharply from 20% per year to 8%. The company has now switched tack to cater for the rapidly growing demand for premium products at the upper end of the market "whose household budgets are more immune to rising inflation and faltering economy". However, at this end of the market Nestlé is up against more competition from Ferrero Rocher and Cadbury. Nandkishore summed up the issue: "the challenge is developing an organisation that is able to manage the extremes of going after the rural market and the affluent" and to operate in a market characterised by wide income disparities.

Source: *Financial Times*, January 14th 2014

Short of a full-blown foreign-payments crisis, there are many degrees of macro-instability that can undermine the commercial viability of an investment and prevent the fulfilment of foreign-currency obligations. A sharp decline in economic growth due to an external shock, a sudden tightening of monetary and fiscal policy, or a political shock that causes a sharp drop in domestic and foreign investment can reduce domestic demand and lower sales and profits. The effects of inflation may be periodically offset by price rises (if there are no price controls), but if the product is exported, this would result in either a loss of competitiveness or the erosion of profit margins. If not curbed, inflation may become entrenched and lead to social and political instability. Eventually, anti-inflationary policies will have to be imposed with a sharp tightening of monetary and/or fiscal policies, weakening consumer demand.

Regulatory and policy uncertainties

Unexpected regulatory changes have become increasingly common micro-level risks that need monitoring. These are highest in highly regulated industries, such as utilities sectors, including power and water, and transport, where there are public subsidies. The deteriorating fiscal position of the sovereign may require cuts in subsidies, involving the foreign investor in politically difficult bargaining. Foreign investors rarely enter these sectors unless there are sovereign guarantees, such as in a power project, take-or-pay guarantees and fixed prices, called power purchase agreements. Even so, these sectors are a political minefield. If there is a change of government, the new regime may not be prepared to uphold the guarantees of the previous regime. Or, as in the Dabhol project (the high-profile failure of the Enron investment in the Indian power sector), the conflict could be between the central government, which is prepared to offer many concessions to attract foreign investors in infrastructure, and the local/state government (see case study 11.2). In the case of US-based AES Corporation, which acquired Telasi, an electricity distribution company in Georgia, the Georgian government gave ironclad guarantees to offset most risks and ensure a high return on investment. But soon AES-Telasi was making losses, caught between industrial consumers' building up arrears on their electricity payments and demands from the Georgian tax office for unpaid taxes.

CASE STUDY 7.2

Russia's state-imposed utility price freeze to hit GDP

The price freeze on Russian utilities is an example of country risks in the transport sector. Vladimir Yakunin, chief executive of state-owned Russian Railways, calls the price freeze imposed on rail transport fares in December 2013 a "purely emotional, political decision". It seems to have come as a surprise even to a domestic state entity and is likely to undermine its revenue stream and disrupt investment plans. Behind this price freeze is the periodic and unpredictable outbreak of political power struggles between the government and the heads of the powerful state enterprises. In this case, the freeze affects Russian Railways and oil and gas giants Rosneft and Gazprom. All three have high foreign-currency debt, thus exposing their international lenders to this regulatory risk.

Source: *Financial Times*, December 15th 2013

Economic policy may change radically as a result of a change of regime. Even without a regime change, taxation and trade policies may be radically tightened as governments try to strengthen a country's fiscal and foreign-payments positions. Unexpected liberalisation of trade policies that increases competition from imports can cause loss of local market share and negatively affect revenues for incumbent firms. Conversely, a tightening of trade policies and increased tariffs would provide protection against external competition but also increase the costs of imported inputs.

Taxation and regulatory fines have become common features of risk-facing multinational business. In the US, fines for foreign banks' non-compliance with its Iran sanctions, lax money-laundering, or other governance breaches have been imposed by US regulators, under political pressure since the 2008 subprime mortgage crisis. The public furore in the UK over the tax-avoidance schemes of Starbucks and Amazon is an example of governments needing to boost tax revenues to improve their fiscal position. Tax investigations can also be political tools used by governments to undermine targeted business entities, as seen repeatedly in Russia. This has also become a dominant policy of the government in Turkey, where tax investigations yielded revenue amounting to 1% of GDP in 2013, including the thinly disguised "routine" Ministry of Finance investigation into Koc Group for siding with the Gezi park demonstrations.

Sector-specific risks

Some sectors are more prone to speculative bubbles and economic and political risks than others. For example:

- **Banking.** The banking sector is very much driven by macroeconomic trends, and hence cross-border transactions with banks include almost every conceivable country risk (see Chapter 5). Banking and finance is also increasingly highly regulated. This leaves investors exposed to regulatory risks as found by many international banks operating in the increasingly highly regulated EU, UK and US markets.

- **New technology.** New-technology sectors that became the focus of investment bubbles include textiles, railways, dotcom companies and subprime mortgages (see Chapter 3). From a bottom-up perspective, a country risk manager needs to be wary of transactions in these overly popular sectors and should try to identify whether a commodity, credit, or stockmarket bubble is forming in the destination country.

- **Cyclical.** There are risks involved in cyclical sectors such as property, construction and associated heavy industries, driven by demographic and credit cycles. Analysis of demography, urbanisation and credit trends in a country is necessary to assess the risks in a housing or commercial property investment. The property and construction sector is often subject to political patronage, typified by lack of transparency in tender processes resulting in high corruption risks.

■ **Commodity price cycles.** These are a critical element in the analysis of risk if a country is heavily dependent on a few commodity exports for its foreign-currency earnings. Cross-border investments and financial transactions in the mining and agricultural sectors are vulnerable to these trends. As discussed earlier in the example of the peaking commodity price cycle and its impact on Australian mining, the risks are not limited to those in the end sector but ripple across the economy into supporting sectors, including suppliers of goods and services to the mining firms. There is also increased unemployment, negatively affecting the regional economy more widely. Cyclical trends can undermine existing contracts, especially in long-term investments, and cause conflicts between governments and investors over changing the terms of the contract.

TABLE 7.1 **Macroeconomic sensitivity of industrial sectors**

Highly sensitive	Medium sensitivity	Low sensitivity
Paper, metals, mining	Telecommunications	Environmental services
Capital goods	Technology & IT	Health care
Automotive	Media & publishing	Pharmaceuticals
Airlines, rail, shipping	Engineering	Utilities
Building materials	Construction firms	Cable TV
Oil & gas		Defence
Chemicals		Branded consumer goods
Retail		
White goods		

Source: Ganguin, B. and Bilardello, J., *Fundamentals of Corporate Credit Analysis*, McGraw-Hill, 2005

Jurisdiction risks

These are risks that arise because of a country's business environment. They can range from a fairly benign but critical lack of knowledge of a country's customs and culture on the part of an investor to the more intractable issues arising from red tape and corruption to environmental and liability risks. A good example of culture and taste risks is that of two global retailers, Carrefour and Tesco, which

Identifying country risk at transaction level **135**

failed to appreciate the importance of local tastes in emerging markets and had to retreat from many jurisdictions as a result. Jurisdiction risks include the rule of law and the independence of the judiciary and the regulatory agencies. The World Bank's Doing Business index ranks countries in terms of ten indicators: ease of starting a business; registering property; dealing with construction permits; trading across borders; paying taxes; getting electricity; access to credit; protecting investors; enforcing contracts; and resolving insolvency. By its own admission, these indicators are limited in scope and do not account for broader business conditions that would include a wider assessment of customs and culture, the quality of infrastructure, conditions in the labour market, the financial system, security of property, macroeconomic stability and general institutional strength. Business institutions are a critical factor in the country risk assessment of a project, especially if it goes wrong and legal action must be taken. The recovery ratio, or "loss given default", is a major determinant in the pricing of any investment.

Labour conditions are a main element of jurisdiction and political risk. Despite the still large rural population, shortages of skilled workers in coastal industrial regions are pushing up wages in China, and the cost increases are forcing many international firms to reconsider their decisions to locate in the country. Labour-relations risks are relevant not only in the establishment and expansion phase of cross-border investments, but also when disinvestment is taking place. This is a major risk as commodity prices fall, leading international mining firms to pare back investment plans. In South Africa, the cuts in platinum mines and 14,000 redundancies initially demanded by Anglo American Platinum required the intervention of the government to resolve; in Zambia, the chief executive of Vedanta, which planned to cut 7% of its workforce in the Konkola Copper mines operation, had to leave the country and the government threatened to cancel the company's mining licence before talks were set up to resolve the issue more amicably.

Related to this is the security risk to companies' assets and international personnel. According to a 2013 MIGA-EIU survey of international firms, civil disturbance accounted for 20% and terrorism for 6% of financial losses incurred over the previous three years.

Inadequate infrastructure is a major performance risk. This includes soft infrastructure, that is the level of education of the workforce and health facilities, as well as hard infrastructure such as roads, ports, energy and telecommunications – as mining companies in Mozambique have found (see case study 7.3).

CASE STUDY 7.3

Mining hazards of the frontier: companies that flocked to Mozambique's coal reserves face significant logistical problems

This story highlights the difficulties of lack of infrastructure in a frontier country, Mozambique, which a few years ago had been hyped as the biggest frontier in mining. It cites the challenges facing Rio Tinto, Brazil's Vale, Anglo American and India's Jindal. The resources (coking coal) are located inland in the Moatize basin in Tete province. There is just one colonial-era single-track railway line to the port of Beira, over 600km away. This is also used for passenger traffic and periodically is the target of a rebel group left over from Mozambique's long civil war that ended in 1992. The other option is to ship the coal on the Zambezi River, navigating its treacherous shifting sandbars and dodging the numerous crocodiles. Both options failed to even remotely reach the targeted amounts to be transported.

For Rio Tinto, the logistical problems of exporting the coal, overly optimistic estimates of recoverable coking coal at the Benga mine and falling commodity prices have caused it to write down $3 billion of Mozambican assets and leave the project. Vale has been forced to delay its export targets to 2017; but it is staying put rebuilding a 900km railway running north from Tete into Malawi and back into Mozambique to the deep-water port it is constructing in Nacala. Jindal is trucking its coal almost 700km to Beira. Meanwhile, Anglo American is reported to have scrapped its plans to acquire a majority holding in Revuboe, a coking coal project in Tete, for $550m.

Source: *Financial Times*, September 11th 2013

Corruption

As country risk analysis has widened its scope to include institutional structures, governance and business environment risks have come into focus. From the point of view of country risk management, corruption is a problem if it undermines a country's ability to pay by eroding public funds. Given the international regulatory framework now in place to prevent corruption, it is also a reputational risk for cross-border investors.

Corruption is a reflection of weak institutions. It is often defined as the abuse of public power for private benefit, implying the involvement of a public sector or political entity. However, it clearly is also endemic among private entities globally, judging by the long list of high-profile corporate governance failures in developed countries and recent attempts to fiddle the LIBOR markets.[1] Public-sector corruption tends to be limited by media scrutiny and the greater transparency demanded of public institutions in the developed world. Corruption in state services and political patronage are more associated with developing countries where social change is rapid, institutional development is sluggish and media freedom is restricted. The weaker the rule of law and market and political institutions, the higher are the risks of corruption, nepotism and crony capitalism.

Cross-border transactions are more prone to corruption in sectors that are dominated by monopolistic or oligopolistic structures and where state licensing is required, such as mining, defence, large infrastructure or construction projects, and utilities sectors. This was the main source of the Licence Raj (the system of licences, regulations and accompanying red tape that were required to set up and run businesses) in India before its liberalisation in the 1990s. Countries or regions where corruption is high tend to export it to the periphery. Smuggling networks also foster corruption along their routes. International sanctions imposed on Iraq spawned global corruption, which infiltrated several US- and EU-based organisations. Similarly, sanctions on Iran have generated smuggling networks that have allegedly drawn in Halkbank, one of Turkey's biggest state banks.

The release of funding by multilateral agencies now increasingly requires measures to ensure good governance of the funds. Policies that reinforce nepotism and cronyism and generate hidden subsidies are being monitored – even if entrenched political interests prevent them being significantly altered. However, a problem with this approach is that what is considered to be corruption in one culture may be a traditional way of doing business in another. In the absence of strong institutions, sometimes it is the patronage networks that provide a measure of certainty and security for local business. Hence the boundary between what is legal and what is not can be difficult to draw using developed-economy governance standards.

Political risks

Nationalisation, expropriation and licence cancellation are ultimate political risks where physical assets are involved in cross-border transactions. Radical nationalist governments, as seen in Argentina, Bolivia, Ecuador and Venezuela in the past decade, have nationalised and expropriated increasing swathes of their economies. But as the example of Rurelec in Bolivia suggests, these risks do not come out of the blue and are preceded by measures that show where the government is ultimately heading (see case study 7.4). It is important to understand political attitudes towards foreign investment in a country. Bilateral and multilateral investment agreements that have accompanied the liberalisation of trade and capital flows have reduced the frequency of these types of draconian measures. But as noted in Chapter 6, increasingly these political risks have been supplemented by a range of other more gradual government measures.

CASE STUDY 7.4

Rurelec plans to sue Bolivia

This is an example of how the assets of a UK-based power company, Rurelec, were nationalised. Interestingly, this was the case despite the investor being familiar with the Bolivian power sector, having advised in its privatisation in 1994 and appointed the chairman of Empresa Electrica Guarachi (EGSA), one of the biggest generating companies. Rurelec acquired a controlling stake in EGSA in 2006.

This was badly timed because in that year Evo Morales was elected president of Bolivia with a radical programme – he nationalised the oil and gas sector in 2006 and the telecoms operator (from Telecom Italia) in 2008. Among the programme's aims was the extension of electricity supply to all parts of the country, especially to rural areas where half the population had no access. The commercial viability of rural electrification, always a problem, would be a difficult challenge for private-sector power companies.

Rurelec's share price did not reflect the risks signalled by these developments and it continued to rally into 2008. Bolivia's withdrawal from the World Bank's arbitration body, the International Centre for the Settlement of Investment Disputes (ICSD), in 2007 also did not seem to raise much alarm. It was thought that EGSA's successful operations would insulate it from these moves. However, on May 1st 2010 the Bolivian government nationalised the three biggest power producers, including Rurelec's share of EGSA, and cut power prices by 50–60%. In 2012, after two years of failed negotiations for compensation, Rurelec resorted to international arbitration at the Permanent Court of Arbitration at The Hague. It is still waiting for a result.

Source: *Financial Times*, March 31st 2013

Expropriation and nationalisation

International investment treaties and increased global integration of supply chains have tended to reduce outright expropriation and nationalisation of assets. But they do still happen. These policies rarely come out of the blue and in most cases can be expected. The most recent example is the Argentine government's seizure of the assets of Repsol, a Spanish energy company, in 2012. This should have come as no surprise as it was preceded by a number of other measures, including the revoking of Repsol's oilfield licences by provincial governments. It also is typical of Argentina's economic policy since its debt default in 2002 (see case study 5.3).

These policies may ease short-term pressures, but are ultimately damaging to the national economy. President Hugo Chavez in Venezuela nationalised pretty much every key sector. But even though ample oil revenues have so far allowed the government to avoid payments problems, they have not prevented debilitating

FIG 7.2 **Financial losses due to political risks**
% total losses, 2010–13

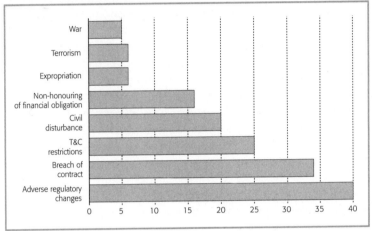

Source: *World Investment and Political Risk*, MIGA, World Bank Group, 2013

inflation, repeated currency devaluations, and shortages of basic food and household goods, causing widespread public protest.

Change of contract

This risk is highest in the extractive sectors where governments try to wrest more revenues from foreign investors. It has come to be called resource nationalism, though it is important to distinguish between radical nationalist rhetoric and attempts by governments to address legitimate concerns. A 2013 study by Paul Stevens and colleagues, *Conflict and Coexistence in the Extractive Industries*, reports a tenfold increase in the number of international arbitration disputes for oil and gas in 2001–10 (correlating with the commodity price boom) compared with the previous decade, with only three recent expropriations – Repsol in Argentina, Rio Tinto in Guinea and First Quantum Minerals in the Democratic Republic of the Congo – costing investors $13 billion. A headline in the *Wall Street Journal* (January 2nd 2014), "Resource nationalism rises and energy sector expands", refers to the expansion of oil and gas production in Africa and notes that South Africa, Mozambique, Kenya and Tanzania and others are preparing legislation for approval in 2014 that aims to increase tax rates and enable state entities to take increased equity stakes in new projects, and demand social investments and job-creation targets.[2]

This risk exists not just in emerging markets but also in developed economies, according to the Frazer Institute's *Annual Survey of Mining Companies*, because:

> [the] contract between government and extractive companies is inherently vulnerable. At the core of the problem is the absence of a practical formula ... to determine an equitable distribution of revenues between the state and companies.

One of the reasons this formula is difficult is that the relationship between a government and a foreign investor changes over the lifespan of a project. This has come to be called the "obsolescing bargain mechanism". The recipient government's bargaining power increases once the investor has sunk its capital in the country. Irrespective of ideological or political attitudes, both sides try to take advantage of these vicissitudes of power. Hence contract renegotiation remains a permanent risk at all stages of an investment in all countries, irrespective of the level of development.

A high-profile project can be the target of political conflicts and associated risks. These include projects in a critical sector to the country, such as a large investment in a power plant, a refinery, or a steel plant, which is respectively crucial to keeping the lights on, reducing the import costs of refined oil, or providing thousands of jobs. A high-profile project in line with the government's policy aims is a good feature of a transaction, as it will mean that the government will try to make sure it happens. But there is a risk that it could become the object of political conflict, with the opposition parties trying to block it. Or the conflict could be between the central government, which needs a successful high-profile investment and local government, which has not been consulted and is trying to wrest more income from the project as happened in the Dabhol power project in India (see case study 11.2). Or it could be that there is local environmental opposition to the project that is being ignored by the central government. Needless to say, if something goes wrong, it becomes a catastrophic high-profile mistake for the investor, probably shutting it out of that country for a long while.

There are also risks associated with investments related to politically important persons, or PEPs. High-level political contacts can facilitate an investment project, but it could easily become a source of reputational risk and liability if corruption allegations against any of these PEPs were to emerge. This is what Tullow Oil found out when it had to suspend drilling off the coast of Guinea because its partner, Houston-based Dynamics, was put under investigation by US regulators for possible breaches of corruption legislation.[3] Or it could leave the foreign investor exposed, if the local high-level contact falls foul of the government and has to make a hasty exit from the country – which happens frequently in autocratic regimes in Central Asia, for example.

CASE STUDY 7.5

Bankia purges 800 external directors

Risks embedded in transactions with politically important persons are shown in a news report on the purge of directors at Bankia, one of the biggest regional savings banks, or *cajas*, in Spain. Bankia was formed by the merger of seven *cajas* and nationalised in 2010. It then had to be recapitalised with a huge €24 billion bail-out in 2012. Reporting from Madrid, Miles Johnson noted that before its rescue the majority of its board were former politicians of the ruling Popular Party, or their family members, or trade union leaders. The bank was a symbol of the "heavily politicised and unprofessional management" of Spain's savings banks, which was based on political patronage and had big concentrations of assets to the property sector. The unsustainability of all this was exposed by the implosion of Spain's property bubble, which has reduced the number of *cajas* from more than 50 to less than 15 and forced the divestment of their control over many industries.

Source: *Financial Times*, September 23rd 2013

Political risk is not just in emerging markets; it is also a major issue for international investors in developed markets, especially when they are entering strategic sectors. US political sensitivity to foreign investment remains high in coastal shipping, airlines and communications. This was illustrated in 2006, when bipartisan opposition in Congress forced Dubai Ports, which had acquired P&O, a UK shipping company, to relinquish to a US company its control over port operations in several cargo and passenger terminals on the Atlantic coast. Nor is it a risk affecting only developed-country multinationals. Emerging-market multinational banks and corporations are only just beginning to integrate political risk into management strategies, learning many hard lessons along the way. An example is Egypt's Orascom Telecom, which having built up Djezzy, Algeria's biggest mobile phone network, faced a demand for $600m in back taxes from the government in 2009.

Conclusion

As the examples in this chapter show, country risk abounds in every cross-border transaction. Many are well known and some, as the discussion of the conflicts that arise between governments and mining companies suggest, are an inevitable part of the business. Others can be due to lack of sufficient due diligence, or too hasty decision-making by investors trying to gain entry in a competitive market. Yet others may suggest the wrong balance between risk and reward. But with the exception of fraud, which is not possible to predict, many of these risks are identifiable and to varying extent can be mitigated (see Chapter 11).

PART 2

Modelling, managing and mitigating country risk

8 Country risk models and ratings

Global debt markets have been vividly reminded recently of how
... violently a country can transition from risk-free to risky status ...
Investors are waking up to the significance of sovereign risk ... but
quantifying the appropriate premium remains difficult.

BlackRock Investment Institute, June 2011

AS NOTED IN CHAPTER 1, the development of probability theory
has helped us to think about and measure risk. The techniques that
were established still provide the basis for risk models used in the
insurance, engineering, nuclear power and oil exploration industries,
among others. But after the first world war, the scientific treatment of
risk, constructed around the laws of probability, gave way to a more
realistic understanding of the need to manage uncertainty. This was
particularly the case in economics because of the difficulty of trying
to impose scientific laws to model the underlying mechanisms of
economic and financial markets.

Previous chapters highlighted some of the specific challenges for
country risk, including the difficulties of predicting the "next crisis",
or forecasting political and geostrategic risks. But this is not to say that
one should give up trying to quantify and model country risks. There
is the old adage: "you can't manage what you can't measure". The
discussion below will assess the different methodologies developed
to measure and manage country risk and proposes a pragmatic
approach using a country risk-rating model that is one input of several
in the overall risk management framework.

Country risk assessment methodologies

Not surprisingly, given the complexity of this topic, there is a wide range of country risk assessment methodologies with different levels of formalisation, each with their strengths and weaknesses.

Qualitative approach and expert judgment

At one end, there is a purely qualitative approach with minimal levels of formalisation. Country assessments are based on expert opinion. Expert opinion can be bought in from external providers or provided by in-house analysts, and can even supplemented by a former ambassador to the country. This is a perfectly legitimate approach. Unfortunately, it is a necessary but not sufficient basis for managing country risk. Although country expertise is crucial, without a formal structure the opinion of an expert can easily be dismissed as being one among others who, often, may not be as well-informed. This approach could also introduce implicit subjective biases, making it difficult to compare risks in different countries consistently.

Formal quantitative methods and the search for a theory of country risk

At the other end is a formal quantitative approach using a variety of statistical, econometric and mathematical models. Some of the most commonly used are discriminant, or logit and probit models, which identify indicators to predict payment crises. Logit and probit are regression models used when the dependent variable is binary. Hence they are particularly suited to cope with the binary features of sovereign default risks (default or non-default), though they do assume that the probability of default follows a normal distribution. Other methods such as principal components models try to simplify the process by reducing the number of indicators.

Some people consider these to be "old school" and emphasise the need to model indirect risks, contagion and spillovers. Laura Kodres, an IMF economist speaking at a country risk conference, summed up the new frontiers in country risk models as having moved on from "normal statistical t-distribution stuff to extreme value theories ... way out there". Since the 2008 global financial crisis, modelling the sovereign probability of default has increasingly combined in-country macro-fundamentals with market data that attempt to capture the interconnectedness of the financial system with the sovereign, also extending this across sovereigns. The difficult task of modelling contagion effects is based on network theory or chaos theory. The latter is a complex mathematical approach which models dynamic systems that are highly sensitive to initial conditions. However, this aspect also makes longer-term prediction using such models impossible. There are also models aiming to quantify black swan events found in the fat tail of probability distributions. These draw on extreme value theory used by insurers that focuses on the statistical distribution of extreme events, such as earthquakes.

These exercises are mostly found in academic circles where the admirable but elusive struggle to devise a comprehensive theory of country risk is conducted. Theoretical efforts in this area have over the years borrowed from general theories of credit and combined them with contract theory, game theory or the theory of the economics of information. Basic finance theory used in credit risk analysis is often used to assess a country's ability to pay; the willingness to pay can be analysed using a welfare maximisation model of the costs and benefits of default. With the increased availability of bond-market data for emerging markets, studies have drawn on a combination of finance and portfolio theories. This analysis is benefiting from new ways of using big data and data mining, thus overcoming the limits of small samples normally associated with sovereign defaults (according to a 2013 Bloomberg study, there have been 251 sovereign defaults in the past 200 years).

All these techniques have their uses. But even the authors invariably feel obliged to add a disclaimer against any causal relationships these models may imply, warning of the "heroic assumptions" that have to be made and that:[1]

> [the] unit of analysis is unavoidably the country. Consequently, it
> is very difficult to identify exogenous variables ... the interpretation
> of many results in the literature is clouded by the inclusion in
> the estimated relationships of many endogenous variables as
> explanatory variables.

Moreover, because there is no comprehensive theory of country risk, the choice of explanatory variables remains ad hoc and many are correlated among themselves. In addition, forecasting abilities of such models are undermined by the use of constant coefficients derived over long periods in history, which will have witnessed sharp structural shifts. Some models try to overcome this by incorporating time-varying coefficients, but they too have to be derived from history. Hence, even if models manage to achieve a good fit in explaining past crises, they have many handicaps that pose barriers to predicting future ones, because each crisis is different. As for the use of market pricing and credit default spreads in predicting crises, financial markets may suggest when an indicator is out of its normal range and is due for a correction (reversion to mean), but they are no better at predicting timing, the trigger point, or the magnitude of crises. Furthermore, default risk is usually only one of the factors driving credit default spreads. Hence most quantitative modelling efforts limit their conclusions to pinpointing correlations and the need for further study.

A midway approach: measuring country risk on a relative basis

The limitations of using econometric and mathematical models to imply causality or predictability have led country risk managers to take a more pragmatic approach. This involves quantifying and measuring country risk on a relative basis and then trying to quantify sovereign default risk. Even if it is not possible to predict payments crises, this measure of the relative riskiness of countries can signal that the risk of a payments crisis has risen, at any given time and for any given country, relative to others. This approach is midway between subjective qualitative analysis and the formal, purely quantitative alternatives that presume some sort of scientific predictability.

This book builds on this pragmatic midway approach. As indicated in Chapters 3-6, it seeks to identify the combinations of global conditions and economic, institutional and political features of countries that seem to be associated with payments crises. This involves the use of a quantitative framework using a country rating model. Rating models essentially consist of a checklist of indicators associated with payments crises which are then quantified to measure the vulnerability of a country to crises relative to others. The proposed model is old school in its emphasis on fundamentals – the underlying causal factors that can result in payments crises. But it is also new in the emphasis and weight given to external push factors and cyclical indicators. Combined with expert judgment, a historical perspective and a focus on the bigger picture, as suggested in Chapter 3, this approach provides a framework for shaping an international investment portfolio and managing country risk.

Country risk indicators

The obvious next question is: what are the indicators of country risk that should be included in a rating model? Over the years, hundreds of indicators historically associated with political and economic crises and defaults have been considered in country risk analysis. The choice of indicators in country risk models has been influenced by economic theory and modelling techniques, the availability of data and computing power, as well as the experience of modellers testing which indicators seem to work best and modifying them. The scope of the analysis and indicators has widened too, from a narrow focus on the sovereign balance sheet in the 19th century, and then the whole country, to the recognition that external global factors have a role to play.

Sovereign balance sheet to development indicators

Until the emergence of development economics, country risk modelling focused on the debt-service indicators of the sovereign using a balance-sheet approach. Decolonisation in the 1930s and 1940s increased interest in economic development. The wider availability of macroeconomic data and computer power encouraged a wave of economic modelling using techniques that had been developed during the second world war. Influential theories, such as Walt Rostow's take-off model, emphasised capital accumulation and stages of development. In-country structural fundamentals, especially industrialisation, were seen as indicators of a country's ability to avoid payments crises, which at the time were mostly associated with the negative effects of commodity price shocks on developing country's exports. In the 1960s, fiscal and current-account deficits were highlighted in Hollis Chenery and Michael Bruno's two-gap analysis model.

Currency crisis models to multiple equilibria

The post-second-world-war optimism that came with Keynesian policies and economic forecasting fizzled out with the breakdown of the Bretton Woods system and the mid-1970s crises. As economic theory tilted towards the monetarists and rational expectations, the approach to country risk became more multifaceted. Inflation and currency crises became a major focus of empirical models following the 1980s Latin American debt crises. These payments crises were associated with policy-induced distortions and country risk model indicators reflected these views. Paul Krugman and Larry Obstfeld, two American economists, modelled the inconsistency between a government wedded to its currency peg, which becomes increasingly unsustainable because of loose fiscal policy, and inflationary pressures. Referred to as first-generation models, these failed to anticipate the Mexico or European exchange rate mechanism crises in the 1990s, which were triggered by sudden changes in international risk appetite and a reversal of capital flows.

This shifted attention from the current account to the capital account in the second generation of models. These explored policy options in a liquidity crisis, such as raising interest rates to defend an exchange rate in the context of a speculative attack on currency pegs (which were still common), and tried to capture the self-fulfilling nature of these crises. Features of the 1990s payments crises in Asia and the subsequent shift to flexible exchange rates by many emerging markets led to the development of the third generation of models. These began to incorporate the role of domestic banking systems and governance and other institutional factors. Off-budget contingent liabilities and private-sector debt indicators were added to ratings models.

There was also recognition of the importance of contagion effects, and studies focused on transmission channels and the importance of market sentiment. But this was limited largely to the examination of how crises spread, rather than on their potential causes. Rating agencies, which had only belatedly downgraded the crisis-struck Asian economies, modified their models afterwards. New indicators were added to track a country's vulnerability to external liquidity conditions, such as foreign-currency reserves to short-term debt, reserves to money supply, or reserves to external financing gap. But the conceptual framework remained the emerging markets and in-country over-borrowing.

Sudden-stop models and push factors

The focus on capital flows and international liquidity was new: a recognition that increased global integration and financial-market liberalisation were amplifying and highlighting weaknesses at country level. It was noted that the potential financial panic generated by volatile short-term capital flows could lead to multiple equilibria, where a country – such as Brazil in 2002 – could be at an unstable equilibrium and, depending on market sentiment, could either continue to service its debts or enter a negative cycle towards default. The term sudden-stop crisis was introduced in 1998 by Guillermo Calvo, who, along with others, produced econometric studies suggesting that "about 50% of the variance of net capital flows in Latin America was due to volatility of variables external to the region".

Yet these results were largely ignored and the overall focus of most country risk analysis continued to be on in-country imbalances. Calvo recounts how following the Mexican crisis of 1994–95, "the financial sector, particularly the central capital markets located in the United States and Europe, did not appear on the list of suspects" as a possible causal factor in many of the analyses by multilateral lenders.

Only now is the causal link between conditions in global centres of finance and payments crises elsewhere being given the attention it deserves. The 2008 global financial crisis, the subsequent euro-zone sovereign debt crisis and the potential impact of the US Federal Reserve's tapering policies on emerging-market growth are focusing minds on the contribution of over-lending to the causes of country

FIG 8.1 **Capital bonanzas and busts**
%

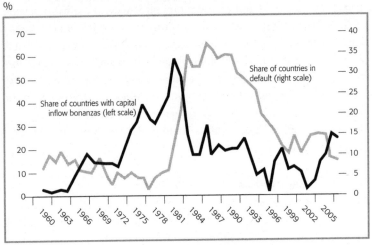

Source: Reinhart, C. and Reinhart, V., *Capital Flow Bonanzas: An Encompassing View of the Past and Present*, NBER International Seminar on Macroeconomics, 2008

defaults. Various studies identify growth differentials between advanced and developed economies, low international interest rates and high commodity prices as being key determinants of the push factors in a global credit boom preceding financial crises (see Figure 8.1).[2] Other historical studies confirm links between waves of sovereign defaults in Latin America in the 19th century with the bursting of global credit bubbles and the subsequent collapse in international liquidity in US and European centres of finance. Sudden-stop models draw on what is being called open-economy macroeconomics, and model the impact of potential shifts in external capital flows on the domestic economy.

Cyclical indicators

The 2008 crisis has also prompted more focus on cyclical factors in models such as the investment cycle, the credit cycle or the housing cycle, especially in the investigation of developed-market financial and payments crises. Awareness of cycles of the global economy and a greater historical perspective can help reduce future uncertainty by eliminating a range of wrong options (see Chapter 3). Because cycles have some consistent features – an initial trough, a cumulative expansion, a peak, a cumulative contraction and a terminal trough – tracking global business cycles and trying to identify associated turning points could impart a predictive angle to models by incrementally chipping away at the levels of uncertainty. However, this again by no means ensures predictability: just as each crisis is different, all cycles are different and unpredictable. As Michael Niemira and Philip Klein suggest in their book, *Forecasting Financial and Economic Cycles*:

> *In all likelihood, the business cycle ... will continue to evolve ... The role of the forecaster and analyst is to ferret out what is enduring and to distinguish it from what is not and to understand how those enduring factors are evolving.*

Rating model structure

The rating model proposed here puts forward an extensive range of indicators that could be included in a rating model. The aim is to provide a forward-looking framework that combines external factors affecting creditworthiness (or the indicators of over-lending) and the domestic imbalances and structural fundamentals associated with over-borrowing:

- In keeping with the direction of analysis in the preceding chapters, from the outside in, the first group of indicators tracks the external push factors. These include indicators of cyclicality and imbalances in systemically important global financial centres.

- The second group includes indicators of country vulnerabilities to external shocks.

- Push factors drive capital flows, but where they go remains closely related to pull factors or domestic economic and institutional conditions. Hence the third set of indicators consists of in-country political and economic features, or fundamentals, that assess a country's ability to pay and willingness to pay.

Many of the indicators in the second and third groups can be found in most country rating models, but those in the first group are usually absent, apart from a few such as Fed or LIBOR interest rates.[3] However, the focus of the analysis has remained on in-country weaknesses and even when focusing on the vulnerabilities, the external drivers of capital flows are excluded from the models and brought in only as part of the textual narrative. The novelty of the rating model proposed here is that push factor indicators are many and are endogenous to the model. This allows the country rating to reflect the changing global conditions incrementally, well before the external shock affects the country data. Furthermore, it would be possible to score the cyclical factors counter-cyclically, downgrading the country in the bubbly stage of a credit crisis as seen from the global credit-growth data. The broad categories of these indicators are listed below:

1 Push factors driving over-lending and cyclical indicators

- Trends in global financial centres (US, UK, EU, China, Japan)
- International interest rates and interbank rates
- International cross-exchange rate relevant to the region
- Credit growth in systemically important economies
- Market volatility indicators
- Rate of change of commodity prices and asset prices
- Electoral cycle
- Global leading indicators (OECD, Baltic Dry indexes)

2 External vulnerabilities

- Trade concentrations, exports and imports
- Access to capital markets
- Savings and foreign-payments imbalances
- Exchange-rate imbalances
- External debt and liquidity indicators

3 Fundamentals causing over-borrowing

Sovereign and policy effectiveness

- Sovereign and fiscal stability indicators, contingent liabilities
- Monetary stability, currency regime and currency status
- Economic policy risks

Economic structure

- GDP growth, volatility and structure
- Economic role of the state
- Financial sector structure, size relative to GDP
- Demographic trends
- Competitiveness and productivity trends

Political and institutional risk

- Domestic political stability
- Exposure to regional or geostrategic risks
- Institutional structure
- Infrastructure and business environment

How to build a model

There are four steps:

- Decide which indicators to use based on the discussion below.
- Set thresholds on each indicator that signal risk levels and score accordingly.
- Assign weights reflecting the level of importance given to each indicator and groups of indicators.
- Add up the weighted scores to give an overall risk score that ranks countries according to cross-border risks. This can be on an ordinal basis, where countries are simply ranked relative to each other, or in absolute terms, where the rating scores reflect risk distance.

Relevance and significance of an indicator

Which of these indicators should be included in the model? And how much weight should they have in the overall score? Using regression analysis, the indicators can be tested to assess their significance over any given time period and groups of countries. Weights can also be derived from these tests. Back-testing the indicators provides valuable information. But depending on the time period and the selection of countries, the results of these tests will show different results. Many empirical studies imply that the current-account deficit, or inflation, or the foreign-debt-to-GDP ratio is not statistically significant, for example. Whether they are statistically significant or not, the decision to include indicators in a rating model should be based on the a priori understanding of country risk as presented in Chapters 3–5 and discussed above. This exercise also departs from the normal discipline of econometrics by ignoring the inevitable correlation between the indicators.

Some indicators, such as the Fed interest rates, may only become significant once a decade. Hence the indicator may or may not have any explanatory power depending on the time period. A study by Paolo Manasse and Nouriel Roubini, *'Rules of thumb' for Sovereign Debt Crises*, comparing the importance of 50 indicators in 1970–2002 and 1990–2002, found that most of the top-ten indicators, consisting of total external debt/GDP and short-term debt/GDP, short-term debt/foreign-exchange reserves (and several variations of these), remained in the top ten; but other indicators, such as current-account balance/GDP, terms-of-trade volatility and openness, shot up in importance when tested in the 1990–2000 period, possibly reflecting the effect of increased liberalisation and global integration of financial markets compared with the earlier decades.

The importance of indicators may change over time. Per-head income has been a strong indicator to differentiate default risks between developed markets and emerging markets. But following the 2008 banking and sovereign debt crises in the developed world and the heavy burden of public debt, Moody's has decided to give more weight to GDP growth as an indicator of a country's ability to grow out of its debt trap. This suggests another important aspect of any quantitative framework: the need for regular review of the model.

Which of these indicators should be used will depend on what you are trying to measure (see Chapter 2). If the aim is to measure the risks of a broad countrywide payments crisis, many of these indicators are needed. For currency risks, a subset can be used. (For example, the Economist Intelligence Unit, which has 60 indicators in its country rating model, uses subsets of these to provide ratings for sovereign, currency and banking-sector risks.) For sovereign default risk, the focus should be on the sovereign balance-sheet indicators. For jurisdiction risk, the bulk of the domestic structural, institutional and political risk factors should be included, and the external indicators of push factors can be excluded. For constructing a short-term early-warning model, high-frequency data of vulnerabilities should be the focus. For assessing long-term country risks, the structural indicators and institutional factors that change slowly over time should drive the model.

One size does not fit all

Not all of these indicators will be relevant for every country in the sample. The model will need to accommodate the differing structure and level of development of an economy. Many model frameworks try to cope with the differences in economic structure by having two (plus two) models: one for emerging markets (with a subset for fragile states) and one for developed markets (with a subset for the euro zone). Another, more advisable, approach would be to have one model with inbuilt flexibility to adjust weights and thresholds to account for different levels of development of the country; the level of global integration or access to capital markets; whether its currency is a reserve currency; whether it is in a currency union; and whether in the past governments have been prepared to default.

Furthermore, the weights on various indicators, such as political risk, could have an interactive element – increasing when political risk deteriorates. The aggregate score on the vulnerabilities indicators could also be linked to the external push factors, so that the more vulnerable an economy is to external shocks, the greater the weight given to the external push factors.

Setting thresholds

How should you set thresholds for countries at different levels of development? At what level is inflation or the current-account deficit or the debt-to-GDP ratio dangerous? Tested across all countries, with the same thresholds and weights, some classic insolvency indicators such as the foreign debt/GDP ratio or the public debt/GDP ratio could be found to be insignificant. This is because developed economies have deeper debt markets and can sustain high levels of debt for long periods. This would suggest that it is necessary not only to weight indicators differently depending on the level of development of an economy but also to impose different thresholds to signal payment problems.

Thresholds may change over time. In the 1970s and 1980s hyperinflation was frequent, with many economies sustaining inflation of over 20% for several years. But more central-bank independence and better understanding of the dangers of inflation have reduced the threshold for danger signals. The same has happened with the public debt/GDP ratio: 60% was considered the threshold for significant risks, but studies based on recent crises show that 35–40% is a better cut-off point.

The thresholds become critical in signalling a payments crisis or default when there is a combination of indicators that are breaching danger levels. One indicator, say the current-account deficit, may look high but not yet signal a crisis. But when this high deficit is combined with other domestic indicators, such as a rapid rise in short-term debt relative to foreign-exchange reserves, accelerating credit growth, budget deficits and unfavourable trends in global markets, it becomes a binding threat to payments stability.

Other technical issues

Granularity

Generally, the more granular the model is the better, since this avoids cliff effects, where the rating suddenly rises or drops. To achieve this, thresholds for scoring indicators should be defined with several bands. This allows the overall risk score (of, say, 1–100) to move more frequently within one category of rating (of AAA to CCC), with the changes in the score giving early warning of pending rating changes.

Level, lagged, net, gross, log or volatility?

The model builders will need to decide on various versions of the indicators suggested: level, lagged, rate of change and so on. A model for measuring risk of sovereign default is affected more by the levels of the various relevant indicators. The early-warning function of a model is enhanced if the rate of change of indicators is tracked. Lagged data may have more explanatory power for some such as interest rates, which can take time to filter through the economy. Also definitions may vary. Some models use net foreign debt, which gives a more generous score on the foreign debt/GDP ratio as it subtracts the central bank's foreign-currency reserves and foreign assets from the total external debt.

Qualitative indicators

Granularity is particularly important for the qualitative indicators, which are mostly used to assess political risk and institutional structure. Qualitative indicators should be kept to a minimum and creative ways of quantifying them should be sought. For example, central-bank independence can be scored qualitatively (scores ranging from very independent to not independent), or inflation over the past five ears could be used as a proxy. On governance and corruption, many models use internationally recognised indexes such as Transparency International. There are also some specialised services which collect data on press freedom, or employee location security risks. Similarly, indicators of the business and financial environment could use the World Bank's Doing Business scores, or the standards set by the Financial Stability Board. These indexes should be used critically, however, and not be seen as the final authority. They may in turn be based on qualitative and subjective scores introducing implicit biases (see below). Qualitative indicators, especially for political risk, need to strike a balance between data that reflect political instability, such as the number of days lost in strikes or the number of terrorist attacks, and data that highlight underlying deterioration in the political environment, such as a worsening of income distribution, a sharp rise in food prices, or unemployment.

Adjustment factors

Models need adjustment factors (add-factors or overrides) because no model is able capture the extreme peculiarities of every country. Add-factors are particularly useful to score outliers, where extreme conditions prevent the normal functioning of the economy. These include fragile states or a country facing international sanctions, such as Iran. However, adjustment factors should be kept to a minimum and they should be tracked with a transparent audit trail. Their overuse signals either the need for a new model or weak analysis. The latter is the case if, for example, the rating is adjusted up (improving) when the problem is not the model but rather overly conservative estimates for GDP growth or another indicator driving the rating.

The time horizon, responsiveness of the model, pro-cyclicality

How forward-looking should the model be? If the time horizon is longer than three years, scenario analysis should be used. The model should signal improving conditions or deterioration early enough for the investing entity – bank, corporation or fund manager – to act. This implies that a forward-looking element should be built into the model that should score according to the forecasts for at least the next 12 months.

A related question is how responsive the model should be. Ideally, country ratings should not move around much. It is bad practice to upgrade a country and allow several investment decisions to be made only to downgrade a few months later. An upgrade should be based on long-term, sustainable structural improvements in the economic, political and institutional factors and a proven resilience to global shocks. Downgrades should come more easily. The worst thing that can happen is that a country is downgraded too late. Thus a conservative bias should be built into the models.

Ratings downgrades and upgrades are often criticised for being pro-cyclical. This is a difficult dilemma because country ratings improve when the investment cycle is in its boom phase because the data driving the model improve, and both deteriorate in the down phase of the cycle. To avoid this, many rating agencies rate through the cycle, which in theory should impart a counter-cyclical bias. However, if a country is moving towards a default, this prompts a large step adjustment (a cliff effect) in the ratings, triggering an overreaction in financial markets. Because of this, rating agencies' rating changes are criticised for mostly acting as lagging indicators.

But country risk management needs to have an early-warning function. Hence it is better practice to rate point-in-time and structure the model to have a forward-looking angle by including leading indicators. These include early indicators of different types of crises. For example, currency crises are mostly preceded by an overvalued currency, and banking crises by a credit bubble or a sharp decline in the currency and asset markets. Early warning is enhanced with the inclusion of factors such as the OECD leading indicators that show possible cyclical inflection points.

The aim is to build a model that signals a downgrade before the peak is reached, and a growth or credit cycle turns, thus preventing the concentration and high risks associated with the "bubbly" part of a cycle. Although not an easy task, this may be possible with the model suggested above. The leading and cyclical indicators are likely to include data on the rate of change of various cyclically driven economic factors, such as commodity prices, property prices and credit growth. The thresholds for these could be set up so that they are scored in a counter-cyclical way. For example, the higher the rate of growth of credit (in relation to GDP growth or other clever ratios) and the longer it goes on, the more of a negative impact it has on the score.

One problem with this is that the model may signal a turning point too early. What if the expected crisis fails to materialise due to an unexpected change in policy, an IMF bail-out, or an improvement in global conditions? This is where the function of even the best models stops, and a management decision has to be taken on when to respond to the signals.

Implicit judgments and prevailing misconceptions

An obvious problem is that this is a predetermined checklist and the indicators may miss the factors that will drive the next crisis. For example, after the 2008 crisis people realised that looking at the official policy interest rates set by central banks was not enough; they also needed to track interbank rates. This is why a model should be only one part of the country risk management exercise.

The choice of indicators is also vulnerable to popular trends in economic philosophy and prevailing misconceptions. As discussed in Chapter 4, in the 1970s it was mistakenly thought that oil producers represented hardly any sovereign risk. Investors and rating agencies overestimated the cushion of EU membership to east European economies and of the currency union to southern euro-zone economies. And the 2008 crisis revealed the dangers of the prevalence of "this time is different" ideas. Hence a healthy scepticism regarding prevailing economic orthodoxy is useful in constructing a model and is a valuable asset in a country risk manager.

The other issue is the implicit subjective judgments and biases about countries that, even in this model, can creep in with the answers to qualitative questions. (In a 2014 paper Unicredit, an Italian Bank, argued that the scoring of the qualitative factors by sovereign ratings agencies introduced large distortions to the scores of the euro-zone periphery sovereigns.) Bullish or bearish biases regarding a country or region are an inevitable part of this exercise. Instituting cross-regional checks on the scoring of qualitative questions or rotating analysts can help deal with these outlook biases. What about political and value judgments? In social sciences it is of course impossible to have a purely objective stance. Our approach and the questions we ask are based on our values. The problem is not so much if there are value judgments but if they are implicit – when they become biases.

In conclusion, if there are all these problems with models, why have one? There are three reasons:

- First, this exercise is hugely educational, as discussion and debate increase management's awareness of risks and create a cohesive framework for assessing risks and opportunities.

- Second, and more important, a systematic methodological framework is necessary to discipline arbitrary subjective judgments about country risks and ensure that the investment decisions are as far removed as possible from subjective biases.

■ Third, it should be remembered that the country risk-rating model is only one component of a set of tools needed for managing country risks.

What next?

Once an approved rating model is built and the ratings produced, what happens next? The object of the exercise is to produce a diversified portfolio that avoids country concentrations (except in the case of the country of incorporation of the business entity, in which case there is no cross-border risk and therefore no country risk – see Chapter 2). This involves mapping sovereign ratings to probabilities of default and setting limits and other controls on country exposures. This is discussed in Chapter 10.

9 Country risk mitigation: global level

THE MITIGATION OF COUNTRY RISK takes place at three levels: global (crisis-prevention policies pursued by international organisations and countries); firm (micro-level risk management by finance and other organisations); and transaction. At the global level, efforts to manage pressures that can cause over-lending and over-borrowing have generated a growing number of international organisations tasked with increased regulation, supervision and international co-ordination of national policies. However, as suggested earlier, even if they can be put off temporarily or dampened, payments crises will occur. Hence this chapter includes a section on debt relief and rescheduling once crises strike and countries default. The result of these efforts is the complex rules-based international system we have today, which has had some success in global policy co-ordination in the aftermath of the 2008 financial crisis, but at the expense of increasingly impinging on national sovereignty, which itself can introduce new types of risks.

This chapter sits uneasily in this section of the book, which contains practical suggestions for measuring, managing and mitigating country risks. However, given the emphasis in previous chapters on global external factors in contributing to payments crises and defaults, it seems necessary to evaluate crisis-mitigation efforts at the international level. Chapter 10 discusses risk mitigation at the firm level with suggestions on best-practice country risk management structures, and Chapter 11 presents mitigation techniques for cross-border transactions.

Crisis prevention, reregulation and risks of international fragmentation

A major element of international crisis prevention is international supervision and regulation of the global economy. Regulation has ebbed and flowed over the years, and since the 2008 global financial crisis there has been another major increase in regulatory controls. Regulators themselves have not gone unscathed, having missed the massive growth of off-balance-sheet financial activities. This increase in regulation came after highly contradictory trends over the past few decades. The liberalisation of trade and financial markets in the 1980s was accompanied by growing reregulation. The current wave of regulation is potentially fragmenting global markets.

During the first globalisation era, the classical gold standard acted as the international regulatory force on domestic policies – as long as governments chose to adhere to it. When crises did take place, it was major central banks, such as the Bank of England, or big, powerful banks, such as JPMorgan, that would act as the lender of last resort. In the 19th century, the US Interstate Commerce Act of 1887 was passed to regulate the railway industry – not a surprising choice given its proclivity to trigger global economic crises. The 1929 crisis and the liquidity squeeze that followed left 12 Latin American and 9 European countries in full or partial default. A wave of regulation followed in the 1930s across Europe. In the US it included the Glass-Steagall Act, which separated commercial and investment banking activities.

International institutions of the time were unable to cope with the level of international economic dislocation. The League of Nations did not have much of an economic mandate. The Bank for International Settlements (BIS), formed in 1930, was largely dysfunctional until after the second world war. The 1933 London Monetary and Economic Conference to co-ordinate policies ended in disputes. Weak political leadership and the depth of the crisis led to a wave of protectionism as the most important international institution, the gold standard, fell apart. New international structures set up after the second world war drew on the lessons of the 1930s. These included the Bretton Woods currency agreement and associated institutions. What these efforts tried to achieve was "the first serious attempt in history consciously to construct an international monetary system that worked for the benefit of all", according to Robert Skidelsky, a British economic historian. These entities functioned in a global economy where capital and finance were still highly regulated and controlled, and cross-border financial flows consisted mostly of aid, multilateral finance and foreign direct investment (FDI). But trade was being liberalised.

The crises of the 1970s prompted policies that aimed at deregulation and liberalisation of the global economy and finance. In the US the share of regulated industries fell from 17% of GNP in 1977 to 6% by 1988. The Glass-Steagall Act was repealed in 1999. In the UK, many nationalised industries were privatised and the Big Bang financial reforms of 1986 abolished the City of London's old system of rules. However, governments also combined privatisation and liberalisation with new systems of reregulation. Regulatory bodies were set up to monitor and control the privatised industries of telecoms, power, water, air, rail transport and so on. In US telecoms industry was mostly deregulated in the 1990s, but the 1996 Telecommunications Act brought in new reregulation. The Big Bang in London was followed two weeks later by the Financial Services Act (FSA), which introduced a new system of regulation.[1]

This combination of liberalisation and reregulation of international finance continued following the 1980s debt crisis with the Basel accords (Basel I) in 1988, new accounting rules such as the FAS-15 in the US and an increased supervisory role for the IMF. Problems of regulatory arbitrage seen under Basel I soon led to the next set of Basel accords. Basel II was released in 2004, but its inadequacies were apparent even before it was fully implemented. Work on Basel III began in the aftermath of the global financial crisis and is still in the process of being implemented (for more on the Basel accords, see Chapter 10)

One of the most powerful new regulatory agencies born after the 2008 crisis is the US Financial Stability Oversight Council (FSOC) and its Office of Financial Research (OFR) as part of the Dodd-Frank Act of 2010. The Dodd-Frank Act is seen as the most significant change to financial regulation in the US since the 1930s. The FSOC and the OFR have powers to oversee not just individual financial institutions but the broader market in which they operate. These include the authority to collect information, using subpoenas if necessary, from any bank or non-bank financial institution and statutory powers to impose corrective measures, such as requiring financial institutions to shrink in size, become less entwined, reduce short-term debt, or set aside more capital.

Numerous international bodies have been set up to co-ordinate regulatory requirements and set international standards. The 1990s Asian crisis led to several task-forces being set up under the G10, the BIS, the OECD, the Institute of International Finance (IIF) and the IMF to study new global regulatory requirements and construct a "new financial architecture". Since the global crisis, the G20 has emerged as a key forum for the international co-ordination of policy and efforts to reduce "spillover" risks, though policy co-ordination seems mostly to happen when a crisis has already struck and at best aims to avert another one. There are now a large number of international organisations to provide guidance and co-ordination functions. The major ones include:

- The Financial Stability Board (FSB), set up in 2009 by the G20 from the previous Financial Stability Forum, is tasked with promoting co-ordination between national regulators and codifying 12 international financial standards.

- The Joint Forum on Financial Conglomerates (JFFC) brings together banking, insurance and securities (International Organisation of Securities Commissions or IOSCO). The banking arm is the Basel Committee on Banking Supervision (BCBS) formed in 1974.

- The International Accounting Standards Board (IASB) is responsible for the International Financial Reporting Standards (IFRS) set up in 2001. The Public Interest Oversight board (PIOB) oversees the International Federation of Accountants (IFAC) formed in 2005 after the Enron, Arthur Anderson, WorldCom and Parmalat scandals.

- Country risk has not been immune to the rise of regulation. The European Securities and Markets Association (ESMA) in the EU and Section 939F of the Dodd-Frank Act in the US are charged with the regulation and supervision of rating agencies.

■ The ESMA is one of three entities in the supervision of the European financial sector. There is also the European Banking Authority (EBA) and the European Insurance and Occupational Pensions Authority (EIOPA).

There are also many other standard-setting organisations that have legal authority. For example, the Financial Action Task Force (FATF) on money-laundering aims for a co-ordinated international response to increasing levels of illicit funds in the global financial system, with the authority to blacklist countries and financial institutions.[2] The recommendations of these bodies generally involve more regulation, but they sometimes have unintended consequences. Some governments arbitrage these criteria, and sometimes policies constructed in London or New York do not work in Dhaka and Kabul, with the regulations criminalising the informal networks that function in developing countries.[3]

In 2013, five years after the 2008 crisis, Christine Lagarde, the managing director of the IMF, saw the task of financial stabilisation as a "mission not yet accomplished", adding that she wanted to see the financial sector as a "Monet painting, not Kandinsky or Pollock". But there is also the risk that regulation is overdone and becomes too prescriptive, generating new forms of risks. The stringent leverage and capital requirements of Basel III and other regulations that restrict business models are already raising concerns that financial regulation has become too prescriptive, too complex. There are also risks that the many differences in national regulations could be arbitraged or could create conflicts leading to global financial fragmentation. While all would agree that the financial sector needs to be simpler, more transparent and more risk averse, the vigour and movement of a Pollock painting may be closer to capturing the risk appetite and innovative skills needed for a dynamic financial sector.

The pendulum may be swinging back. In early 2014, the bogeymen of the 2008 crisis – securitisation and the originate-and-distribute model – were once again being promoted as the solution to the lacklustre growth in developed markets. *The Economist* reported

"Back from the dead: the return of securitisation", referring to the three-letter abbreviations – ABS (asset-backed securities), CDOs (collateralised debt obligations) and other forms of repackaged debt backed with once considered risk-free triple-A rated assets as collateral – that had become demon words.

Evolving role of the IMF: multilateralism versus regionalism

The IMF has been given a crucial role in these international crisis-prevention efforts, but it seems to be struggling. It began operations in 1947 tasked with maintaining exchange-rate stability in a world of mostly fixed exchange rates and capital controls. Initially, it was mainly European economies drawing on IMF facilities. France was the first to borrow, and lending to the UK, when the pound was hit by a speculative attack during the Suez Canal crisis in 1956, established the IMF's role as an episodic international lender. It survived the collapse of the international monetary regime in the 1970s and reinvented its role as a crisis manager. In these early years, IMF lending peaked during the gold pool crisis of the mid-1960s and the oil shocks of the 1970s. The loans had few policy conditionalities, being structured only to ensure that the fund was repaid.

This changed radically in the 1980s. The onset of the developing-countries debt crisis in the 1980s and the recognition that it was mainly emerging markets that would tap IMF credit lines led to financing being increasingly linked to policy reforms to ensure debt sustainability.[4] The IMF provided large bail-out packages (such as the $50 billion lent to Mexico) to prevent a liquidity crisis turning into a solvency crisis and was allowed to lend into arrears (when Brazil and Argentina halted interest payments in 1986–87). In 1989, as the Berlin wall fell, the IMF expanded its role to assist with the transition of the former Soviet economies. The membership of the fund rose to 172 and its staff expanded nearly 30%, marking the heyday of the institution.

During the 1990s Asian crisis there was another expansion of the IMF's role, including enhanced surveillance and monitoring of countries' performance. The aim was to devise policies to avoid emerging-market financial crises and to prevent crises in the volatile periphery from destabilising the centres of global finance. Thus the IMF tasks had moved on from a funding role to one of crisis prevention.

But the conditions of emergency lending by the IMF in the Asian crisis were criticised for forcing the pace of structural reform and capital account liberalisation, too optimistic growth forecasts and insufficient attention to banking-sector vulnerabilities. These criticisms led to a reformation of the IMF's *Guidelines for Conditionality* to restrict its focus to its core areas of macroeconomic stabilisation. The Asian crisis also generated the perception that the IMF was being "instrumentalised" by the US and its financial institutions. The Asians reacted with a proposal to establish their own regional monetary fund, but this was rapidly shot down by those who thought it would dangerously fragment international multilateral co-operation. The IMF also had its critics in the US, who worried about moral hazard. Milton Friedman argued that the rescue of Mexico in 1994–95 encouraged irresponsible lending and that "had there been no IMF, there would have been no East Asian crisis".

After the 2008 crisis, efforts at crisis mitigation reverted to developed markets. There have been radical changes in policy recommendations, allowing the use of selective capital controls, which had been frowned upon in the 1990s. To cope with financing demands, the IMF's lending capacity was almost tripled to $700 billion (still on a temporary basis). A new flexible credit line facility was introduced with the ability to disburse very large sums quickly, not tightly constrained by quotas as in the past.

But this time the size of the loans made to euro-zone economies attracted criticism in the G20 forum, increasing demands for changes in the country representation on IMF's decision-making bodies to better reflect the growing weight of emerging markets in the global economy. There was also criticism of IMF's pre-crisis surveillance, especially of the euro-zone banking sector, and the repeated and large revisions in growth forecasts for Greece. The debates over the fiscal multiplier revealed confusion about how austerity policies worked. Some of these seemed to be a repeat of mistakes previously seen in the 1990s Asian crisis, but others apply to the economics arena as a whole. No one really knows how prudential policies, fiscal multipliers or monetary policy work in today's integrated global economy.

It has also seemed that IMF support helps gain time but may not always avert default. A 2014 Moody's report showed that half of sovereign defaults in 1983–2012 had been preceded by an IMF programme in the two years prior to their default. It also seems to take the intervention of the US Treasury (as in the case of the Brady Plan) and/or other major creditor governments to ultimately resolve a debt crisis. This was the case in the 1980s when the intervention of several US Treasury secretaries was needed to construct the Brady Plan, finally resolving the debt overhang that caused a lost decade for many indebted developing countries. In 1997, it required bilateral support from the US Federal Reserve, the Bundesbank, the Bank of England and the Bank of Japan to pressure 200 commercial banks to roll over a critical volume of short-term debts coming due in South Korea. (At this point in late December 1997, almost all of South Korea's foreign-currency reserves were depleted. This experience no doubt contributed to the massive build-up of reserves in East Asia.)

The IMF is in another period of retrospection and will have to be reformed. It was established by only 45 nations gathered at Bretton Woods; now the membership is 188. The founders of the Bretton Woods system had taken it for granted that private capital flows would never resume the prominent role they had in the 19th and early 20th centuries. Yet global capital flows had surpassed 19th-century levels as a share of global GDP in the late 1990s. The IMF was originally set up to lend to members facing current-account difficulties where capital flows were managed by capital controls. It is also revealing that the G20 proposal in 2010 to increase the voting power of bigger emerging markets such as China, Mexico, South Korea, and Turkey is still awaiting congressional support in the US, the IMF's largest voting member with a 16.75% share. US objections centre on the old moral-hazard issues, but there are also worries that changing the IMF's voting formula will increase the clout of countries with different economic and geopolitical interests from the US.

The travails of the IMF show how difficult it has become to cope with the volatility caused by large capital flows and recurring financial crises over the past three decades. We now have a paradoxical situation where there are wide networks of international organisations and efforts to manage and mitigate global crises. At the same time, there is increased public scepticism about these efforts, combined with the growing reluctance of many governments to give up more sovereignty. The weakening of the legitimacy of the IMF has led many governments to avoid or procrastinate in tapping IMF credits. These have included Angola, Egypt, Hungary, Turkey, Ukraine and others, which seek instead bilateral loans from China, Russia or the Gulf regimes, which are prepared to make finance available with fewer economic strings in exchange for more political and strategic allegiances.

Overlaying these trends there is the increasing heavy-handedness of major powers in international forums, as well as efforts by these powers to establish their own regional forums for co-ordinating and managing international affairs. These contradictory forces are most apparent in the euro zone. The resolution of the euro-zone crisis has depended on the establishment of the European Stability Mechanism (ESM), a regional monetary fund – an idea that had been rejected previously when it was mooted in Asia. In Asia, there is now the Chiang Mai initiative, establishing currency-swap lines among members. Other regional groupings abound, including the Andean regional fund, FLAR, the Community of West African States (ECOWAS) and the Arab Monetary Fund. These regional forums are an expression of the difficulty of global multilateral management, making way for smaller, more manageable institutions. But there is a risk that all these trends could fragment the multilateral international system.

Debt restructuring: voluntary versus market-based burden sharing

Debt restructuring is the second arm of international efforts to deal with payments crises, once a crisis strikes. The restructuring of cross-border defaulted debt has evolved from the colonial-era political and/ or military interventions, to the major debt relief of African nations by the Paris Club, to the current focus on private-sector involvement to avoid problems of moral hazard and find a speedy and orderly way of restructuring country debts.

CASE STUDY 9.1
Greece: a historic debt restructuring

The Greek debt restructuring agreed over the course of 2011, covering €206 billion of Greek government debt, was the largest ever debt restructuring. An estimated 74% loss in net present value (NPV) terms was agreed with 84% (97% with the activation of collective action clauses or CACs) of private creditors, designed to give Greece up-front debt relief of €106 billion (50% of Greek GDP).[5] However, this was criticised for being too little, too late, and Greece needed another bail-out within six months. It was late because the euro-zone treaties explicitly stated that there would be no bail-outs of member countries by other members and it took a year for Angela Merkel, the German chancellor, and Nicholas Sarkozy, then the French president, to agree an orderly debt workout process at the Deauville summit in October 2010. This departure from the previous position and the announcement that the private sector would need to bail in had a negative effect on the markets, and there were panic sales of not only Greek but also other indebted euro-zone countries' bonds. Paradoxically, despite its large size, the first bail-out was too little because the deep recession in the Greek economy and the further bail-outs required left the country with a debt/GDP ratio, as projected by the IMF in 2014, of 174% – not far from where it had been prior to the debt write-off. Worse still was the impact on the Cypriot banking sector, which had large holdings of Greek sovereign bonds; a bail-out of Cyprus was required in 2013.

The Paris Club

This has been the main international organisation involved in debt relief. The Paris Club of official bilateral creditors was founded in 1956 following a series of meetings in Paris to negotiate Argentina's default. At the time, financial flows to developing countries mostly took the form of multilateral lending and bilateral aid credits. In the 1980s, politically strategic countries such as Egypt, Jordan and Pakistan received major debt relief from the Paris Club. The same logic extended debt relief to former communist countries in transition and those affected by the first Gulf war in the 1990s.

The debt-relief operations of the Paris Club evolved further with the HIPC (heavily indebted poor countries) initiative in 1988 to deal with debt overhang in poor countries. This began with Toronto terms, proposing a 33% debt relief, but the realisation that more generous terms were needed to help overcome the debt trap for about 42 countries, mostly in sub-Saharan Africa, led to reductions of up to 80% of eligible debt with the 1996 Lyon terms.

Thus since its formation, the Paris Club has not only shed its core principle of not negotiating already rescheduled debt, but its operations have evolved from being a debt-collection mechanism to being a creditor-controlled mechanism for debt forgiveness. This evolution of Paris Club activities has created tension between official (and taxpayer funded) and private creditors.

Bondholder committees and the London Club

Early bondholder committees were formed during the waves of international lending and defaults in the second half of the 19th century. The Corporation of Foreign Bondholders of Great Britain, formed in 1868, and the Association Nationale des Porteurs Français de Valeurs Mobilières, formed in 1898, aimed to give UK and French creditors more negotiating power when defaults occurred and also to control financial middlemen. In the 1930s, with the UK and the US governments beset with their own problems, efforts to establish international co-ordination in debt restructuring failed to take off. In recent years, bondholder committees have formed sporadically, for example the Global Committee of Argentina Bondholders, though this was never formally recognised by the Argentine government.

The other private-creditor forum, the London Club, was formed in 1976, initially to negotiate the restructuring of loans to Zaire, which was the first to default after the international commercial bank lending bonanza of the 1970s. Its bank advisory committee negotiates on behalf of all banks affected. In the 1980s and 1990s there were more than 100 debt restructurings under the London Club umbrella. Most were considered successful, though some took a long time and were extremely complex, such as the 1983 Yugoslav debt restructuring, which required 30,000 documents to be signed in eight international financial centres.

The rapid growth of private-sector international capital flows in contrast to the relative decline of official lending in recent decades put the spotlight on private creditors to better manage the restructuring of defaults. The IMF bail-outs of the 1990s led to much discussion about the moral hazard that this was creating by making international private creditors more irresponsible. Furthermore, big write-downs taken by official bilateral creditors have increased the pressure on private creditors to bail in or burden share. This has become a central point of debate in the euro-zone sovereign crisis.

However, the private-sector creditors have not escaped unscathed. Of the $120 billion of commercial debt restructured in 1998–2010, some of the bigger ones included Russia ($31.9 billion with 50.8% losses – or reductions in NPV – in 1998), Argentina ($43.7 billion with 76.8% losses in 2001) and Iraq ($17.7 billion with 89.4% losses in 2005). The losses also varied widely, from as low as 9–11% on Uruguay's pre-emptive restructuring of its $3.1 billion debt in 2003, Pakistan's in 1998 and the Dominican Republic's in 2004, to over 70% on the debt restructurings of Argentina, Iraq and Serbia-Montenegro. Meanwhile, the Greek debt restructuring of €206 billion, the biggest in history, had losses of 74% in NPV terms (see case study 9.1).

Voluntary market versus statutory debt rescheduling

This brief review of the wide range of private-creditor losses in the past, and the more recent experience of Greece's debt relief and Argentina's debt-restructuring debacle, highlights the many problems of the market-based voluntary sovereign debt workout process: delayed, costly, unpredictable and disorderly. Other ways to make market-based restructuring more automatic and make it easier to impose losses on the private sector, such as some version of CoCos (contingent convertible notes, or debt convertible into equity if a pre-specified trigger event occurs), are thought to possibly increase contagion risks, widening and deepening the crisis. Hence there have been calls for a rules-based regime that is automatic, transparent and minimises resort to official funds and litigation by hold-out creditors.

Proposals for reforming the debt-restructuring process are based on either arbitration panels with different degrees of formalisation or a statutory framework. Along these lines, the idea of an international bankruptcy code based on the US corporate or municipal bankruptcy laws has been discussed for a long time. Most recently, a version of this has been proposed for the euro zone, the European Crisis Resolution Mechanism (ECRM), which is a fully statutory framework that is legally binding and requiring treaty changes. Somewhat less formal is the IMF's sovereign debt restructuring mechanism (SDRM), proposed initially in 2002 by Annie Kruger, when first deputy managing director of the IMF, which does not require a supranational legal entity but rather the creation of a forum that would function as an arbitration panel with the IMF providing interim financing. Both would require voting by a supermajority of creditors on the basis of aggregation across all claims. This is more powerful than collective action clauses (CACs), which require voting on each individual instrument.

The debate on debt restructuring and resolution remains in flux, caught up in the political backlash from the taxpayer-funded bank rescues in the UK and the US and the deep recession in the peripheral euro-zone economies of Cyprus, Greece, Ireland and Portugal triggered by their bail-outs. As yet there have been no moves towards formal statutory systems of debt restructuring or the establishment of an international bankruptcy court, which would breach many aspects of national sovereignty. And even if it were accepted, how would it be enforced?

Conclusion: whither sovereignty?

International co-operation can work. But some of the most successful recent examples, such as the concerted currency intervention by the G7 to support the yen after the Japanese earthquake and tsunami in 2011, have happened in the heat of a crisis, rather than to prevent one. Crisis-prevention efforts can work. But the structures and regulations that have been set up can also create unforeseen risks:

- Risk that the rules-based system is becoming too complex. The regulation involved in the current international rules-based system may have become too complex. Some experts warn that a rules-based international system can be destabilised, especially during global transitions of power. Moreover, the vulnerability of the system increases with the degree of complexity of the rules and anxiety among countries that one particular power may instrumentalise the rules to its advantage. There is also growing scepticism about the efficacy and viability of international rules and regulatory bodies. Some observers now promote uncertainty, or rather flexibility, as a better way of reconciling the highly flexible functioning of global markets with the interventionist agendas of rules and conventions set by inter-governmental bargaining.

- Risk of global economic fragmentation as multilateral bodies are supplanted by regional ones. The multilateral entities set up in the 1940s need to be reformed if they are to cope with the radical changes in the global economy. The old multilateral institutions based on the concept of sovereignty, such as the UN, the World Trade Organisation and the IMF, seem to be struggling with their tasks. They are being supplanted by new regional or ad hoc groupings, such as the G20 and the new trade blocs in the making in Asia, with China at its centre, across the Pacific (the Trans-Pacific Partnership or TPP) and across the Atlantic (the Transatlantic Trade and Investment Partnership or TTIP), with the US at its centre.

- Risk of increased impingement on national sovereignty. As the discussion about regionalism and debt rescheduling suggests, the solutions could potentially fragment the global economy and further impinge on national sovereignty. But compared with the 19th century, this time around national sovereignty is mostly constrained by rules-based systems imposed by multinational or regional entities, not colonial governments.[6] While policy and economic management at national level is becoming ever more restricted by global integration and large capital flows, authority is being usurped at regional and global level.

These growing constraints on national sovereignty, and the opposition to them, have been most apparent in the EU. The banking union framework agreed in 2014 further limits euro-zone governments' control over their national banking sectors. Even though euro-zone members had already accepted the loss of a significant amount of autonomy in managing their economies, the debt-relief packages for Greece, Ireland, Portugal and Cyprus took this to new heights. An inquiry by the Economic and Monetary Affairs Committee of the European Parliament into the workings of the European Commission, IMF and European Central Bank troika concluded that too often national parliaments were left out of the equation, and the way the troika worked hindered national ownership of economic reforms.

What consequences does this have for country risk management? Chapter 1 made the point that country risk management was an endeavour that arose with the establishment of national sovereignty as new nations came into being with the process of decolonisation. New nations are continuing to emerge, this time with the fragmentation of the 19th and 20th century ones. At the same time, sovereignty is being constrained by the size and volatility of global capital flows and is chipped away by the very institutions that have been tasked with crisis prevention and regulation of the global economy to manage this volatility. Hence it may be that trends in the global economy, decisions by international and regional entities and geostrategic risks become important determinants of country risk, increasingly pushing the focus of country risk analysis to the international level.

10 Integrating country risk into management structures

JUST AS THERE ARE NO MAGIC FORMULAS for predicting payments crises and political risks, so there are no magic enterprise-level organisational structures to make sure that country risk is appropriately managed. The structure that will work best depends on the sector, the type of cross-border business and the size of the investing institution. Informal structures may be suitable for smaller companies and banks, and the level of formality is likely to have to increase with the size of the organisation.

Given the close integration of the global economy today, it is crucial that country risk should not become a stultified, rigid, box-ticking exercise. Yet the impetus of regulatory requirements for risk management threatens to encourage just this. Several surveys of business executives suggest that for many firms, the reason for having risk management is that they are told they are required to have it. Effective risk management requires not rigid rules, but flexibility. Internal organisational risk structures have to be flexible and capable of responding to risks arising at unexpected times and places. More important than rigid rules, the internal culture of an organisation is crucial for this. An open and debating culture with independent-minded people is likely to signal risks earlier, giving management time to respond to them.

Earlier chapters described the historical development of the concept of risk and its management. Country risk management, in particular, emerged as a widely used systematic process after the second world war. Multinational companies were the first to grapple with these risks, which were seen mostly as political risks caused by the nationalisation and expropriation of foreign assets by newly independent nations. The breakdown of the Bretton Woods system in the 1970s and the ensuing currency volatility brought a new focus on management of international financial transactions, as treasury departments grappled with currency risks. The increase in international loans by commercial banks in the 1970s, and the wave of sovereign defaults in the early 1980s, increased the focus on country risk management in the financial sector.

Around this time, risk management in general benefited from the wider availability and greater power of computers, mathematical techniques such as the capital asset pricing model (CAPM) and risk adjusted return on capital (RAROC), and new derivative products to hedge risks. Risk management departments moved from small teams at the edge of the finance department to centre stage as independent risk-control functions in banks and corporates.

The 1990s Mexican, Asian and Russian crises, from early 2000 the scandals of Enron, WorldCom and Arthur Andersen, and the various probes into the financial sector following the dotcom bust created an additional incentive for risk management and provided the political impetus for a series of regulations. In the US, the Sarbanes-Oxley Act, passed in 2002, was seen as the most significant reform for corporate governance and risk management since the creation of the Securities and Exchange Commission (SEC) in the 1930s.

In finance, the increase in regulation came in several stages around the Basel accords from the mid-1980s onwards. It gathered speed in the aftermath of the 2008 financial crisis and frames country risk management at firm level. International regulatory co-ordination of national regulations is now conducted by the Financial Stability Board (FSB – formerly called the Financial Stability Forum), which was set up by the G20 in 2009. Among its tasks is to focus on reducing the moral hazard generated by the too-big-to-fail, systemically important financial institutions (SIFI), of which there are about 30, mostly US and European investment banks and a few Chinese and Japanese ones.

Regulation and the internal organisation of country risk in finance

Basel I

The regulation and management of risk in finance has been institutionalised with the Basel accords, which were initially proposed in 1988. The Basel Committee was set up in 1974 to ensure a level playing field for internationally active financial institutions. But the financial crises of the early 1980s switched its focus to regulation and crisis prevention. Basel I, which came into effect in 1992, introduced the concept of risk-weighted assets (RWA – the measurement of bank assets weighted according to risk) to calculate the minimum capital requirements to cope with unexpected losses without causing broader systemic problems. Sovereigns were considered to be low risk and had 0% weights if they were OECD members; exposures to all other sovereigns had to have 100% weightings. The former included Mexico when it became a member of the OECD in April 1994, the first developing country to join, and it became risk-free just before its financial crisis.

Basel II

The late 1990s debt crises led to a new round of regulation known as Basel II, which came into effect in 2004. Basel I had been criticised for being too schematic and lumping many different risk grades together. Basel II aimed to be more differentiated and used credit ratings to determine the risk weight of financial products. It gave banks the option to use publicly available external ratings (the standardised approach) or to use their own internal models (the foundation and advanced internal ratings-based approach) to calculate RWA and the total capital that must be put aside to meet the 8% hurdle for the capital/assets ratio. Table 10.1 shows the standardised risk weights that were specified for sovereign entities by Basel II, which Basel III has not changed (these also assume a loss given default or LGD of 45% and maturity of 2.5 years). At the discretion of their national supervisors, banks were allowed to give a lower rating to their own sovereigns. Basel II also refers to broader criteria such as access to foreign currency risks (that is, transfer risks) to be considered in assigning internal sovereign ratings:

> [T]here must be an ongoing monitoring of economic and political developments in the countries rated. The political dimension must include the possibility that a sovereign might be unable or unwilling to repay its obligations, or may not have access to foreign currency.

TABLE 10.1 **Sovereign ratings and risk weights: standardised approach**

Credit rating	AAA to AA−	A+ to A−	BBB+ to BBB−	BB+ to B−	Below B−	Unrated
Risk weight, %	0	20	50	100	150	100

Source: Bank for International Settlements

Shortly after the start of Basel II, it was realised that there was rampant regulatory arbitrage and that RWA encouraged securitisation and other innovations to shift high-risk exposures off balance sheet to reduce capital requirements. The accords were also criticised for being pro-cyclical, creating the impression that the zero risk-weighted assets were risk-free, and encouraging portfolio concentrations in low risk-weighted assets like government bonds and mortgages. There was also concern that different national regulators interpreted these guidelines differently – for example, defining capital more generously, thus giving their banks a competitive edge.

Basel III

These criticisms resulted in a new round of measures even before Basel II came fully into effect. From 2009 onwards, new proposals, called Basel III, sought to address these issues by introducing a liquidity coverage ratio to try to avoid the build-up of excess leverage seen in the 2008 crisis, and capital buffers and dynamic provisioning to reduce pro-cyclicality. By early 2014, most member jurisdictions had issued the final set of Basel III capital regulations. Despite an extended implementation deadline of 2019 to gradually phase in the liquidity and capital requirements, many banks appear to be implementing them sooner. This has caused concern that the regulations are undermining the expansion of credit and growth out of the crisis. Basel III is still a work in progress. Debates continue over how to strengthen the regulators, what to do about perverse financial incentives, how to manage non-bank financial institutions within the shadow banking sector and too-big-to-fail entities, the co-ordination of cross-border resolution regimes, and derivatives markets reforms.

A blame game over regulation of sovereign exposures

The re-pricing of sovereign risk in the euro zone since 2009 focused attention on the regulation and supervision of sovereign risk and revealed some of the problems of this increasingly prescriptive regulation. At the peak of the euro-zone crisis, Basel accords were criticised for the concentration of sovereign assets on bank balance sheets and for allowing zero risk weights for highly rated sovereigns. A blame game started among different regulators, with the chairman of the International Accounting Standards Board (IASB) calling this the biggest accounting scam in history. Basel officials in turn blamed national and regional – EU – regulators. They pointed to a Brussels directive that allowed the assigning of zero-risk weights to the sovereign debt of EU members and noted that the 2011 European bank stress tests revealed that only 36 out of 90 participating banks were applying an internal model for rating sovereigns.

The situation in the US, where Basel II had not yet been fully implemented, was even worse. The old Basel I directive of OECD/ non-OECD distinction was still being widely applied. US regulators had never really liked the Basel accords and limited Basel II to apply to only the internationally active US banks. According to remarks made by the US comptroller of the currency, John D. Hawke Jr, the initiative on capital ratios, the fundamental principle of the Basel accords, had come not from bank supervisors themselves, but rather from lawmakers reacting to the rather abrupt deterioration of the US banking system in the late 1970s. The loss of faith in RWA has led to the search for a more effective and simpler tool, the leverage ratio, which is being implemented more strictly in the US than in Europe.

This episode exposed the fault lines in the regulatory treatment of sovereign risk. It shows how the proliferation of national and regional rules with different regimes can increase risks of regulatory arbitrage and lead to unintended consequences. It also confirms worries that Basel III is too prescriptive, and combined with national regulations is adding a complexity bias when what is needed is to simplify. When regulation becomes complex and prescriptive, risk managers focus on the risk of not meeting the regulation rather than managing the real-world risks. It is on this aspect that Jacques de Larosière, one of the wise men of EU finance, observed: "after every financial crisis, there is a tendency to overdo the reregulation", arguing that to return Europe to growth again it needed a more "market-financed economy".

CASE STUDY 10.1

Regulating the external rating agencies

While country risk in the broad sense has not been an explicit focus of regulation, some aspects have come under more scrutiny. One of these is issues relating to rating agencies. In the US, the main criticism has focused on the overoptimistic ratings given to structured products containing subprime mortgages. In the EU, concerns focused on the belated and sharp sovereign debt downgrades at the peak of the euro-zone crisis of several economies, including Greece, Ireland, Italy, Portugal and Spain. This has accelerated regulatory scrutiny. But these problems were nothing new. The same criticisms of the main regulatory agencies had been made in the 1990s as the Asian crisis unfolded and several Asian economies suffered sharp multi-notch downgrades of their investment-grade ratings. Investigations had been launched into rating agencies by the US SEC and the EU Committee of European Securities Regulators (CESR) after the collapse in 2001 of Enron, a Houston-based energy, commodities and services company, following an extensive accounting fraud that also took down its accountancy firm, Arthur Andersen.

At the root of the problem, however, are two quite different factors. One is the business model of issuer pays, which characterises the biggest rating agencies. The second is not the fault of the rating agencies but of the regulators, which have increasingly embedded ratings in the regulation. And that is not all: the creation of the status of nationally recognised statistical rating organisation (NRSRO) by the SEC in 1975 established a monopolistic sector structure by giving only three agencies NRSRO status until a few years ago. Efforts have been made at several levels – EU, US, UN, G20 – to reform this sector and increase regulatory scrutiny to reduce conflicts of interest, ensure the independence of the ratings process, increase competition in the sector and reduce the hardwiring of regulations on ratings. The solution is to reduce overreliance on credit rating agencies by encouraging enterprises to generate their own ratings internally. Hence the trend is towards increased use of internally generated risk analysis of investments and financial instruments, including country and sovereign ratings.

The Basel accords have not addressed country risk in the broad sense, focusing on only sovereign risk and treating it as just another credit risk subject to all the requirements commensurate with the underlying credit risks. But they have provided a framework for integrating country risk into the overall risk management exercise. The use of internal risk models and the increased granularity of risk assessment required by Basel regulations also imposed a more systematic and quantified approach to the management of country risk. The calculations used by management to meet the required capital/asset ratio, as well as the calculations of the rate of return on a transaction, began to take into account country risk using the country rating as an input. Thus the higher the country risk, the higher the return had to be on the cross-border transaction to cover for the increased capital to be put aside. Moreover, national regulators have increased regulatory oversight of cross-border exposures. For example, the UK's Financial Services Authority (FSA – the precursor of the Prudential Regulation Authority or PRA) required historical records to be kept so as to verify whether the country risk assessment responded appropriately to political and economic events; and during the euro-zone sovereign debt crisis country exposures were subject to regulatory scrutiny.

Country risk management in multinationals

The management of risk in non-financial organisations has followed similar trends. In the US, the regulatory impetus on risk management in corporations came with the Sarbanes-Oxley Act of 2002, which required high levels of disclosure to avoid mainly fraud risks, with the internal audit departments being the key nodes. International standard-setting organisations, such as the Foreign Terrorist Asset Tracking Centre (FTAT) and the Extractive Industries Transparency Initiative (EITI), have expanded the regulatory restrictions on cross-border business. The concept of enterprise risk management (ERM) provides the most comprehensive framework for multinationals, though reports suggest this is not widely used. ERM aims to cover the management and mitigation of all risks from operational, IT and workplace safety, to political and security risks and natural catastrophes. For multinationals, the management of country risk – in addition to traditional risks such as exchange rates and political and macroeconomic volatility – also includes supplier risks in the globally connected production process.

The types of risks facing multinational enterprises have changed over time. In the past decade, the focus was less on political risks and more on environmental, governance, operational and reputational risks. There have also been growing demands for social responsibility to be added to risk management portfolios, particularly in mining companies (see case study 11.1). Following a lull in classical political risks such as nationalisation and expropriation, it appears that political risk is back, but with a change of form to risks arising from regulatory and contract renegotiation. Moreover, regime-change risks (as seen in the Arab spring countries) and geostrategic risks (as seen in Ukraine) seem to be increasing, resulting in heightened country risks for cross-border investments.

The management of country risk for non-financial organisations has two distinct (though related) stages. The first is similar to that of financial institutions, where decisions must be made on which country to invest in. This is done by conducting a thorough country risk analysis as suggested in Chapters 4–6 and possibly using ratings to incorporate a country risk premium in various capital budgeting and cash-flow calculations. The second is the subsequent management of country risks facing the international subsidiary. Once a multinational has put bricks and mortar on the ground it is committed to stay, although future investment plans can be altered to some extent. This internalises the risks and puts country risks into a different perspective compared with cross-border transactions by financial entities.

The tools: basic organisational structures for managing country risk

While many of the regulatory initiatives can be criticised for being too prescriptive, there are some exemplary guidelines that leave sufficient room for initiative. One is the Principles for an Effective Risk Appetite Framework agreed in November 2013 – one of 12 standards set by the FSB. These principles are for managing risk in the broad sense. They are at a high enough level to be shaped according to the specific features of the business entity, taking into account its business model, resources and organisation. They could have universal applicability, including for non-financial entities. They also provide enough flexibility to cope with the changing economic and regulatory environment. Hence they provide a useful basis for the organisation of a management framework for country risk. The main elements include:

- an effective, explicit statement of risk appetite;
- setting of risk limits in line with the defined risk appetite;
- clear definitions of the roles and responsibilities of the board and senior management.

Using these broad principles, here are some suggestions of best practice for organising country risk management. While some of the technical aspects of the proposals apply mainly to financial institutions, the broader risk management structure should be applicable to multinational companies too.

Define country risk appetite

This refers to the articulation in written form of the maximum risk that an institution is willing to accept, or avoid. This appetite statement should include some more-difficult-to-quantify risks such as reputation risk and those arising from money-laundering.

The risk-appetite definition should be in line with business strategy and the desired rating of the enterprise as a whole. The statement should ideally include quantitative expressions, such as $100m of capital or $200m of earnings, of what managers are prepared to lose (and are able to live with, presumably without being sacked) to

FIG 10.1 **Expected and unexpected losses**

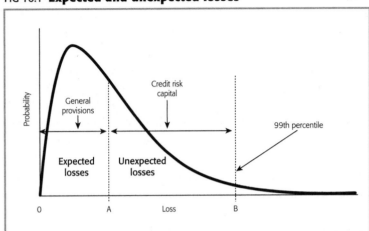

Source: Author

achieve their business strategy and rating targets. The loss referred to here is unexpected loss, as expected loss is already reflected in the pricing of the transaction. In Figure 10.1, expected loss is the area under the curve up to A on the x-axis. This could then be translated into maximum country risk appetite in the form of country limits.

The risk-appetite statement should be in line with business strategy and take into account normal and stressed market and macroeconomic conditions. This may require stress testing of various worst-case global scenarios for the business to make sure it is operating within the defined risk appetite. For example, if the business is in commodities, a stress test for a sharp drop in commodity prices as seen in the 2008 global financial crisis should be applied; if it has high exposure to the property sector, there should be a stress test of property prices; and if there is high concentration in one or several countries, there should be a stress test of various macro-crisis conditions specific to those countries.

Country risk limits

The next step is to translate the aggregate risk-appetite statement to set country risk limits for countries where operations or financial investments are located. For country risk management, exposure limits can provide a ceiling for maximum exposure to a country. These limits can then be disaggregated to the business line, legal entity and specific risk categories.

This is where the country ratings proposed in Chapter 6 come in handy once more, particularly the sovereign rating mapped to its probability of default. This is fine with sovereign ratings as sovereign defaults are discrete events. (Also, as explained in Chapter 1, countries do not default; it is the borrowing entities within a country that do. This may include a large swathe of borrowers in addition to the sovereign. But even in the worst defaults, such as Argentina in 2001, trade finance lines remained open.) However, depending on the statistical models used, there may not be a sufficient number of sovereign defaults to derive probabilities, hence many models use banks' credit probability of default (given the close correlation between banking and sovereign defaults) as proxy.

For a financial entity, the country limit can be determined by a function that takes into account the maximum risk appetite, the total economic capital and the probability of default as implied by the sovereign rating. This can be derived using sophisticated portfolio optimisation models or kept to a simple equation. The crucial link here is the calibration of the sovereign probability of default to capital. The limits are higher if the country rating is better; the limits also rise when a bank's capital increases and vice versa. The formula can be adjusted for other considerations, including whether the country is considered core or non-core. The function can be specified to reduce the limit exponentially for countries with sovereign ratings beyond a certain risk level. The country limit can be further constrained by a GDP cap, for example exposure must not be greater than X% of GDP. This is useful for countries with a small GDP but high ratings, such as Botswana or Cyprus.

This approach to setting maximum country limits ensures that there is a direct link between the analysis of the conditions in the country, investment strategy towards that country and the financial capacity of the investing entity. If country risks are increasing, this is reflected in a deteriorating sovereign rating and the probability of default associated with that rating. Thus the country limit is reduced, alerting businesses to hold off on new transactions and become more discriminating.

For example, if the initial country limit was $300m and there were several transactions in the pipeline that could have absorbed it all, the reduction of the limit to $200m would force the business to choose only the best and least risky of them; the weaker country rating may already have eliminated some deals because they can no longer achieve the return on investment required or absorb too much capital. If the country limit of $300m was already fully utilised, the lower limit would imply that the business try to reduce existing exposures.

Country limits can be disaggregated with a higher share of the country limit given to lower-risk transactions, such as trade finance, or for trading-desk limits in liquid markets (issuer risk). The allocation of limits requires balancing many interests. This can include managing conflicts between different business lines that want a higher share of the country limit.

Country risk management is not just about avoiding risks. This framework should also help identify and encourage management to focus on opportunities in countries that are being upgraded. In this case, the limit would be increased and tenor limits (limits on the maturity of the transactions) eased to allow for longer-term lending and project finance. Senior management may also decide to go above the model-generated limit if the country is considered strategic.

The sovereign rating as ceiling

Basel I had stipulated that the sovereign rating of a country would be the best rating in that country. Since then the Basel accords, in their bid to differentiate more between relative risks, have dropped this requirement. There was recognition that some private entities such as multinational companies and exporters could have better access to foreign exchange. Hence they would not be as exposed to the transfer and convertibility (T&C) risks.

Depending on the strength of this feature, some counterparties could be allowed to pierce the sovereign ceiling, with better ratings than the sovereign. Risk managers need to be sparing in the use of this option, looking for stringent conditions that include a couple of features from the following: high offshore foreign-exchange earnings (combined with low foreign-exchange debt); relatively liquid assets held offshore; committed credit lines from international banks; a track record of debt repayments during a sovereign payments crisis; and expectations of preferential treatment from the sovereign.

While non-financial organisations can pierce the sovereign rating, financial institutions' ratings should remain capped by the sovereign given the historical close link between sovereign and banking crises. A few exceptions include some central and multilateral banks, such as the World Bank, the European Bank for Reconstruction and Development (EBRD), the Asian Development Bank (ADB) and others which, due to their preferential lender position and multilateral funding sources (see Chapter 11), are rated based on the strength of their balance sheets irrespective of the country where their headquarters reside. For example, the rating of the African Development Bank, with headquarters in Tunis, was not affected by the political and economic instability following the downfall of the Ben Ali regime which led to the loss of Tunisia's investment-grade rating.

TABLE 10.2 **Controls: tenor (loan maturity) limits, watch listing, exposure reports, limit breaches**

How country limits can be disaggregated	Some useful controls
Country limits for banks	**Tenor limits**
Primary (lending)	**Limit breach reports and breach policy**
Pre-settlement (derivatives)	**Watch-list categories:**
Issuer (trading)	Green: Germany, China, UK
Inventory	Amber: Angola, Tunisia
Business line limits	Red (limits suspended): Pakistan, Greece

Tenor limits

Assuming there is a sufficiently rigorous management information system in place to track cross-border exposures, the next question is how to control country exposure. In addition to country exposure limits, it is important to set tenor limits (maturity of the transaction) to show how confident the country risk team is about the time perspective of its outlook for the country. If a country seems to have a reasonably sustainable political and growth outlook, longer-term tenor limits can be applied. If the situation is volatile and unpredictable, tenor limits for new transactions may be cut to 12 months or less.

The tenor limit is a powerful control instrument. However, it is a double-edged sword, being highly pro-cyclical. While it makes sense from the point of view of the individual lender or investor to cut tenor limits at critical times, this only makes conditions worse for the borrowing country or entity just as its ability to meet its debt-service payments is weakening.

Once country exposure and tenor limits have been set, the next task is to have a system in place which ensures regular review of limits and exposures and has systems in place to control breaches.

Watch list

A watch list is used to warn a business not to take new positions in a country placed on the watch list without various levels of approval – that is, delegated authority to use the country limit is either restricted or suspended. For example, a country such as Ukraine is downgraded, the limit cut and it is placed on a watch list. A large transaction which had been in the pipeline is finally ready to complete, yet there is not enough country limit to go ahead. In this case the transaction would have to be referred to higher-level management to take the final decision. If the transaction had been on the books before the country limit was cut but is now causing a breach of the lowered limit, management may be asked to make new arrangements with borrowers or partners. If this fails, provisions may have to be taken against possible losses.

Limit breaches

Many organisations produce daily country exposure reports. Real limit breaches should not be tolerated – for example, if a trader takes a position in a watch-listed country without prior approval. But exposure reports can throw up many "false" breaches of limits. If someone enters the wrong decimal point, that will show up. Other things that frequently arise include: the wrong currency conversion; the trade not netting; the exposure appearing in the wrong country; unresolved bugs in the collateral algorithm. Because the country portfolio is usually much smaller in terms of items than the credit or market risk portfolio, country limit breaches are more easily identifiable. Country exposure reports provide ultimate control of a business's international exposure.

Independence of the country risk function

Roles and responsibilities

Since the 2008 crisis, regulators have been more insistent on the involvement of senior managers in risk management, so various high-level committees and reports have had to be established. There have been extensive discussions on the responsibilities of the board of directors, the chief executive officer, the chief financial officer, the chief

FIG 10.2 **Main constituents of the country risk management matrix**

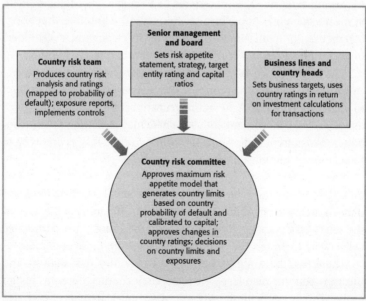

Country risk team
Produces country risk analysis and ratings (mapped to probability of default); exposure reports, implements controls

Senior management and board
Sets risk appetite statement, strategy, target entity rating and capital ratios

Business lines and country heads
Sets business targets, uses country ratings in return on investment calculations for transactions

Country risk committee
Approves maximum risk appetite model that generates country limits based on country probability of default and calibrated to capital; approves changes in country ratings; decisions on country limits and exposures

Source: Author

risk officer, the internal auditor and the business line head. A parallel process has affected country risk. The fairly flat reporting matrix in which country risk was managed has widened and deepened to involve senior management and the board. Their most important role is to make sure that there are enough resources to establish systems that correctly report and measure country exposures, and to give sufficient authority and support to the country risk function.

Figure 10.2 is an organogram of the main constituents of the country risk management matrix. In addition to senior management, including risk management heads, the most important constituents on the business side are the country managers of the international subsidiaries and the heads of main business areas. On the risk side are country risk managers and other risk management heads, including legal risk, credit and market risk.

Management conflicts

The independence of the country risk managers – those who actually analyse, quantify, model, report and control country risk – is essential to prevent extensive risk procedures becoming a box-ticking exercise to meet regulations. Some form of country risk committee that brings together senior management, the country risk team and stakeholders from business lines is a crucial link in this structure.

The country risk team can come under pressure from several constituents. For example, country and business managers may want to upgrade a country. Higher ratings mean that the business can price its transactions more competitively. There may be similar pressure for better ratings from senior management, who see this as one way of being more economical in the use of capital.

These internal conflicts intensify when a country is being downgraded and limits have to be cut. If the limit is reached, decisions may be needed on which transactions to offload. It is the role of the senior risk managers specifically and the country risk committee collectively to protect the country risk team from these pressures.

There may be a tug of war between country risk analysts and business country managers, who feel their country deserves higher limits. This is particularly difficult, as country managers can also claim to be closer to the ground and hence know the country better than the analysts, who may be located on the other side of the world and visit only once a year. But the converse is more frequently true: it can be difficult for the person on the ground to have the detached perspective required to see developments clearly. That said, there are country managers who can see the situation deteriorating and, instead of wishful thinking and just hanging in there, warn the centre ahead of time.

Then there are the traders who know the market and are chafing against the country limits or the reluctance of the country analyst to upgrade the country. There is an inherent conflict here because of the different time horizons the two functions work with: 12–18 months for country risk analysts compared with 1 week–3 months for trading desks, which take short-term positions (if longer, their positions could be considered stuck). As long as the market is liquid enough, often a short trading position should be allowed even if the country risk managers continue to have a negative view of the country. But markets can suddenly lose liquidity, so this can be a difficult conflict to manage with no easy answers (see case study 10.2).

CASE STUDY 10.2

Trader versus country risk: Iceland and Hungary

Iceland mid-2008

The Icelandic economy, with the top three banks' assets at 11 times GDP and a massive property and credit bubble, was an early casualty of the US subprime crisis. By the end of June 2008, the Icelandic krona had collapsed by 36% against the euro, trading at Ikr125 compared with Ikr91 at the start of the year.

The trading desk requested a country limit, arguing that it was a good time to take a position as the currency had already depreciated so radically that the only movement now was likely to be up. It was also argued that the repayments due from the three heavily leveraged Icelandic banks (Kaupthing, Glitnir and Landsbanki) for the rest of the year had already been funded. The country risk desk had earlier put Iceland on a red watch list and after some discussion the trade was not permitted. Although no one could foresee the US and UK banking shocks that would come in autumn 2008, this typical trading logic was extremely high risk, ignoring the deterioration in the global environment.

Hungary January 2012

With foreign debt at around 150% of GDP, Hungary's economy was one of the hardest hit by the global crisis, suffering a double-dip recession in 2009 and in 2012. The incoming Fidesz government in April 2010 did not renew talks with the IMF and opted for unorthodox policies, including the renationalisation of private pension funds and ad hoc taxes on banking, telecom, retail, and energy companies. A law was passed that curbed the central bank's independence, and a fiscal council set up to supervise government policy was shut down. This was the last straw for the EU, as Hungary had been under the excessive deficit procedure since its accession to membership in 2004. In January 2012, the European Commission threatened to suspend EU budget allocations to Hungary unless fiscal policy was tightened. The forint then collapsed to Ft320 per euro, almost 20% lower than a year earlier.

At this point traders wanted to take positions in the forint, betting that Hungary would have to mend fences with the Commission. The country risk desk disagreed, wary of the vulnerabilities of the Hungarian economy (such as large currency mismatches) and tensions in the euro zone. But the traders were allowed to take a small position – and they bet right. By June 2012 Hungary had come out of the excessive deficit procedure, having shifted into a tight fiscal stance. This, together with the improved global risk appetite and strong capital flows into emerging markets, strengthened the forint to Ft277 per euro by August 2012. But from a longer-term perspective the country risk team was also right: the exodus of capital from emerging markets in 2013 sent the forint back down to Ft307 per euro by early 2014.

Establishing the authority of country risk managers

Given the above points, it is fair for country risk managers to ask: how do we make sure we are listened to? (This question came up at a workshop on country risk organised by the Institute of International Finance in New York in 2013.) In addition to the country risk team, there are many other sources of country expertise in firms with international operations: the local country teams; the traders who specialise in these markets; the treasury team, which follows currency movements and manages liquidity or collateral; corporate finance; credit teams, which deal with the private sector; not to mention the senior manager who has just been on a "wonderful visit to the country, has met the finance minister, and is very impressed", and so on. There is also a vast amount of information and data available online. In this crowded information market, it is not easy to establish the authority of the country risk team. It obviously helps to get it right more often than not. But given the difficulties of predicting country events, there are other ways of ensuring that country risk managers are listened to. Besides reading this book and understanding its principal recommendations, there are some rules of thumb:

- construct a good argument and put your experience behind it;
- quantify and use models, but do not be driven entirely by them;
- if the situation is too volatile, hedge your argument or use scenario analysis – but also give your best guess;
- establish a transparent process of analysis, management and control of country risks appropriate to the organisation;
- educate staff in the approach to country risk – communicate clearly and often;
- escalate concerns to stakeholders – engage senior management and establish good lines of communication;
- warn of risks early enough, but don't only be a Cassandra – highlight investment opportunities in countries where the crisis has bottomed out;
- help transactions in high-risk countries through the approval process by finding the appropriate risk mitigants, as suggested in Chapter 10.

Why you cannot outsource country risk management

This chapter has provided a snapshot of the regulatory framework that has come about and, in that context, best practice for the organisational structure of country risk management. Over the past decade, the country risk function has moved from a fairly simple, informal process to a more complex rules-based one covering an increasingly broad range of topics. This has been partly in response to the growing integration and volatility of the global economy, as explored in Chapter 2; and partly because of increased regulatory requirements as governments have realised they have to do something about corporate governance problems and contain financial crises.

This increase in regulatory requirements brings into country risk management the same risks that are found in overall risk management. One is the pro-cyclicality reinforced by the regulations around the country risk management process. Another is that it becomes a box-ticking exercise to meet the regulations, rather than a genuine effort to manage country risks. And worse still is that it turns into an exercise in regulatory arbitrage. This was one of the factors highlighted in the investigation into losses of more than $6 billion at JPMorgan in 2012 in highly complex derivative trades by a London trader nicknamed the London Whale. A contributory factor, according a US senate subcommittee report, was tinkering with the bank's internal models and calculating risk differently to reduce risk-weighted assets on the balance sheet. But according to Jamie Dimon, chief executive of JPMorgan, before the 2011 incident some banks had far more aggressive risk-weighted asset calculators than JPMorgan did.

Managing country risk requires resources, expertise and internal management information systems, which all incur costs. Hence accountants will ask whether any of this can be outsourced. The scope of country risk has expanded, making the possibility of outsourcing more difficult than ever. In the past, it was mostly about nationalisation and expropriation. Then came currency risks with the collapse of the Bretton Woods system. To these were added institutional and governance weaknesses. Then it was noticed that global capital flows were creating havoc with national economies and contagion became a major feature of payments crises. The experience of the 2008 global financial crisis, the increase in the range of cross-border financial products and new regulations have further widened the focus of country risk to include operational functions such as payments systems, risks arising in clearing houses, custody, and collateral and inventory management.

Not all enterprises are subject to all these risks, of course. It makes sense to have specialist service providers – whether for data, for a skeletal ratings model that can be customised internally to suit the business, or for political risk analysis. Some informational aspects of country risk can be outsourced. But what cannot be outsourced are the internal culture, professional integrity, accumulated knowledge and interest in country risk, and the tradition of being responsive to the challenges. So the answer is no, it is not possible to outsource country risk management. It is a process that needs to be deeply embedded in the way an enterprise works.

11 Country risk mitigation at transaction level: the final defence

CHAPTER 6 SHOWED how to identify the country risks in a transaction: transfer and convertibility risks (risk of capital controls); exchange rate and interest-rate risks; macroeconomic risks caused by volatility in economic growth; sector-specific risks; political and policy risks; jurisdiction risks (country-specific business environment and management risks); and reputational risk. These will reflect a combination of global external shocks and home-grown vulnerabilities.

In a well-structured risk management process, the country risk analysis presented in Part I and the rating models should flag these risks and warn of deteriorating conditions that could cause payments problems. As discussed in the previous chapter, the risk management structures in an organisation should, in turn, ensure that there is an effective and timely management response. This should have triggered decisions to downgrade, reduce country limits, or place the country on a watch list, putting on hold any new transactions.

But what happens to the existing in-country exposure, including physical assets? Country risk mitigation at transaction level, which anticipates and tries to mitigate these risks, is the last point of defence. It is also the only way of coping with unanticipated shocks of the tail risk, black swan variety (the unknown unknowns).

There is no single way of mitigating all country risks in a transaction. And most risk mitigants (except comprehensive credit guarantees) provide only partial cover against some aspects of country risks – although this can be extended by structuring the investment and constructing composite hedges from many different instruments to reduce risks. But even so, there will be some residual risks that are impossible to reduce. Case study 11.3 on financing telecoms investments in Afghanistan and Palestine shows how composite mitigants can be used to de-risk successful transactions in high-risk jurisdictions. In contrast, the Dabhol power project in India (case study 11.2) shows how despite including a number of risk mitigants, the broader political and global risk shocks undermined the viability of the high-profile investment project. Mitigating risks in transactions ultimately has a price in terms of the extra management time, or simply the purchase of insurance. But, in addition to the benefits of reduced risks, many of these structures can translate into better risk rating for the transaction (see Chapter 8), thus lowering capital requirements.

The process

Incorporating risk mitigants in a transaction is an iterative process requiring co-ordination between the country risk, credit risk, operational, legal and business teams. It involves a debate between business and risk managers to ensure that the preparation stage of a transaction builds defences against potential country risks and that its pricing reflects the risks. It is the responsibility of the country risk management team to identify and propose mitigants for country risks and that of the business team to negotiate the terms. In addition, the credit, legal and operational teams must make sure that the proposed structures are embedded in the transaction with an effective legal structure.

Below are some of the key steps in this iterative process.

Check reputation risks

- Are the country, the name of the organisation, or the names of any individuals on any international sanctions lists?
- Has the country been delisted from any standard-setting international organisations such as the Financial Action Task Force (FATF)? The US has an extensive list of specially designated nationals and blocked persons issued by the Office of Foreign Assets Control (the most recent, issued in June 2014, had 592 pages, with the president of Belarus, Alexander Lukashenko,

related entities and persons taking up seven pages). This has become an increasingly complicated exercise and will need legal and compliance involvement.

■ Are any politically exposed persons involved? The "know your client" (KYC) team can assist in answering this question, but country risk team expertise is needed to decide what risks could arise from the political connections of the individuals.

If there are reputational risks arising, it could be the end of this deal and it goes no further. But it may not be that straightforward. For example, in Belarus, there are EU sanctions against top political figures and some government entities. Yet there was sufficient international demand for a sovereign bond issued in 2012. If the business team insists on going ahead, the final decision on the transaction should be escalated to a reputation committee, which includes senior management.

Consider the broad country risks and vulnerabilities

■ How vulnerable is the country to global shocks such as commodity price fluctuations or a sudden stop in capital flows?

■ Is the country dependent on one main export market (such as Mexico on the US), or does it have close financial links to another country (such as Cyprus on Greece)?

■ At which point on the credit cycle is the country: is there a credit bubble in the making, or a highly contested election coming up? These two factors could mean increasing financial sector risks and heightened volatility in economic policy and exchange rates.

Talk to credit analysts about the main credit parameters of the transaction

■ How sensitive is the cost structure to a depreciation of the currency? It will be very sensitive if the import content of the inputs is high.

■ If producing for the local market, how vulnerable are revenues to country events and what is the growth outlook?

■ Does the investment generate export revenues? Is it in the extractive sector and mostly producing for export?

■ The credit approval process should include a sensitivity analysis of the transaction to basic macroeconomic drivers such as exchange rate, interest rates, growth and commodity prices.

Other risks to be considered include:

■ Transport, infrastructure and environmental risks and business environment risks specific to the country.

■ Political sensitivities – public subsidies, regulatory instability, contract renegotiation risks, key sector and employer risks. If the transaction is a high-profile transaction in a key sector providing much needed employment, for example, it could become a political target for the opposition and in turn create reputational risks (see case study 11.2).

Once the specific country risks relating to the transaction are identified, possible mitigants should be discussed.

Go back to business with proposed structures

The structures that mitigate risks often have a cost, but the business team should have an incentive to incorporate them because of their positive impact on the rating and capital requirements of the transaction.

Consider the level of exposure set for the country and sector

If the country limit is full, other exposures may need to be reduced. Deciding on what transactions constitute an optimal risk-reward mix in the investment portfolio is the role of the portfolio managers and beyond the scope of this book.

If the whole transaction will not fit within the limit, the business team may have to bring new participating investors into the deal to share the risks (and rewards). Or a hold level less than the value of the loan or investment may be considered with a strategy to distribute the loan. This tactic of originate and distribute has a bad reputation, because it has been seen to have encouraged investors to take higher risks and has become a target of scrutiny by regulators, with a view to ensuring that a floor is set on how much of a transaction must be held on the books. If the business team is keen to distribute the bulk of a transaction, maybe it should not be approved in the first place.

Approve or reject

Sometimes the best mitigant is to say no and reject the transaction, if there are simply too many risks and not enough mitigants. It is bad form to take on a transaction that seems likely to need to tap its political risk insurance. It is also possible that, on the basis of their mandate, the country risk managers reject the transaction, but then it is escalated to senior management to take the final decision.

There is also a legal get-out available to say no at the last minute, even though contracts may have been signed: the MAC (material adverse change) clause. Such a clause inserted into a contract covers against dramatic changes if a project is approved, but has been progressing slowly before it is finally executed or closed. Sometimes transactions take a long time to gestate, especially in jurisdictions with many stakeholders and regulations, such as the EU. Or a project may take a long time because it is in a jurisdiction where there is no credible government and a caretaker regime is unable to make decisions, such as in Egypt after the fall of the Mubarak regime. The MAC is a sweeper clause that protects the lender, investor or acquirer from having to continue if a material adverse change or some unforeseen dramatic event has occurred. There are many legal issues surrounding the wording of these clauses and their implementation that cannot be discussed here, but they have been useful in providing that ultimate protection.

Commonly used country risk mitigants

There are several ways of mitigating country risks at transaction level:

- **Structuring.** This is where each type of risk is identified and isolated and an appropriate mitigant is found to possibly reduce it. However, this can result in complex structures, involving multiple levels of securitisation and distribution of risks that end up in the shadow banking sector. It is good practice for risk managers to be suspicious of structures that promise to have eliminated country risks. Also some structures merely enhance the reward profile but do little to reduce the risks. This is a big topic and the focus here is on the basic principles.

- **Buying protection or insurance against country risks.** This can take many forms, including political risk insurance from private insurers or public insurers such as export credit guarantee agencies, and the use of credit default swaps (CDS – an agreement that pays compensation to the buyer of the CDS linked to an underlying loan in the event of loan default) or other derivatives. However, buying protection does not reduce the risk of default, expropriation, licence cancellation, and so on – it only makes it less costly if these risk events do occur. In credit analysis parlance, it does not lower the probability of default, but it does lower the loss given default. The use of CDS and other derivatives to hedge country risks is at the transaction level here. These instruments are also effectively used to manage the risk profile of the overall investment portfolio where a long position in one country or currency can be offset by short positions, so that the net exposure is minimised. This is the task of market risk managers and not within the scope of this book.

- **Co-financing.** This can be with multilaterals that have preferential lender status or official export credit guarantee agencies that provide other valuable risk mitigants.

- **Operational risk mitigation.** This is mostly relevant to mitigating country risks in direct investments and involves operational risk mitigation for longer-term commitments. As indicated previously, once a physical investment is made in a foreign country, the country risks become internalised and part of the day-to-day operational management of the local firm.

Structures embedded in transactions for mitigating risks

Structured financing of cross-border investments took off in the aftermath of the 1980s sovereign debt crisis when access to financial markets became blocked for many emerging markets for almost a decade.

Offshore debt-service accounts

Payments risks arise because of the cross-border aspect of transactions. The most common way of reducing these risks is to locate the source of repayment offshore, outside the country of risk. Many risks can be reduced, including transfer and convertibility, exchange-rate risks and others relating to the availability of foreign currency for debt repayment or profit repatriation. It is possible to do this if the transaction is in an exporting sector. The structure most commonly used is an offshore debt-service account, where a proportion of the proceeds of the export revenues are deposited to be used for servicing the debt. Oil and commodities exporters often use such accounts. The residual here is the possibility that the government will redirect the export revenues or impose export-revenue-repatriation restrictions on private-sector exporters. There are different degrees of security on different types of offshore collection accounts. A debt-service reserve account, with the funds pledged to lenders and held with a highly rated institution abroad, is considered the most secure.

Future-flow financing

If the transaction is not in the export sector and its earnings are in local currency, and if the government is involved, it may be possible to direct other offshore receivables to a debt-service account. This is often called future-flow financing, where future export receivables can be linked to repayments on a project without export revenues. For example, a transaction in a country with no access to financial markets could be made possible by linking credit-card receivables from tourism payments to a debt-service account specifically to repay a loan to, say, upgrade the urban waste-water treatment system. Both this technique and the offshoring of debt-service accounts involve an assessment of the reliability of the future export receipts and an assessment that the government will not redirect the export earnings. One of the earliest examples of this structure was in Mexico, where the government gained access to international financial markets in the early 1990s by pledging the revenues from the international calls of Telmex, the state telecoms company.

Collateral and guarantees

Another structure that helps mitigate some debt repayment or profit repatriation risks is the holding of collateral in a highly rated institution offshore. Regional banks often do this. Collateral held in a bank in a country with a relatively stable banking sector, such as Kenya, could enable trade or other project finance lines to be extended to more high-risk countries in sub-Saharan Africa with which Kenya has trade and investment flows, such as South Sudan. A similar option is to get suppliers or the parent company involved in the transaction to provide debt-service guarantees. This works if the parent entity is located in a lower-risk country. For example, a Malaysian company building an airport in Myanmar with a licence to operate it gives guarantees from the parent company in Malaysia to step in if loan repayments from the Myanmar project are interrupted. Or a UK construction company borrowing to expand into projects in Africa provides a guarantee from the parent company in the UK to cover the debt-service risks of the African projects.

There are also sovereign guarantees where the central government guarantees the debt service of a loan or investment relating to a semi-sovereign or sub-sovereign entity, such as state industries or local or municipal authorities. The judgment call on sovereign guarantees becomes purely a country risk decision where the solvency of the government's finances, its contingent liabilities, the general tone and direction of policies, and its past history in meeting foreign-debt obligations all have to be taken into account. But even if all these boxes are ticked, there can be conditions, such as a regime change, when the guarantees granted by the previous regime are ignored. This was what many investors found when, in the midst of the Asian crisis, the Suharto regime in the Philippines collapsed. The generous terms that the regime, which was steeped in corruption, had given foreign investors were seen as too favourable by the incoming government, which chose to renegotiate them to boost political support.

Other structures

There are other structures for adjusting the financial conditions of a loan or a project that provide credit enhancements to improve the reward profile, even though they do little to reduce the risks. Hence they are not strictly risk mitigants, but they do open financing possibilities for projects in some countries that otherwise would be closed. Dual currency repayments remove at least some part of the repayment risk arising from currency problems –though not transfer and convertibility risks. These can take the form of repayment of the principal in foreign currency while interest payments are in local currency allowing the creditor to potentially gain from higher local currency interest rates and enhance the reward profile of the transaction. There are also put options where the pricing of the transaction can be adjusted or its tenor can be changed, bringing forward the repayment profile, linked to a specific event such as a sovereign rating change. The problem with this is that it makes it harder for the borrower to repay just when the conditions of its repayment become more difficult. It is pro-cyclical and the sort of structure that helps pass a transaction through committees, but in reality offers little real protection.

Buy protection: risk transfer instruments

It is possible to buy credit guarantees that cover the full debt service in the event of a default. These are mostly available for projects in highly rated countries. The discussion below focuses on the more common partial guarantees for political risks across a wide range of rating grades.

Political risk insurance

The most common way of insuring against country risks is through political risk insurance (PRI). This is a line of insurance that protects against non-commercial risks, or losses caused by specified political risk events. It is provided by private-sector and public-sector entities and purchased by firms engaged in international trade, direct investments, or financial loans. More recent product developments include insuring cross-border private equity. In the context of PRI,

FIG 11.1 **Historical trends in expropriations, by sector**
Number of events

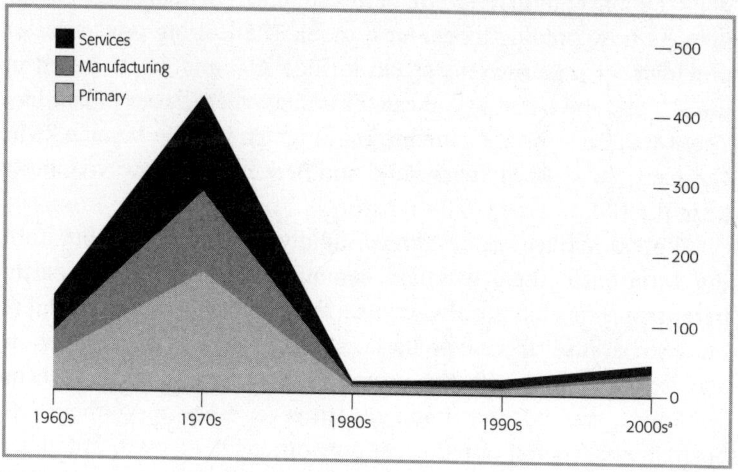

a Estimate.
Source: Hajzler, C., *Resource-based FDI and Expropriation in Developing Economies*, Economics Discussion Papers, No. 1012, University of Otago, September 2012

political risks are arbitrary or discriminatory actions, taken by home or host governments, political groups, or individuals, which have an adverse impact on cross-border flows. The bulk of the PRI market consists of insurance against country risks in short-term, low-value trade transactions. Insurance on direct investments and cross-border finance of projects or commercial loans that are longer term (often up to 15 years) can be as high as $800m for a single project.

Public-sector insurers include multilateral development banks and their associated insurance agencies, such as the World Bank or the Asian Development Bank, and the Multilateral Investment Guarantee Agency (MIGA). These usually offer partial coverage to ensure risk sharing with the private sector on projects that meet their development objectives. There are also national development agencies, such as the US's Overseas Private Investment Corporation (OPIC) and Germany's KfW, and national export-credit agencies, such as the UK's Export Credits Guarantee Department (ECGD) and China's Sinosure, and others that are members of Berne Union. This group will provide cover to support their national firms, be they suppliers, investors or lenders. Public-sector insurers have historically been the major source of PRI for longer-term cross-border investments, but many large private insurers now provide longer-term cover. The leading private-sector providers, or underwriters, of PRI include AIG and Zurich based in the US, and the Lloyd's syndicate of underwriters based in London. There are also reinsurers, the biggest of which include Munich Re in Germany, Swiss Re in Switzerland and Berkshire Hathaway/General Re in the US.

The PRI market has developed rapidly since the 1970s, but until the 2008 crisis, there was less demand for PRI. This was partly because insurers did not always meet the expectations of the insured, but also because classical political risk in the form of nationalisation and expropriation, with the exception of a few countries such as Venezuela, was not that frequent. However since 2009, there has been an acceleration of PRI cover outstripping the growth of foreign direct investment into developing economies. In 2012, Berne Union members issued $100 billion of investment insurance, triple the amount in 2005.

There are several reasons for this. On the demand side they include instability in the Middle East, high-profile expropriations in Latin America, contract renegotiations in resource-exporting countries, and last but not least the use of PRI to reduce capital constraints by financial creditors and investors. On the supply side, provision of new products, lengthening of tenors insured and new private-sector entrants into the PRI market have increased the capacity of PRI markets. Data published by the Berne Union show that in 2012, its members had $1.8 trillion of collectively insured assets, or 10% of international trade. Including commercial and political risks, since 2008 Berne Union export-credit insurers have paid out $22 billion in compensation payments. In 2012, the top three countries where claims arose included the US and Italy (see Table 11.1).

Although the wording of insurance contracts should be carefully scrutinised, in principle PRI coverage can be comprehensive. The main things covered are expropriatory action, currency inconvertibility or non-transfer risk, political violence and breach of contract. It is notable that of all these items, a 2013 MIGA *World Investment and Political Risk* survey of investors suggested that "PRI was most effective in relation

TABLE 11.1 **Berne Union claims paid in 2012**

Type of insurance	Country	Amount, $m
Investment	Libya	27
	Vietnam	24
	Brazil	10
Medium- and long-term export credit	Iran	501
	Libya	457
	US	231
Short-term export credit	Italy	201
	US	167
	Iran	111

Source: Berne Union

to political violence and expropriation risks, and less so in cases of breach of contract and adverse regulatory changes".

- **Expropriatory action.** This can take the form of confiscation, expropriation, nationalisation and deprivation, commonly known as CEND. Expropriation refers not just to outright seizure of assets but also creeping expropriation, where politically motivated policies can interfere with an organisation's ability to generate revenues. For example, the expropriation by Iraq of the Kuwaiti Airways fleet during the invasion of Kuwait in 1991 resulted in a $230m payment within 30 days to the Kuwaiti government, which had taken out PRI insurance for its aircraft. (The insurer managed to fund its payment with the possession and sale of the aircraft after the war.) CEND cover could also include insurance against tax disputes and blocked bank accounts if it can be shown that this was politically motivated.

- **Currency inconvertibility or non-transfer risk.** Brokers charge a high price for this type of cover because there can be many reasons for claims to arise. While an active blockage by a government and central bank of conversion of local to foreign currency is a clear event and not often encountered, passive blockage in the form of delays can be frequent. But this is not covered. Moreover, the insurance will not cover pre-existing

FIG 11.2 **Breach of contract events by sector**
Number of events

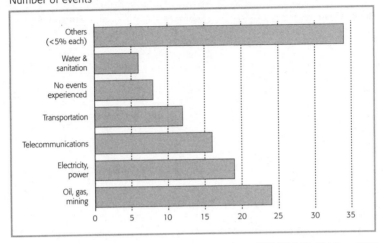

Source: MIGA-EIU, *Political Risk Survey*, 2013

conditions. For example, in 2012 it was well known that payments by Egypt's state oil company, EGPC, had extensive delays, which had become longer since the overthrow of Hosni Mubarak in 2011 and the political uncertainties that persisted. PRI would not cover this for any international investor or lender to the EGPC. Lastly, unless accompanied by capital controls that prevent currency transfer, insurance will not cover against devaluation risks. These need to be mitigated by using either the structures referred to above (see structuring a transaction), or local-currency loans and hedging with cross-currency swaps, if the country has sufficiently developed financial and capital markets.

- **Breach of contract.** This is useful in the case of investments or projects where the host government changes the conditions of the contract. Cover can also be extended to regulatory risks. These types of country risks are commonly seen in mining projects, utilities (especially power) and other infrastructure investments (see Figure 11.2). The insurance claim is triggered if the investor is prevented from going to arbitration by the host government, or if the arbitration award is in the investor's favour but the host government does not pay. However, this is cover is expensive and there can be disagreements about whether the government action is politically motivated. Similar cover, called contract frustration, is available specifically for risks that arise in trade-finance contracts with public entities. This broad term covers many trade risks, from non-payment to import/export cancellation.

Credit default swaps and derivatives to hedge risks

A credit default swap (CDS) is another form of insurance, with a focus on insuring against the default of a specific borrower. The purchaser of a CDS buys the option to sell the security to the institution issuing the CDS if the borrower defaults. Like PRI, CDS cover does not reduce the probability of default; it only reduces loss given default. The price of the insurance is the CDS spread expressed as a percentage of the notional amount insured.

CDS spreads are therefore closely monitored to glean the market perception of borrower's probability of default. But this assumes liquid CDS markets, which may not always be the case for emerging-market borrowers. At the peak of the 2008 crisis and the southern euro-zone sovereign crisis in 2010, CDS spreads reached stratospheric levels. Post-mortem studies show that, although government bond spreads and CDS spreads were driven by similar factors – macroeconomic fundamentals, deterioration in global risk sentiment, spillover risks and liquidity – CDS spreads had a greater tendency to overshoot.

Credit default swaps are useful, but these types of products can give investors a false sense of security and lead to the underpricing of risk. Losses on CDS were the cause of the $85 billion government bail-out of AIG in 2008, and it was in reference to the CDS market that Warren Buffet, an American investment magnate, warned of "weapons of financial mass destruction". CDS markets had mushroomed in the past decade, with annual CDS notional value (face value, not market value) outstanding peaking at $58.2 trillion in 2007, compared with $6.4 trillion in 2004.[1] This raised questions about whether the market was being dominated by speculative trades as opposed to actual hedging of risks. In 2012, European financial regulators voted to ban the "naked" selling of CDS when the CDS does not link to the holding of the underlying security.

Sovereign CDS are also often bought to cover for the default of a semi-sovereign entity, a state bank or a state enterprise. But to have a payment, this assumes that the sovereign will have defaulted by the time the state entity defaults, which is not necessarily the case. If the semi-sovereign entity that defaults is the biggest bank in the country or the national oil company, that may be a plausible expectation, but not if it is a state cement or telecoms company.

Many other derivatives are used to hedge against specific risks. These can be attached to the transaction to hedge unexpected exchange-rate, interest-rate and commodity price risks. Forward and future contracts are commonly used to hedge currency risks. A futures contract's daily marking to market (valuing the asset based on its daily market price) involves an adjustment of a margin account put up by the borrower, increasing the amount in the account if the exchange rate moves against the borrower. Thus, assuming there is a liquid market that provides this information, such a hedge can also help reduce counterparty risk. These hedging instruments are not allowed to be used in countries that are worried about currency volatility, or have capital controls or other restrictions. In this case, non-deliverable forwards (NDF)[2] are used to hedge local-currency exposure. These hedges can be a condition precedent for the transaction to proceed, to show that the borrower is hedged against the risks and that the derivatives are under International Securities and Derivatives Association (ISDA) guarantees. For example, if a loan transaction is to an airline, part of the condition for the loan could be that the borrower hedges its fuel costs (that is, it insures against a rise in the price of oil). Or if the project involves a coffee producer, a commodity price hedge (to insure against a fall in the coffee price) could help mitigate these risks.

These mitigants – PRI, CDS and NDF – are often referred to together as risk transfer instruments. Essentially, they transfer the risk of the host country to the country of the insurer or the provider of the hedging instrument. Given the problems of securitisation and the originate-and-distribute model of business, risk transfer has gained a bad reputation since the 2008 crisis. But even before the crisis, there were limits to the use of these instruments for risk mitigation. In relation to PRI, although the cover seems comprehensive, difficulties in defining trigger events have caused problems with claims. For example, in the case of creeping expropriation, where the government enacts various policies that undermine the viability of the project, it can be difficult to prove that this was politically motivated or that it was targeting that specific investment. Furthermore, if a lender or an investor makes a claim, they have to turn over the asset to the insurer. The cost of PRI can also often discourage business, especially if the deteriorating conditions in a country make it apparent that such a risk mitigant is needed.

In relation to CDS and NDF markets, their domination by speculative trades is a problem, as is the possibility of the market freezing (so that the parties cannot price) just when the crisis occurs. Despite these weaknesses, most studies show that they do provide important completeness to many asset markets, enhancing liquidity and reducing pricing distortions. Often the problem is not so much the hedge instrument itself but the inadequate systems and controls of the risk management framework. A classic example is the rogue trader who sank Barings bank, Nick Leeson. He was in charge of trading, but he also kept his own books where he covered up his losses.

Multilateral participation

Probabilities of default or repayment problems can be reduced in transactions that have some participation – or co-lender status – from export-credit agencies and multilateral investment banks. The latter include the World Bank or its private sector-arm, the International Finance Corporation (IFC), or regional multilateral banks such as the European Bank for Reconstruction and Development (EBRD), the African Development Bank, the Asian Development Bank, the Andean Development Corporation (CAF) and the Inter-American Development Bank. These multilateral banks and their associated public-sector insurers often have more leverage with the host country governments at the receiving end of the loan or investment. Country risk mitigation comes with these entities' preferred-creditor status in debt repayment in the event of payments difficulties. Host governments are less inclined to default on loans to multilateral banks, as this would have major negative consequences for access to capital markets.

These multilaterals will also provide partial loan guarantees on the late maturities of long-term infrastructure projects. Multilaterals frequently structure these projects as guarantor of record together with private insurers, which allows them also to benefit from the multilateral umbrella. Project or long-term infrastructure finance can often be structured in two tranches, known as A/B loans. The A-loan will consist of multilateral and other bilateral official lenders and the B-loan component will have private-sector participation but under the umbrella of the A-loan risk mitigants, which usually include public-sector PRI. This type of co-financing is often the only way of getting private-sector participation in long-term finance in high-risk countries. The participation of multilateral funders ensures not only the provision of extensive information and analysis, but also supervision of the project and the administration of debt-service collections. In the financial sector, the umbrella of public-sector PRI and preferential-lender status that comes with multilateral participation can mean that private-sector creditors can put aside less capital in relation to the loan, enabling the project to meet various internal risk/return hurdles.

Operational risk mitigants for direct investors

Risk mitigation in direct investments decisions often involves long-term commitment and physical assets, which internalises the risks. These longer-term risks can be managed by structuring risk mitigation around four options: avoid, reduce, transfer, retain.

The risk can be avoided by deciding against the investment, the loan, the merger or whatever because the risk is too high (the "say no" option). At the other extreme, management can retain or decide to live with the risk, but also take measures that may help to insulate the enterprise. This is common in oil and other extractive-industry companies, for example, which often have to operate in highly unstable jurisdictions. A good example is Zimplats (see case study 11.1), which is one of the few international investors to have remained in Zimbabwe despite the civil strife and economic dislocations of the past decade. Furthermore, borrowing in local currency by subsidiaries is one way of living with exchange-rate volatility and also insulating against it.

Between these two extremes, investors can try to reduce or transfer the risks. Transferring risk involves the use of insurance (see above). But producers can also transfer some of the risks to customers by, for example, passing on the higher costs resulting from devaluation through higher prices. Direct investors have other tactics with which they can reduce the risks, such as entering a market gradually to first develop familiarity, forming joint ventures with local partners, engaging with local community organisations, developing relationships with local and national political figures (though this can also be a liability) and setting up plants or retail outlets in multiple locations. The 2013 MIGA-EIU *World Investment and Political Risk Survey* of tools and mechanisms used to mitigate political risk listed gradual entry into markets, use of joint ventures and political/economic risk analysis as the top three most common mitigants used by around half of the survey participants. PRI and CDS were used by only 15% and 12% of participants respectively.

CASE STUDY 11.1

Implats and Zimplats: coping with political risks

Implats (Impala Platinum Holdings), a South African-based platinum group metals (PGM) miner and refiner, and Zimplats produce platinum from the two biggest seams in the world, the Bushveld Complex in South Africa and the Great Dyke in Zimbabwe respectively. Both have developed tactics to operate under conditions of severe civil strife.

In the 2013 *Implats Integrated Annual Report*, of the ten strategic risks identified, six relate to political and macroeconomic risks. These include the customary operational risks such as sensitivity to global PGM price fluctuations, volatility of the rand/dollar exchange rate and labour unrest. There are also more-difficult-to-mitigate political risks, such as uncertainty regarding political and regulatory risk, and maintaining a social licence to operate. The measures adopted in response to these risks, according to the annual report, include:

Maintain regular contact with government officials. Ensure full legal and regulatory compliance in a continuously changing environment. Investing in community and social development initiatives … Maintain sound and mutually beneficial relationships with communities and the general public.

Under Zimbabwean legislation the state is granted a significant shareholding in all extractive companies as part of the country's indigenisation process. But the management tactics adopted by Zimplats go further, including taking on roles normally filled by the state such as building roads and power stations. Social development initiatives include investments in health, education and accommodation. Across the border, the South African government has ruled that all mines should have a Black Economic Empowerment (BEE) partner and should engage in activities that would normally be regarded as the responsibility of the municipal government. By shirking such duties, a large company like Implats runs the risk of losing its mining licence; but by carrying them out it insulates itself from most government threats, since the state becomes partially reliant on the company for providing basic public services.

But there are downsides to this strategy which, while managing some political risks, raises new risks. As the widespread strike action that has affected this sector in South Africa shows, these social policies do not provide a cushion against industrial-relations conflicts. Moreover, the community begins to expect from the corporate entity the basic services and infrastructure that should have been provided by the state. Local problems with infrastructure and service delivery are now blamed not on the government, which can in principle be voted out of office at the next elections, but on the corporate entity. Thus community members unhappy with their living conditions decide that blocking a mine's entrance is more likely get them better services than lobbying far-off politicians. In South Africa's recent past, this has resulted in mining stoppages and increased operating costs.

Strengths and weaknesses of some mitigation measures

Here are some hypothetical examples of the strengths and weaknesses of mitigation measures.

Five-year loan to a UK-listed oil exploration and production company in Kazakhstan

The loan is to be partly repaid by a new share issue in London. This looks like a good structure that seems to eliminate country risks. The share issue is to take place in the UK and will repay the loan. The risk is that the share issue cannot take place due to adverse events in Kazakhstan or a stockmarket downturn in the UK. It may have to be postponed or scaled down in size, and thus will be unable to cover the loan.

Seven-year loan to a Spanish airport operator for an airport in Egypt, with parent guarantees from the Spanish firm

In 2010, no one predicted the fall of the Mubarak regime in early 2011. All that country and political risk assessment could do was highlight the risk of a disruptive change of regime. Hosni Mubarak was known to be suffering from ill health and grooming his son, who was reported to be disliked by the Egyptian military, for succession. The political risk assessment would also have highlighted the potential political vacuum that results when long-running autocratic regimes collapse. Hence the prudent policy would have been to take out PRI to cover against political violence, expropriatory actions and currency inconvertibility in such an event. Parent guarantees from the Spanish construction firm would not have given much comfort, because in 2010 the euro-zone sovereign risk crisis was at its peak and Spain's property bubble was still deflating, putting many Spanish construction companies at risk.

An Asian construction-equipment company working in several African countries

The company has deposits with the creditor bank's subsidiary in Hong Kong and the business team says the transaction should have Hong Kong's Asian rating. But it should have some blended average rating of the African countries it is exposed to. Unless the Asian construction firm can give parent guarantees, there is no basis for rating the transaction from its home country. The fact that the construction firm is a depositor in the creditor bank is irrelevant, as the bank would not have any legal access to the deposits.

A seven-year amortising fixed for floating swap to a mining company in Bolivia

The swap is on the back of a loan to the Bolivian company for capital expansion by a Chinese bank. There is also an off-take contract with a Chinese steel company, which pays into an offshore account for the metal delivered. All this sounds impressively complicated and there seem to be some good risk mitigants. The offshore account will reduce currency risks and the off-take contract makes exports seem fairly safe. The swap reduces the risks of rising interest rates for the borrower as it swaps fixed rates for floating ones. The main risk is political, such as expropriation and nationalisation by the radical Morales regime in Bolivia. Hence PRI would be useful, possibly from Sinosure. There is also a risk that a slowing Chinese economy and falling demand from heavy industry may undermine the off-take contract, especially given the long (seven years) tenor of the transaction.

CASE STUDY 11.2

Country risks in infrastructure finance: the Dabhol power project[3]

This is the story of how a high-profile project went belly up. Tolstoy's saying about "happy and unhappy families" comes to mind when considering cross-border project funding. Successful projects are all successful in the same way; but unsuccessful projects fail in all sorts of different ways. Of all the high-profile, problem-ridden infrastructure finance projects, such as the Channel Tunnel (Eurotunnel), the Bangkok Elevated Road and Train System (BERTS) and the Chad-Cameroon Pipeline, the Dabhol power plant project in Maharashtra, India, must be one of the longest running and most educational, illustrating myriad country risks.

Dabhol back in the news

In January 2014, there were reports of financial difficulties at Ratnagiri Gas and Power (the reconstituted Dabhol Power Corporation), following the halting of power production in March 2013 because of lack of allocation of gas supplies from Reliance Industries gas fields in the Bay of Bengal. Since October 2013, Dabhol had difficulties servicing its debt, thus increasing risks for the banking sector, which is reported to have Rs8,500 crore (around $1.5 billion) of exposure to the plant. Dabhol's financial problems included non-payment of bills by the Maharashtra State Electricity Distribution Company (Mahadiscom).

Indian power problems

Unreliable electricity supply has been a major constraint on economic growth in India; the blackout in July 2012 in northern India was the largest so far. Issues include unsustainable subsidies, a culture of non-payment of bills not just by the poor but also by state enterprises, and high levels of theft and loss from the grid (about 25% compared with a global average of 15%). On the generation side, problems include shortages of inputs such as coal (the primary source of electric power controlled by a state monopoly), planned gas supplies from the Bay of Bengal, environmental opposition to tapping hydroelectric sources, and slow development of nuclear and renewables. Institutionally, bureaucratic turf wars between numerous ministries responsible for electricity, coal, oil and gas, and nuclear and renewable energy are further complicated by the conflicts between the federal and state authorities, especially if different parties are in power.

Attempts at reform of the Indian power sector began in the early 1990s in order to attract private domestic and foreign investment into the sector. But political inertia and bureaucratic conflicts, as well as problems at Dabhol, delayed major change. In 2003 the Electricity Act was passed and the Central Electricity Regulatory Commission was created. The aim was to curb the powers of state entities by removing the state monopoly on transmission and distribution, and to create a national power market by unbundling the functions previously in the hands of state electricity boards. Although private electricity generation has grown rapidly, implementation of the law has been patchy due to resistance from state entities. Consequently, regulatory uncertainty has remained high, further undermining investment.

Dabhol becomes a political football

Dabhol was built in the 1990s with Enron as project leader and Bechtel and GE as contractors, providing an initial $279m of equity. There was also $643m of loan finance from Bank of America, the Overseas Private Investment Corporation (OPIC) and the Export-Import Bank of the United States (Ex-im

Bank), as well as the Industrial Development Bank of India and other Indian banks. The project – a build-own-operate (BOO) model with a lease of 20 years – was eventually completed and is still India's biggest gas-fired plant with a generation capacity of 1,967 megawatts. But from the start the Dabhol project was beset with problems.

The initial problems included the opaque bidding process through which Enron won the contract. The power purchase agreement (PPA) had been signed without being cleared by the Central Electricity Authority, and the Indian government had agreed to counter-guarantee the project before it was announced. The original contract included a PPA at the elevated price of 7 US cents per kilowatt hour, but the Maharashtra State Electricity Board (MSEB) was selling electricity at only 3.4 US cents/kwh; it was also thought that the take-or-pay agreement would increase the state's electricity costs by displacing cheaper coal-fired generation at peak times. Environmental issues had not been addressed. In 1992, the World Bank criticised the project as too big and too expensive.

There were also political problems. The initial commissioning of Dabhol took place when the Congress Party was in power in New Delhi and Maharashtra. But in 1995 the Shiv Sena and Bharatiya Janata Party (BJP) won the Maharashtra state election; and Dabhol was a focus of political controversy in the election campaign. In 1996, a BJP-appointed commission halted Phase I after $300m had been spent. Enron initiated arbitration proceedings in London, but settled at a renegotiated electricity price. By 1999, Phase I had become operational and Phase II was almost complete. In that year the Congress Party returned to power in Maharashtra and, with costs at Dabhol climbing to $2.8 billion, took a critical stance towards the previous renegotiations by the BJP. Dabhol became a football, bouncing between political parties and the federal and state authorities.

The macro-environment was also working against the project. The agreement to price the electricity in dollars transferred the currency risks away from Enron, leaving the burden with the MSEB and Dabhol. Soaring international oil and gas prices weakened Dabhol's commercial viability. By 2001, the MSEB began to default on its payments, Dabhol was shut down and another renegotiation began. At this point Enron, beset with corporate governance and financial difficulties in the US, bailed out of the project, leaving GE, Bechtel and OPIC to pursue a long litigation battle with the Indian government.

Enron and the other investors knew that this was a high-risk project. Mitigating some of the risks was $160m of commercial cover and $231m of political risk insurance from Ex-im Bank and OPIC. Legal advisers had structured the PPA with state and federal government guarantees and for any arbitration to be under English law. Yet for all parties involved, including the Indian government, the project was a huge and costly failure because the terms agreed were not realistic. Enron, GE and Bechtel were too aggressive and the Indian government made too many concessions in its bid to attract big-ticket foreign direct investment into the sector. Enron underestimated the strength of local activists and the level of political scrutiny of this high-profile project. Moreover, legal contracts are only good if they are held to, but Enron failed to understand the strength of the state electricity institutions and the potential conflicts with the federal authorities.

CASE STUDY 11.3

Mitigating country risks: Roshan in Afghanistan and Wataniya in Palestine[4]

Two telecoms transactions that might never have happened

Roshan is the brand name for Telecom Development Company Afghanistan, the leading GSM (global system for mobile communications) provider in Afghanistan, which was awarded a 15-year GSM licence in 2003 and now provides coverage for 65% of the population in all 34 provinces. A $65m loan was arranged in 2006 to finance Phase III of its network expansion plan. The loan (A/B structure) included the participation of multilateral banks, export credit agencies and an international and regional commercial bank. It was the first time private commercial funding was extended for a project in Afghanistan in the post-Taliban era.

Wataniya Palestine Telecom is the second GSM operator in Palestine. The $285m project was to fund the launch and initial rollout of infrastructure in the West Bank region. It was 70% equity funded by the majority shareholder Qatar Telecom and the Palestine Investment Fund. The remaining 30%, or $85m, was a syndicated loan lead managed by Standard Bank, the London subsidiary of a Johannesburg-based regional African bank, which included three local Palestinian banks, Bank of Palestine, Commercial Bank of Palestine and Quds Bank; Ericsson Credit AB, the credit arm of the Swedish telecoms equipment manufacturer; and the International Finance Corporation (IFC). Exportkreditnamden (EKN), the Swedish Export Credit Guarantee Board, and GuarantCo, a specialist guarantor of infrastructure financing in low-income countries, acted as guarantors.

Country risk mitigants
Wataniya

- 100% PRI and partial commercial insurance from EKN for the three-year commercial tranche
- Multilateral umbrella with the participation of the IFC for the $30m tranche and seven-year term
- $30m local commercial bank funding guaranteed by GuarantCo with a seven-year term
- $20m five-year equipment supplier credit from Ericsson with 100% PRI and partial commercial cover by EKN
- High-profile political commitment with the main shareholder, Qtel, having experience in high-risk jurisdictions

Roshan

- Multilateral umbrella – $30m six-year-loan Asian Development Bank (ADB) facility with 100% PRI
- $30m commercial facility (with ADB as lender of record) from international and regional commercial banks – Standard Bank and National Bank of Pakistan
- DFI (development finance institutions) facility $20m six-year loan with PRI and commercial risk cover from Proparco (the French development agency, DEG (Germany) and FMO (Netherlands)

These transactions are good examples of combined public-private funding for projects in high-risk jurisdictions, although it is the public-sector institutions that, through their guarantees, shoulder the bulk of the risks. The involvement of private commercial funding became possible only through an extensive array of country risk mitigants, especially in the Wataniya transaction. Both the transactions were also structured with a debt-service reserve account and both benefited from high-level political support.

Wataniya country risks

The country risks in this project are all too evident. Palestine was not a universally recognised sovereign state. There was no national currency, with the Israeli shekel, the Jordanian dinar and the US dollar circulating in the economy. The position of the Palestinian government seemed fragile, and there were deep differences between the government and Hamas. Country-specific sector risks included control of bandwidth by the Israeli telecoms authorities and risks of a trade embargo on equipment imports. The GSM market was dominated by the state-owned Palestine Telecom's Jawwal and the newcomer would also face competition from Israeli operators. There was no telecommunications law. Although the loan facility would be governed by English law, security documentation was covered by local law. The Palestinian legal system was a complex blend of British, Egyptian, Jordanian and Ottoman laws, reflecting the history of the territories.

The negotiations began in a positive atmosphere following the May 2008 Palestinian investment conference held in Bethlehem, which was followed by agreements between Israeli and Palestinian authorities to attract more foreign investment into Palestine. The Wataniya telephony licence covering the West Bank was listed in the framework investment plan presented by the Office of the Quartet (the US, EU, UN and Russia). Hence despite the evident political risks, the investment had high-level political support.

The launching of retaliatory missile attacks by Israel on the Gaza strip in December 2008–January 2009 came on the eve of the launch of the loan facility. But the loan went ahead because of the high commitment to the project, which would be one of the largest and the first internationally and privately funded investments in Palestine. It also helped that the loan team had had experience working in high-risk jurisdictions, having previously worked on the Roshan project in Afghanistan. Furthermore, Wataniya's main shareholder, Qtel, was an operator with experience in places such as Cambodia and Laos. In the end, it was not the missiles but the disputes over the release of bandwidth that created the biggest operational problems.

Roshan country risks

The country risks in this project included acute security risks, including Taliban attacks on the telecoms towers and field engineering staff. There was a good legal framework set by the Telecoms Law passed in 2005, which provided protection against expropriation and allowed international arbitration for settling disputes with foreign investors. The Ministry of Communications had been successful in establishing a regulatory framework with which to attract local and foreign private capital investments. It was this law that enabled Roshan to raise several rounds of international finance for its expansion plans, with the most recent one being in 2013. The project also benefited from the long-term commitment to Afghanistan of the Asian Development Bank (ADB) and the experience of the Aga Khan Fund for Economic Development (AKFED), Roshan's major shareholder, in other high-risk jurisdictions and its successful track record negotiating with the government authorities since winning the GSM licence in 2003. However, there were still several policy risks. Roshan became one of the biggest taxpayers into the government budget and this attracted increasing scrutiny by the authorities. The AKFED report refers to the dirigiste tendencies among high-level policymakers in Afghanistan who looked at the private sector with some degree of suspicion. Roshan has had to negotiate its way around sudden demands (including an attempt to impose a levy just before the signing of the 2006 facility) from the Afghanistan Telecommunications Regulatory Authority (for a lower price) and the Ministry of Finance (for higher taxes).

12 Conclusion: how to stop being surprised all the time

THIS BOOK BEGAN with a brief history of risk drawing on Peter Bernstein's *Against the Gods: The Remarkable Story of Risk*. It ends with a quote from his concluding chapter, "Awaiting the wildness":

> *Wars, depressions, stockmarket booms and crashes, and ethnic massacres come and go, but they always seem to arrive as surprises. After the fact, however, when we study the history of what happened, the source of the wildness appears to be so obvious to us that we have a hard time understanding how people on the scene were oblivious to what lay in wait for them.*

The analysis presented in previous chapters should help reduce at least some of the surprise elements in country risk. Below is a summary of the main points.

Have a historical perspective

Focus on the big picture and look for the causes of over-lending as well as over-borrowing. Every topic in this book has been presented in its historical context, beginning with the concept of managing risk, which came with the Enlightenment when people began to think they had some control over their lives. Country risk management came about with the emergence of sovereign nations where the actions of sovereign governments forced international investors to manage their cross-border risks.

In recent decades, the liberalisation of capital markets and the growing size of financial flows relative to most national economies have become important drivers of currency, payments, banking and sovereign debt crises. These conditions have also greatly reduced the room for national policy options. Accompanying all this is an extensive and complex web of international regulation and standards, which reinforce the narrowing of sovereignty. Hence management of country risk requires attention not just to the home-grown country risks that drive over-borrowing, but also to external risks arising from the global trends that drive over-lending.

Don't fall for the "this time is different" syndrome

The inability of many policymakers and regulators to see the 2008–09 global financial crisis coming has justifiably generated much discussion about why many economists failed to predict it. There have been numerous different answers, including one from Alan Greenspan, who served as the chairman of the US Federal Reserve from 1987 to 2006. He thought it was lack of focus on human behaviour: "if economists (can) better integrate animal spirits into our models, we can improve our forecasting accuracy". This seems to somehow deflect responsibility. Another more down-to-earth answer is that economists and regulators did not fully understand the extent of the evolution of the financial system and the emergence of shadow banking, which involved massive growth of the repo market and securitisation over a 30-year period.

More broadly however, there is a realisation that economics has become "history-less". It was this absence of historical perspective that lulled people into thinking that the "great moderation" of the past decade could continue. A 2013 conference at the Bank of England, "Teaching Economics after the Crisis", concluded that "greater awareness of economic history and current real-world events" was needed. (A survey conducted by the Society of Business Economists in January 2013 confirmed that financial history is an essential topic while advanced mathematics scored low.) Others who did know their history were thinking "this time is different" (borrowing from the title of Carmen Reinhardt and Kenneth Rogoff's book). The IMF, in a review of financial crises by Stijn Claessens and Ayhan Kose in 2013, concluded:

Given the commonalities, it should be possible to prevent crises. Yet that seems to have been an impossible task. This suggests that future research should be geared to beat the "this time is different" syndrome.

Understand the new shape of political and geopolitical risks

One response to this narrowing of scope for independent national policy has been to seek greater international co-ordination of policies through multilateral financial institutions such as the IMF, standard-setting bodies such as the Bank for International Settlements and the Financial Stability Board, and inter-governmental forums such as the G20. These are part of the rules-based multilateral system that the bigger powers vie to use to their advantage, and which creates new risks. Another response has been for increased regionalism, potentially fragmenting the global economy and the multilateral system. And yet another, not yet dominant response is for national policies to turn inwards, introducing various levels and forms of defensive protectionism. This has been more evident in the aftermath of the 2008–09 crisis, with increased government intervention in the economy through bank nationalisations, involvement in industrial policies, immigration and capital controls, and increased financial and corporate regulation. This is turn has increased political risks, which had been thought to have receded a decade or so ago. But political risk is now back with different forms.

Try to quantify risks, but know the limits of economic and political models

This book does not pretend to have all the answers. It has been made clear that predicting payments crises is difficult, no matter how sophisticated the model is. But it is still useful to try to quantify country risks in some sort of formal model. Even if you cannot predict the future, rating models can show which countries are more prone to crises than others at any given time. This, combined with an understanding of the cyclical global context and a historical perspective, can provide a useful framework for managing cross-border risks and opportunities.

Identify the drivers of political risks and potential triggers of natural catastrophes

Dealing with political risks, such as geopolitical risks, is difficult because they develop slowly over time. But even political risks of the black swan variety do not come from nowhere. There are ample signs, if you are prepared to see them, that help pinpoint the risks, as shown by the example of Ukraine (see case study 6.2). If the risks can be identified, measures can then be taken to mitigate them.

This is the case even with catastrophic disasters such as the one at the Fukushima Dai-ichi nuclear power plant in Japan in the wake of the Tohoku earthquake and tsunami in 2011. An independent investigation concluded that this tragedy was the culmination of a complacent safety myth that had built up around Japan's nuclear energy plants, the lack of independence of the Nuclear Safety Commission, which had an unhealthily close relationship with TEPCO, the nuclear power company, and the inertia created by the extensive network of interests around nuclear power. Even TEPCO admitted that the accident was a human-generated disaster.

Know that payments crises and defaults will always be there

Payments crises and defaults are not only difficult to predict but will always be there. International efforts at crisis prevention mostly focused on emerging markets before the 2008 global recession. Policy advice to emerging markets focused on managing their demand for international borrowing and there was little interest in the effect of over-lending from the global financial centres – the push factors – on payments crises. The 1980s developing-countries debt crisis prompted tighter regulations to manage the supply of international lending, with BIS risk-based capital rules that raised the level of capital that a bank had to hold against loans to non-OECD countries. But this resulted in filling bank balance sheets with the sovereign bonds of OECD members. Since the 2008–09 global financial crisis and the euro-zone sovereign debt crises, developed-market crises have taken centre stage. International crisis-mitigation efforts include counter-cyclical and macro-prudential policies to reduce vulnerability to crises; an enhanced role for the IMF; changes in the structure of multilateral institutions to ensure broader representation of rising emerging markets; and new forums such as the G20 to discuss and hopefully co-ordinate national policies.

But is all this likely to work? There are several reasons to be sceptical of these counter-crisis measures, especially in mitigating financial crises:

- **History doesn't repeat itself and every crisis is different.** Between 2003 and 2008, many economists thought the disorderly correction of the growing US current-account deficit (the global imbalances) was the biggest global risk. There was too little consideration of the deteriorating financial-sector balance sheets, the possible links between monetary policy and the global imbalances, and the credit boom and asset bubbles.

- **Warnings don't help much.** Most credit, housing and other asset bubbles and the build-up of unsustainable debt are a long time coming and visible. The question is how to manage this and when to intervene. One way is with official warnings. But this rarely works. Charles Kindleberger and Robert Aliber, in *Manias, Panics, and Crashes*, note the "Cassandra-like" warning from Paul Warburg, a founding member of the US Federal Reserve System, in February 1929 that US stock prices were too high; the markets paused briefly and resumed their rise until the panic finally set in at the end of October. Another example is the 1970s lending boom which ended with widespread defaults by the early 1980s. In 1977, G10 central bank governors invited 57 international banks to voluntarily agree to regulate lending decisions based on a checklist of the creditworthiness of sovereign borrowers. They were told to mind their own business and that sovereigns don't default.

- **Difficulties of tracking financial developments and containing credit bubbles.** Many studies show the near impossibility of using monetary policy to control monetary

growth. Financial innovation always manages to develop new
money substitutes, which are not being tracked or regulated
and are off balance sheet. Some devices such as securitisation
that are seen as risk reducing for an individual financial entity
may increase systemic risk. The impact of fiscal, monetary and
macro-prudential policies to contain credit bubbles and the
effectiveness of multilateral bail-outs are not well understood.
IMF bail-outs may not prevent default, as shown in Russia
in 1998. When the bubble bursts, central banks have to make
critical judgment calls. The decision to let Lehman Brothers
collapse in 2008 at the height of the US financial crisis was
the wrong call from a financial stability point of view. The
independence of central banks is crucial, but sometimes it is not
enough.

■ **Lack of data is not the problem.** Analysts, regulators and
decision-makers will never have enough data because the
indicators that need tracking – the activities on the margins – are
always evolving. Data on economic and political fundamentals
and key market indicators essential for country risk managers
are now widely available. In the financial sphere, however, there
has been the paradoxical situation of investors having more data
than ever as a result of the IT revolution but less transparency
and visibility in the markets.

Countries can move out of the debt-default cycle

If you cannot do much about global crises, crisis prevention is not
that reliable and regulation can make things worse, are countries
condemned to payments crises forever? The answer is no: countries
can learn to manage their economies to avoid the debt-default cycle
– for some periods of time.

A historical view of debt and financial crises shows that newer
nations are more likely to default than older ones. This is because
over time and in specific periods of history, older nations have
learned how to manage their national economies. Looking as far
back as the 17th century, Carmen Reinhart and Kenneth Rogoff argue
in their book *This Time is Different* that it took time for new nations

to establish economic and political institutions that could steer the economy without overreliance on debt. They introduce the concept of national economies "graduating" from the debt-default cycle as they develop. Early serial defaulters in the 14th–18th and the first decade or so of the 19th centuries were France, Austria and Spain. But from about the 1820s, although Spain and Portugal continued regularly to default on their debts, France and Austria had graduated from this position, defaulting only once. Meanwhile, in the 19th century the number of serial defaulters expanded to include newly independent nations such as Colombia, the Dominican Republic, Greece, Mexico and Venezuela.

It seems more difficult to graduate from recurrent banking and financial crises. Out of 66 countries in the sample, only Austria, Belgium, Portugal and the Netherlands managed to escape banking crises between 1945 and 2007. But this extended period of graduation came to an end for some in this select group with the euro-zone crisis, in which Portugal was bailed out and Belgium had to rescue several large banks.

The wide use of sovereign ratings is imposing some discipline on policies against over-borrowing. Although there have been justifiable criticisms of rating agencies (see case study 10.1), many emerging markets are now included in sovereign ratings. This has made governments more aware that deteriorating ratings mean higher borrowing costs and public criticism of their economic policies. This was seen in Russia in 2008–09: despite the sharp erosion of its foreign-currency reserves, it was generally thought the government resisted imposing capital controls to preserve its investment-grade rating.

Policies can cushion against global shocks

At the receiving end of capital flows …

Chapter 5 concluded that, ultimately, it is policies that determine the outlook for a country, and presented a list of rogue policies that weaken the ability to pay. Conversely, countries can bolster their defences against external shocks by having the political flexibility to generate policy options and strong institutions. Deep capital markets, high levels of foreign-currency reserves, flexible currencies and diversified export markets also help. Other policies that can cushion national economies and help countries come off the fragility list include (see also case study 4.3 on the effects of tapering):

- **Domestic mechanisms to provide more resilience to capital flow volatility.** In Chile and Malaysia, the domestic private sector with accumulated foreign assets (pension funds in Chile and multinational companies in Malaysia) repatriated them at times of crisis, offsetting foreign capital outflows.
- **Exercising self-restraint.** Counter-cyclical fiscal rules, when combined with fiscal transparency and an independent government audit agency, can impose discipline on governments.
- **Counter-cyclical funds.** Resource exporters accumulate export revenues in sovereign funds in the boom years to provide a spending cushion when commodity prices fall.
- **Maintaining room for policy manoeuvre.** Countries with large domestic markets, such as China and India, are more insulated from global shocks in comparison with, say, Singapore. But the bigger economies need to have policy room to respond to an externally generated crisis, which can be provided by counter-cyclical fiscal policy. These economies cannot rely on stimulating domestic demand growth if credit indicators are flashing red.
- **Middle ground convergence.** In response to the "trilemma" problem (capital markets, monetary independence and exchange-rate stability), some emerging markets, mostly in Asia, have opted for middle ground convergence with international policy norms, with partial liberalisation of capital flows to establish an element of control over exchange rate and monetary policy.
- **Macro-prudential policies to avoid the build-up of credit bubbles.** These are being used by bigger emerging markets whose currencies appreciated, export growth faltered and current-account deficits widened as a result of developed economies' quantitative easing policies.

... and in the international centres of finance

The policy measures above address the problems of mostly emerging-market economies on the receiving end of capital flows. But policies in the international centres of finance and other strategically big economies, such as China, should also be considered. For the first time, the possible negative impact of tapering has resulted in a potentially constructive debate. Emerging-market policymakers have been calling for strategic economies to be more mindful of the impact of their policies on the rest of the world. This was initiated by the governor of the Central Bank of India, Raghuram Rajan, who criticised the growing dysfunction of the G20 process and the attitude of advanced economies that wash their hands and say, "we'll do what we need to and you do the adjustment". Others advised the Fed to take account of the external impact of its actions to the extent that these feed back into the US economy. Through trade and financial linkages, financial and economic distress in foreign markets can come home to roost. With these comments emerging-market policymakers are not trying to shirk their responsibility for their own country's problems, but are simply highlighting the interconnectedness of the global economy and the larger share now represented by emerging markets.

Follow regulatory requirements but don't box-tick: look at the underlying risks that need managing

Over a decade ago, following the 1998 Russian default, Alexandre Lamfalussy asked in his book *Financial Crises in Emerging Markets* whether:

> destruction in the world of finance implies a greater risk of systemic instability than it does for, say, manufacturers of engineering products or microchips. It may well do so. Hence ... the financial markets ought not to be left to their own devices.

Although this is a strong argument to try to regulate and manage financial markets, how and when to intervene in the ever-evolving world of global finance remains a challenge. Some regulatory rules have increased pro-cyclicality. Others have become too complex and prescriptive, creating a complacent box-ticking attitude to risk. Regulation may induce a false sense of security, such as the Basel accords which allowed creditors to build up massive exposures to southern European sovereigns, with consequences all too evident a few decades later.

Keep risk management organisational structures flexible and guard the independence of the country risk function

Country risk analysis and management has developed over time, learning from each crisis. But has this resulted in improved country risk management? Also, if crisis is endemic to finance and the market economy, can country risk management achieve anything? The answer to both of these questions is yes, because not all countries are as vulnerable to external shocks or prone to home-grown crises as others. Crises also take different forms in different countries, though there are similar patterns. It is important to know what kinds of global crises are building up, which countries are crisis-prone and what kind of analysis is needed to manage country risk. One of the most important components of country risk management is the identification of risks at the transaction level, but it can be missed as it may fall in the grey area between country and credit risk functions. Supporting this process is a flexible risk management structure and, most importantly, the independence of the country risk management function as outlined in Chapter 10.

No easy formulas

This book outlines a step-by-step approach to define, analyse, identify, model, mitigate and manage country risk, moving back and forth among four levels: global, country, enterprise and transaction. The analysis shifts between an abstract, theoretical approach to risk in general and the practical management of country risk.

There are not many books on country risk. Some older books reflect the thinking of the time – the analysis is good but it soon becomes dated as countries and crises move on and change in content and form. This book tries to overcome this problem by adopting a historical perspective and a taking longer-term view on the possible evolution of global and country risks.

There are no easy formulas for managing country risks: not at the global and country level with policies seeking to mitigate crises; not at the enterprise level where risk management can become a box-ticking exercise; and not at the transaction level where there are no easy mitigants of country risks. This is because country risk varies depending on the type of investment and the nature of the enterprise, the target countries for investment and the historical features of the global economy. Hence this book should be seen as a guide to how best to approach country risk and tailor it to suit different purposes at different times.

Notes and sources

1 Introduction

Notes

1   The first known demographic census is said to have been conducted by the Babylonians in 3800BC. In 2500BC Egypt conducted a census to count the number of men available to build the pyramids.

2   Niall Ferguson makes the point in his book *The Ascent of Money* that the "imposition of British rule (as in Egypt in 1882) practically amounted to a 'no default' guarantee; the only uncertainty (being) the expected duration of British rule".

3   See *Foreign Bonds: An Autopsy* by Max Winkler for a detailed account of "unwise lending" as a major cause of defaults in the late 19th century through to the 1920s. First published in 1933, reprinted in 1999 as a Business Classic by Beard Books.

4   One of the earlier writings on political risk is by Dan Usher, "Political Risk", in *Economic Development and Cultural Change*, July 1965.

5   In Russia, the Bolsheviks nationalised all foreign-owned assets upon seizing power. The Turkish republic, founded in 1923 with the collapse of the Ottoman empire, was more pragmatic. For example, the 30 or so foreign power companies established in 1910 were eventually bought out by the Turkish government in the 1930s for failing to make the longer-term investments necessary to expand production – a familiar theme.

6   There is the case of Bayer Aspirin which was expropriated by the US government and auctioned for $5.3m in 1918 and sold to Sterling Drug Inc. Bayer AG did not manage to retrieve its full rights to the brand name until 1994 and with a payment of $1 billion.

7   Nestlé began local production of chocolates in Japan in 1934. It survived the state requisition of its plant during the war years, to regain its assets and start production once the war ended. See Donze, P.Y. and Kurosawa, T., "Nestlé coping with Japanese nationalism: Political risk and the

strategy of a foreign multinational enterprise in Japan, 1913–45", *Business History*, Taylor & Francis, 2013.
8   The Brady Plan restructured the debt with around 30–50% haircuts, and provided the debtor countries with the option of buying US guaranteed bonds at favourable prices to use as collateral. As well as countries in Latin America, Bulgaria, Poland, Morocco, Nigeria and Philippines were included in the plan.
9   Michael Bouchet, Ephraim Clark and Bertrand Groslambert cite Paul Krugman's "A model of balance of payments crisis", *Journal of Credit, Money and Banking* (August 1979) as an early theoretical underpinning to the many papers which then followed, such as Graciela Kaminsky and Carmen Reinhard, "The Twin Crises: The Causes of Banking and Balance-of-Payments Problems", *American Economic Review* (June 1999).
10 The global outcry against the role of US multinationals – especially International Telephone and Telegraph (ITT) – in the overthrow of the government of Salvador Allende in 1973 was a critical turning point in defining the limits of political intervention by international business at the time.

Sources

Bernstein, P.L., *Against the Gods: The Remarkable Story of Risk* (Wiley, 1996).
Bouchet, M., Clark, E. and Groslambert, B., *Country Risk Assessment: A Guide to Global Investment Strategy*, Wiley, 2003.
Freely, J., *Aladdin's Lamp*, Random House, 2010.
Ferguson, N., *The Ascent of Money*, Penguin, 2009.
McKinsey Global Institute, *Financial Globalisation: Retreat Or Reset?*, March 2013.
MIGA, *World Investment and Political Risk*, 2009.
MIGA, *World Investment and Political Risk*, 2011.
O'Rourke, K.H. and Williamson, J.G., *Globalization and History: The Evolution of a Nineteenth-Century Atlantic Economy*, MIT, 1999.
Solow, R., "How did economics get that way and what way did it get?", *Daedalus*, Vol. 126, No. 1, 1997.
Taleb, N., *The Black Swan: The Impact of the Highly Improbable*, Penguin, 2010.
Toksöz, M., *A linear programming approach to current planning issues of electricity supply in Turkey*, DPhil thesis, University of Sussex, 1979.
Tugendhat, C., *Multinationals*, Penguin Books, 1971.
Waiber, M., "Sovereign defaults before international courts and tribunals", *Cambridge Studies in International and Comparative Law*, 2011.
Winckler, O., *Arab Political Demography: Population Growth, Labour Migration, and Natalist Policies*, Sussex Academic Press, 2009.

2 Definitions of country risk

Notes

1   Calverley, J., *Country Risk Analysis*, Butterworths, 1990. Those approaching country risk from a credit background seem to like referring to this also as "collective debtor" risk, defined as economic and political events that adversely affect the creditworthiness of all debtors within a country.
2   Meldrum, D., "Country Risk and Foreign Direct Investment", *Business Economics* (January 2000), quoted in Bouchet, Clark and Groslambert (op. cit.).

Sources

Bernstein, op. cit.
Investopedia, www.investopedia.com
Knight, F.H., *Risk, Uncertainty, and Profit*, Houghton Mifflin Company, 1921.
Van Efferink, L., Kool, C. and Van Veen, T., *Country Risk Analysis*, NIBE-SVV, 2003.

3 Causes of country risk at global level: excessive lending

1   Some analysts put it more strongly. An Institute of International Finance report published in the midst of the 2008 crisis stated: "[T]hese capital flow cycles have taken over from policy makers as the key drivers of the global cycle." (Suttle, P., *Global Capital Flows and the Global Business Cycle*, Special Briefing, IIF, September 29th 2008.)
2   Quoted in Max Winkler, op. cit.
3   The absolute numbers are staggering, though relative to the projected GDP of developing countries this is less dramatic at between 6% and 11%, depending on the assumptions made about global growth (the historical peak was 9% of emerging markets GDP in 2007).
4   Assets under management by firms (including sovereign wealth funds) based in developing countries doubled their level over the past decade, but this was still only 5% of total managed assets. (Towers Watson, *The World's 500 Largest Asset Managers*, October 2012.)
5   This is highlighted by Peter Nolan in *Is China Buying the World?* (Polity Press, 2012) where he shows how industrial consolidation since the 1980s has led to the emergence of giant "system-integrator" firms with production facilities across the globe that control more than 50% of global market share in large commercial aircraft, automobiles, IT and beverages.
6   For example, it is not commonly known that industrial production declined 28.8% from its cyclical peak in July 1929 for over a year before the first wave of bank failures began in November 1930. (See Miron,

J. and Rigol, N., *Bank Failures and Output During the Great Depression*, NBER Working Paper No. 19418, September 2013.) Ben Bernanke, in a speech at an IMF conference, compared the financial panic of 1907 with the 2008 crisis, noting that the financial panic that struck in October 1907 was preceded by a recession that had already begun earlier in the year in May. (*The Crisis as a Classic Financial Panic*, 14th Jacques Polak Annual Research Conference, Washington DC, November 8th 2013.)

7   For a comprehensive discussion of cycles see Michael Niemira and Philip Klein, *Forecasting Financial and Economic Cycles* (Wiley, 1994) and *World Business Cycles* (The Economist Books, 1982 – unfortunately, an update is yet to be published).

8   See Grilli, E. and Maw Cheng Yang, "Primary Commodity Prices, Manufactured Goods Prices, and the Terms of Trade of Developing Countries" (*World Bank Economic Review*, Vol. 2, No. 1, 1988, updated in 2007). The secular decline of commodity prices in the 1960s became a major focus of development studies around the Singer-Prebisch theory that the terms of trade worked mostly against developing countries that mainly exported commodities.

9   See "Commodities traders call end of 'supercycle'" (*Financial Times*, June 26th 2013), which reports that the cancellation of investments in new mining projects weakened the Australian dollar and affected several sectors including mining-equipment manufacturers, service industries such as warehousing, transport and logistics, and firms that provide temporary housing to mining workers. Particularly badly affected were regions that depended on these activities, such as Perth, where mortgage defaults were expected to begin.

10 See "Betting the house" (*The Economist*, April 6th 2013), which quotes Edward Glaeser's paper on US housing booms, *A Nation of Gamblers* (NBER, 2013), arguing that easy credit was a "common thread in America's property history, but low interest rates are unfairly maligned" and that house prices rise in periods of low and high rates of interest. It suggests that policies such as mortgage securitisation first introduced in the 1920s and zero down-payment mortgages and federal guarantees in the 2000s played a bigger role.

11 See Dyer, P., "Demography in the Middle East: implications and risks" (in *Transnational Trends: Middle Eastern and Asian Views*, Pandya, A. and Laipson, E., eds, Henry L Smithson Centre, July 2008). Dyer quotes Henrik Urdal, who found that "when youth make up more than 35% of the adult population, which they do in many developing countries, the risk of armed conflict is 150% higher than in countries with an age structure similar to most developed countries" ("The Demographics of Political Violence", in Brainard, L. and Chollet, D., eds, *Too Poor for Peace? Global Poverty, Conflict, and Security in the 21st Century*, Brookings

Institution Press, 2007). Although I find this formula too precise for such a complicated relationship, the broad point seems relevant.

Sources

"Capital flows: powered down", *Financial Times*, January 6th 2014.

"The slumps that shaped modern finance", *The Economist*, April 12th 2014.

Bruner, F., Didier, T., Erce, A. and Schmukler, S., *Gross Capital Flows: dynamics and crises*, Discussion Paper No. 8591, Centre for Economic Policy Research, October 2011.

Claessens, S. and Kose, A., *Financial Crises: Explanations, Types, and Implications*. Paper presented at IMF Conference on "Financial Crises: Causes, Consequences and Policy responses", September 14th 2012.

Drehman, M., "Total credit as an early warning indicator for systemic banking crises", *BIS Quarterly Review*, June 2013.

Gordon, R.J., *The American Business Cycle: Continuity and Change*, University of Chicago Press, 1990.

IMF, *Global Financial Stability Report*, April 2006.

IMF, *Global Financial Stability Report*, April 2007.

Kaminsky, G. and Vega-Garcia, P., *Varieties of Sovereign Crises: Latin America 1920–1931*, NBER Working Paper No. 20042, April 2014.

Kindleberger, C. and Aliber, R.Z., *Manias, Panics, and Crashes: a History of Financial Crises*, Palgrave Macmillan, 2011.

Lamfalussy, A., *Financial Crises in Emerging Markets: An Essay on Financial Globalisation and Fragility*, Yale University Press, 2000.

Minsky, H., *The Financial-Instability Hypothesis: Capitalist Processes and the Behavior of the Economy*, 1982 (http://digitalcommons.bard.edu/hm_archive/282).

Motianey, A., *SuperCycles*, McGraw Hill, 2012.

Reinhard, C. and Rogoff, K., *This Time is Different: Eight Centuries of Financial Folly*, Princeton University Press, 2009.

Reinhart, C. and Reinhart, V., *Capital Flow Bonanzas: An Encompassing View of the Past and Present*, NBER International Seminar on Macroeconomics, 2008.

Subramanian, A. and Kessler, M., *The Hyper-globalisation of trade and its future*, Working Paper, Peterson Institute for International Economics, Washington, DC, July 2013.

Toksöz, M., *Turkey to 1992: Missing Another Chance?*, Special Report No. 1136, Economist Intelligence Unit, September 1998.

Winkler, M., *Foreign Bonds: An Autopsy*, first published in 1933, reprinted in 1999 by Beard Books.

Wolf, M., "Why the future looks sluggish", *Financial Times*, November 19th 2013.

World Bank, *Global Development Horizons*, June 2013, Washington DC.

4 Payments crises: country vulnerabilities

Notes

1   See Meier, G.M., *Leading Issues in Economic Development*, Oxford University Press, 1994.
2   See World Bank, *Global Economic Prospects* (January 2014), where it is noted that "global factors ... together account for about 60% of the increase in capital inflows between 2009 and 2013" to emerging markets.
3   For more on this see Kindleberger and Aliber, op. cit., last chapter, "The lessons of history".
4   For more on these themes, see Toksöz, M., "The GCC: prospects and risks in the new oil boom", in Nugee, J. and Subacchi, P. (eds), *The Gulf Region: A New Hub of Global Financial Power* (Royal Institute of International Affairs, 2008)

Sources

"Global Recovery and Monetary Normalisation: Escaping a Chronicle Foretold?", 2014 *Latin American and Caribbean Macroeconomic Report*, Inter-American Development Bank, March 2014.

Bowman, A., *et al*, *Central Bank led capitalism?*, Centre for Research in Socio-cultural Change, University of Manchester, 2012.

Calvo, G., "Capital flows and capital-market crises: the simple economics of sudden stops", *Journal of Applied Economics*, 1(1), 1998.

Elson, A., *Globalisation and Development: Why East Asia Surged Ahead and Latin America Fell Behind*, Palgrave Macmillan, 2013.

European Commission, *Alert Mechanism Report 2014*, Brussels, November 13th 2013.

Flandreau, M., *Caveat Emptor: Coping with Sovereign Risk Without Multilaterals*, CEPR Discussion Paper No. 2004, October 1998.

IMF, *Global Financial Stability Report*, No. 4, 2012.

IMF, *World Economic Outlook*, April 2014.

Kindleberger and Aliber, op. cit.

Krugman, P., *Currency Regimes, Capital Flows, and Crises*, Paper presented at the Jacques Polak Annual Research Conference, IMF, Washington, DC, November 2013.

Lamfalussy, op. cit.

Nowzad, B., "Lessons of the Debt Decade", *Finance and Development*, March 1990.

Ortiz, G., *Recent Emerging Market Crises: What Have We Learned?*, Per Jacobson Lecture, Bank for International Settlements, 2002.

World Bank, *Global Economic Prospects*, January 2014.

5 Payments crises: in-country causes

Notes

1 However, this is somewhat deceptive as it reflects outsourced production processes by the world's biggest multinational industrial firms, which dominate key manufacturing sectors based in these countries.

2 Despite the deadly factory accident in 2013 in Bangladesh, a McKinsey study showed that its garment industry remained the number one choice for international retailers such as Walmart. Bangladesh's minimum wage at $39 per month is only a quarter of China's (*Wall Street Journal*, September 17th 2013).

3 On a trip to the Uyu Tolgoi copper mine in the Gobi Desert in Mongolia in 2011, I talked to Australian and Mongolian engineers who had just finished assembling a massive coal-washing plant on site and asked what was the most difficult challenge they faced. The answer was: "Just getting the equipment here."

4 The Fund for Peace, based in Washington, DC, produces a failed states index, which in 2013 listed Somalia, the Democratic Republic of Congo, Sudan, Chad, Zimbabwe, Haiti, Afghanistan, Yemen, Iraq and the Central African Republic in its top-ten troubled countries, strangely omitting Syria.

5 An example of the spread of mobile banking is the M-pesa system set up in Kenya, which is reported to be handing up to 100bn Kenyan shillings ($1.1 billion) of transactions per month with around a third of Kenyan GDP passing through it. (Birch, D., "The future is mobile and African", *Prospect*, May 2014.)

Sources

Berg, A. and Sachs, J., "The debt crisis: structural explanations of country performance", *Journal of Development Economics*, Vol. 29, 1988.

Byblos Bank, *Country Risk Weekly Bulletin*, September 26th 2013.

Calverley, J., *Country Risk Analysis*, Butterworths, 1990.

De Luna-Martinez, J. and Vicente, C.L., *Global Survey of Development Banks*, Policy Research Working Paper 5969, World Bank, February 2012.

European Securities and Markets Authority, *Trends, Risks, Vulnerabilities*, March 12th 2014.

Ferguson, N., *Too Big to Live: Why We Must Stamp Out State Monopoly Capitalism*, Centre for Policy Studies, October 2009.

Government of India, *A Hundred Small Steps: Report of the Committee on Financial Sector Reforms*, Planning Commission, New Delhi, 2008.

Haglund, D., *Blessing or Curse? The rise of mineral dependence among low- and middle-income countries*, Oxford Policy Management, December 2011.

IMF, *Global Financial Stability Report*, April 2014.

Lazzarini, S., Musacchio, A., De Mello, R. and Marcon, R., *What Do Development Banks Do? Evidence from Brazil, 2002–09*, Working Paper 12–047, Harvard Business School, December 2011.

Rethinking Central Banking, Committee on International Economic Policy and Reform, September 2011.

Tett, G., "West's debt explosion is real story behind Fed QE dance", *Financial Times*, September 19th 2013.

World Bank, *Global Financial Development Report*, Washington, DC, 2013.

6 Political and geopolitical risks

Notes

1   The score of the factor-driven economies is the average of 58 countries categorised as factor driven (eg, Sierra Leone) and transitioning to efficiency driven (eg, Saudi Arabia); efficiency-driven economies are 53 consisting of the efficiency driven (eg, Indonesia) and transitioning to innovation driven (eg Mexico), and 37 economies in the innovation-driven category. (World Economic Forum, *The Global Competitiveness Report*, 2013–14, Geneva, 2013.)

Sources

Acemoglu, D. and Robinson, J.A., *Why Nations Fail*, Profile Books, 2013.

Bremmer, I. and Keat, P., *The Fat Tail: The Power of Political Knowledge for Strategic Investing*, Oxford University Press, 2009.

Das, U., Papaioannou, M. and Trebesch, C., *Sovereign Debt IMF, Restructurings 1950–2010: Literature Survey, data, and Stylized Facts*, Working Paper 12/203, 2012.

Dormandy, X. and Kinane, R., *Asia-Pacific Security: a changing role for the United States*, Chatham House Report, April 2014.

El-Erian, M., "Tranquil markets underprice geopolitical risk", *Financial Times*, March 24th 2014.

Hanson, P., *Reiderstvo: Asset Grabbing in Russia*, Chatham House and University of Birmingham, March 2014.

Jakobsen, J., "Old problems remain, new ones crop up: political risk in the 21st century", *Business Horizons*, No. 53, Kelley School of Business, Indiana University, 2010.

Moody's Investor Service, *Proposed refinements to the Sovereign Bond Rating Methodology*, December 17th 2012.

OECD, *The Emerging Middle Class in Developing Countries*, Development Centre Working Paper, No. 285, 2010.

Reinhart, C. and Rogoff, K., *This Time is Different: Eight Centuries of Financial Folly*, Princeton University Press, 2009.

Weiss, M., *Iraq: Paris Club Debt Relief*, US Congressional Research Service, January 19th 2005.

7 Identifying country risk at transaction level

Notes

1 The London Interbank Offered Rate (LIBOR) is the average interest rate calculated by leading London banks for interbank lending.
2 The Canada-based Frazer Institute publishes an annual survey of mining companies and the business environment in 90 countries to assess how the mineral endowment of a country and public policy such as taxation and regulation affect exploration and investment. In 2012/13, the ten "least attractive jurisdictions for investment", according to its policy potential index, included (from the bottom) Indonesia, Vietnam, Venezuela, Democratic Republic of Congo, Kyrgyzstan, Zimbabwe, Guatemala, the Philippines and Greece.
3 "Tullow steps up transparency in reporting", *Financial Times*, March 24th 2014. The report also reveals that Tullow Oil is to become the first international oil company to disclose its tax, royalty and other payments on a project-by-project basis in line with EU directives.

Sources

"Mining Cuts rile African Hosts", *Wall Street Journal*, December 6–8th 2013.
Alon, I. and Herbert, T.T., "A stranger in a strange land: Micro political risk and the multinational firm", *Business Horizons*, 52, 2009, Kelley School of Business, Indiana University.
Bouchet, Clark and Groslambert, op. cit.
Heinsz, W.J. and Zelner, B.A., "The hidden risks in emerging markets", *Harvard Business Review*, April 1st 2010.
MIGA, *World Investment Trends and Corporate Perspectives*, 2013.
Stevens, P., Kooroshy, J., Lahn, G. and Lee, B., *Conflict and Coexistence in the Extractive Industries*, Chatham House Report, Royal Institute of International Affairs, November 2013.
Vernon, R., *Sovereignty at Bay: The Multinational Spread of US Enterprises*, Basic Books, 2013, as quoted in Jakobsen, op. cit.
World Bank, *Ease of doing business and distance to frontier, Ease of doing business index: ranking methodology*, 2014.

8 Country risk models and ratings

Notes

1 Eaton, J., Gersovitz, M. and Stiglitz, J., "The pure theory of country risk", *European Economic Review*, Vol. 30, Issue 3, June 1986.

2   See Reinhart, C. and Reinhart, V., *Capital Flow Bonanzas: An
Encompassing View of the Past and Present* (NBER International Seminar
on Macroeconomics, 2008). Also Accominotti, O. and Eichengreen, B.,
*The Mother of All Sudden Stops: Capital Flows and Reversals in Europe,
1919–1932* (Berkeley Economic History Laboratory Working Paper, 2013/7),
which compares the current euro-zone crisis with the sharp decline in
capital inflows to Europe in 1929 to find push factors are better than pull
factors at explaining the surge and subsequent reversal of capital flows
into Europe in 1924–31. Also Forbes, K. and Warnock, F., *Capital Flow
Waves: Surges, Stops, Flight, and Retrenchment*, NBER Working Paper No.
17351, August 2011. An older study that anticipates the coming risks is
Kamin, S., Schindler, J. and Samuel, S., *The Contribution of Domestic and
External Factors to Emerging Market Devaluation Crises: an Early Warning
System Approach*, where a probit model is used to conclude "domestic
factors have maintained a relatively steady contribution to vulnerability
... but that the external shock and external balance variables have
exerted greater swings over time" (International Finance Discussion
Papers 711, Board of Governors of the Federal Reserve System,
September 2001).

3   The IMF's *World Economic Outlook* (October 2012) models indicators that
may have contributed to the post-crisis resilience of emerging markets.
Included among the four sets of indicators are external shock factors
that include the S&P volatility index, US ex-ante real interest rate, terms-
of-trade indicators, sudden-stop (capital flows) indicators and advanced
economy recession indicators.

Sources

Artis, M.J., Bladen-Hovell, R.C. and Zhang, W., "Turning points in the
international business cycle: an analysis of the OECD leading indicators
for the G-7 countries", *OECD Economic Studies*, No 24, 1995.

Bhatia, A., *Sovereign Credit Ratings Methodology: An Evaluation*, IMF Working
Paper, October 2012.

BlackRock Investment Institute, *Introducing the BlackRock Sovereign Risk
Index*, June 2011.

Bloomberg, *Quantitative Approaches to Modelling Sovereign Risk*, 2013.

Calverley, op. cit.

Calvo, G., "Capital flows and capital-market crises: the simple economics of
sudden stops", *Journal of Applied Economics*, 1(1), 1998.

Calvo, G., "The Mayekawa Lecture: puzzling over the anatomy of crises
– liquidity and the veil of finance", *Monetary and Economic Studies*,
November 2013.

Chenery, H. and Bruno, M., "Development alternatives in an open
economy", *Economic Journal*, Vol. 72, 1962.

Claessens, S. and Forbes, K. (eds), *International Financial Contagion*, 2001, Springer US.

Coons, J. and Fratzscher, M., *Capital Flows, Push versus Pull Factors and the Global Financial Crisis*, paper presented to the 2011 Sloan Global Financial Crisis Project Conference, NBER Working Paper No. 17357, August 2011.

Cukier, K. and Mayer-Shoenberger, V., "The rise of Big Data: how it's changing the way we think about the world", *Foreign Affairs*, May–June 2013.

Embrechts, P., Resnick, S. and Samorodnitsky, G., "Extreme Value Theory as a risk management tool", *North American Actuarial Journal*, Vol. 3, No. 2, April 1999.

Hubbard, D., *The Failure of Risk Management*, Wiley, 2009.

Hyun Song Shin, *Pro-cyclicality and the Search for Early Warning Indicators*, IMF conference on "Financial Crises: Causes, Consequences, and Policy Response", Washington, DC, September 14th 2012.

IMF-FSB Early Warning Exercise, "Design and Methodological Tool-kit", September 2010.

Kaminsky and Vega-Garcia, op. cit.

Kodres, L.E., *Early Warnings of Sovereign Risk: Accounting for Systemic Risk*, presentation at IIF Conference on Country Risk, February 11th 2013.

Krugman, P., "A model of balance of payments crises", *Journal of Money, Credit and Banking*, 1979.

Krugman, P., *Currency Regimes, Capital Flows, and Crises*, paper presented at the 14th Jacques Polak Annual Research Conference, Washington, DC, November 2013.

Manasse, P. and Roubini, N., *"Rules of thumb" for Sovereign Debt Crises*, IMF Working Paper, 2005.

Mendoza, E. and Yue, V., *A Solution to the Disconnect between Country Risk and Business Cycle Theories*, NBER Working Paper No. 13861, March 2008.

Moody's Investors Service, *Proposed Refinements to the Sovereign Bond Rating Methodology, Request for Comment*, December 2012.

Niemira, M. and Klein, P., *Forecasting Financial and Economic Cycles*, Wiley, 1994.

Unicredit, "The damaging bias of Sovereign Ratings", Unicredit Global Themes Series, Economics Research, March 26th 2014.

Van Efferink, Kool and Van Veen, op. cit.

Williamson, J., "Is Brazil Next?", Peterson Institute of International Economics, *International Economics Policy Briefs*, No PB 02–7, August 2002.

9 Country risk mitigation at global level

Notes

1 According to one study "the FSA may have revolutionised life in the City even more than the Big Bang, for in matters of regulation it replaced the informal with the formal, the flexible with the rigid, and the personal with the legalistic". Vogel, S., *Freer Markets, More Rules*, Cornell University Press, 1996, quoted in Hunt, B., *The Timid Corporation*, Wiley, 2003.

2 These included Pakistan and Yemen, but also big emerging markets with deep capital markets and high levels of capital flows such as Indonesia and Turkey. In relation to the latter, the weakening of the rule of law in recent years would appear to have been compounded by the underground activities and smuggling generated by the international sanctions on Iran. (www.fatf-gafi.org/topics/key/fatf-public-statement-oct-2013.html)

3 See Mahdavi, P., *Gridlock: Labour, Migration, and Human Trafficking in Dubai* (Stanford University Press, 2011) for an example of how laws made in Washington, DC, can have unforeseen consequences elsewhere in the world. The US Trafficking Victims Protection Act has created a moral outcry about sex workers and resulted in the criminalisation of immigrant women, also weakening their social support organisations.

4 Peter Kenen notes in *Refocusing the Fund: A Review of James M. Boughton's Silent Revolution: The International Monetary Fund, 1979–1989* (IMF staff papers, Vol. 50, No. 2, 2003) that only a quarter of the IMF's total disbursements "involved little or no conditionality" but this had more than doubled to about 60% by the mid-1980s and continued to rise.

5 Net present value (NPV) is the sum of future income (interest and principal) on a bond discounted at the agreed market rate. A collective action clause (CAC) allows a supermajority of bondholders to agree to debt restructuring that is legally binding on all bondholders.

6 This is not always the case. The bail-out of Mexico in 1994 was a construct of the US Treasury and the Fed, given the vulnerability of US banks. The conditionality imposed on Mexico almost harked back to the 19th-century bail-outs of Egypt and Ottoman Turkey. It required that Mexican oil revenues would be held as collateral by the Federal Reserve Bank of New York and advance ratification had to be obtained from the US Treasury of all tranches released as well as approval of how the funds would be utilised.

Sources

"And the Walls came Tumbling down", interview by Atish R. Ghosh with
    IMF official historian James Boughton, *Finance and Development*, Vol. 49,
    No. 1, March 2012.

"Back from the dead", *The Economist*, January 11th 2014.

"Obama's IMF gambit", *Wall Street Journal*, March 25th 2014.

Aggarwal, V.K. and Granville, B. (eds), *Sovereign Debt: Origins, Crises and
    Restructuring*, Royal Institute of International Affairs, 2003.

Blundell-Wignall, A. and Atkinson, P., "Thinking beyond Basel III: necessary
    solutions for capital and liquidity", *OECD Journal, Financial Market
    Trends*, Vol. 2010, Issue 1.

Boughton, J.M., *Northwest of Suez: The 1956 Crisis and the IMF*, IMF Staff
    Papers, Vol. 48, No. 3, 2001.

Callaghy, T.M., "The Paris Club and International Economic Governance", in
    Aggarwal and Granville, op. cit., 2003.

Das, U., Papaioannou, M. and Trebesch, C., *Restructuring Sovereign Debt:
    Lessons from Recent History*, IMF Working Paper, August 2012.

Eichengreen, B. and Park, B. (eds), *World Economy after the Global Crisis*,
    World Scientific Books, 2012.

Eichengreen, B., *Historical Research on International Lending and Debt*,
    University of California at Berkeley and NBER Working Paper No.
    90–153, December 1990.

European Parliament, "EU/ECB/IMF Troika needs fixing, but ministers must
    shoulder responsibilities", press release, February 25th 2014.

Granville, B., *Sovereign Debt Crisis Resolution: The Benefits of the Uncertainty
    Principle*, The Business Economist, 2002.

IMF, *About the IMF: History: Globalisation and the Crisis (2005–present)*,
    (https://www.imf.org/external/about/histglob.htm).

James, H., "Cosmos, chaos: finance, power and conflict", *International Affairs*,
    Vol. 90, No. 1, January 2014.

Lagarde, C., *Managing the New Transitions in the Global Economy*, speech at
    George Washington University, October 3rd 2013.

Mody, A., *Sovereign Debt and its Restructuring Framework in the Euro Area*,
    Bruegel Working Paper, 2013/05, August 2013.

Skidelsky, R., "Inventing the world's money", *New York Review of Books*,
    January 9th 2014.

Subacchi, P. and Jenkins, P., *Preventing Crises and Promoting Economic
    Growth, a Framework for International Policy Cooperation*, Royal Institute
    of International Affairs and Centre for International Governance
    Innovation, 2011.

Viscusi, W.K., Vernon, J.M. and Harrington, J.E., *Economics of Regulation and
    Antitrust*, MIT Press, 2000.

Winston, C., "Economic deregulation: days of reckoning for
microeconomists", *Journal of Economic Literature*, 31, September 1993,
quoted in Viscusi, Vernon and Harrington, op. cit.

10 Integrating country risk into management structures
Sources

"Beyond Basel", *The Economist*, April 12th 2014.
"Treatment of sovereign risk in the Basel capital framework", *BIS Quarterly
Review*, December 2013.
Basel Committee on Banking Supervision, *The New Basel Capital Accord*,
Consultative Document, January 2001.
Blundell-Wignall, A. and Atkinson, P., "Thinking beyond Basel II: necessary
solutions for capital and liquidity", *OECD Journal: Financial Market
Trends*, Vol. 2010, Issue 1.
Bremmer and Keat, op. cit.
Carney, B.M., "What ails the European economy?", interview with Jacques
de Larosière, *Wall Street Journal*, March 11th 2014.
Ganguin, B. and Bilardello, J., *Fundamentals of Corporate Credit Analysis*,
McGraw-Hill, 2005.
Hannoun, H., *Sovereign Risk in Bank Regulation and Supervision: Where Do
We Stand?*, speech at Financial Stability Institute High-Level Meeting,
Abu Dhabi, UAE, October 26th 2011.
Hawke, J.D. Jr, speech at Centre for the Study of Financial Innovation, March
13th 2003.
Henry, D. and LaCapra, L.T., "JPMorgan and other banks tinker with risk
models", *Reuters*, March 18th 2013.
Hubbard, D., *The Failure of Risk Management: Why It's Broken and How to Fix
It*, Wiley, 2009.
IMF, *Global Financial Stability Report*, April 2014.
Shapiro, A., *Multinational Financial Management*, Wiley, 2006.

11 Country risk mitigation at transaction level: the final defence
Notes

1   International Securities and Derivatives Association (ISDA), *CDS
Market Summary: Market Risk Transaction Activity*, ISDA Research Notes,
October 2013. The notional value outstanding had declined every year
since 2007 to $25 trillion in 2012, mostly reflecting early termination of
economically redundant derivatives (a process called compression). But
this should not be interpreted as a decline in CDS market activity, which
is reported to have been stable in 2011–12 and to have risen in the first
six months of 2013, according to the latest data.

2   Non-deliverable forwards (NDF) are futures contracts where the
    two sides settle the difference between the agreed NDF rate and the
    prevailing market rate on the agreed (notional) amount where the
    underlying notional amount is never intended to be paid, hence "non-
    deliverable" forward.
3   The early phases of the Dabhol project are drawn from *Power Play: A
    Study of the Enron Project*, by Abhay Mehta (Orient Longman, 1999) and a
    Harvard Business School case study by Louis Wells, "Enron Development
    Corporation: The Dabhol Power Project" (July 6th 1998).
4   These case studies are based on the author's experience and interviews
    with the project team at Standard Bank. Also useful was a paper
    presented at the June 2007 Enabling Environment Conference by the Aga
    Khan Fund for Economic Development (AKFED), *The Government and the
    Private Sector Working Together to Create the Afghan Telecommunications
    Industry*.

Sources

Bremmer and Keat, op. cit.
Claessens and Kose, op. cit.
Dages, B.G., *Overview of Country Risk Transfer Instruments*, Federal Reserve
    Bank of New York, May 2005.
Heinz, F.F. and Yan Sun, *Sovereign CDS Spreads in Europe: the Role of Global
    Risk Aversion, Economic Fundamentals, Liquidity and Spillovers*, IMF
    Working Paper, January 2014.
Henisz, A. and Zelner, B., "The hidden risks in emerging markets", *Harvard
    Business Review*, April 1st 2010.
MIGA, *World Investment and Political Risk*, 2013.
Wagner, D., *Managing Country Risk*, Taylor & Francis, 2012.

12 Conclusion: how to stop being surprised all the time

Sources

"India's Raghuram Rajan hits out at uncoordinated global policy", *Financial
    Times*, January 30th 2014.
Aizenman, J. and Ito, H., *Living with the Trilemma Constraint*, NBER Working
    Paper No. 19448, September 2013.
Bernstein, op. cit.
Buiter, W., "The Fed's bad manners risk offending foreigners", *Financial
    Times*, February 5th 2014.
Gorton, G., *Misunderstanding Financial Crises: Why We Don't See Them
    Coming*, Oxford University Press, 2012.
Greenspan, A., "Never saw it coming: why the financial crisis took
    economists by surprise", *Foreign Affairs*, Nov/Dec, 2013.

IMF, "The yin and yang of capital flow management: balancing capital inflows with capital outflows", *World Economic Outlook*, October 2013.

Independent Evaluation Office of the IMF, *IMF Performance in the Run-up to the Financial and Economic Crisis: IMF surveillance in 2004–07*, February 2011.

Independent Investigation Commission on the Fukushima Nuclear Accident, *The Fukushima Daiichi Nuclear Power Station Disaster*, Bircher, M.K. (ed.), Routledge, 2014.

Kindleberger and Aliber, op. cit.

Lamfalussy, op. cit.

Reinhart and Rogoff, op. cit.

Teaching Economics After the Crisis: Report from the Steering Group, summarised in The Business Economist, Vol. 44, No. 1, 2013.

Index

Page numbers in *italic* refer to case studies and figures.

A

A/B loans 218, 225
ability to pay 155, 184, 235
Abu Dhabi 74
ADB (Asian Development Bank) 193, 211, 217, 226, 228
adjustment factors 162
advanced economies, structural risk 79, *79*, 80-1, *81*
advanced emerging economies 81-2
AES Corporation *131-2*
Afghanistan 14, 105, 107-8, 109, *109*
    Roshan telecoms project 203, 225, 226, *227-8*
Africa 13, 96, 97, 140, 174, 209
    defaults 1, 42
African Development Bank 193, 217
aid 58, 168
AIG 212, 215
Albania 88
Algeria 143
Aliber, Robert 41-2, 233
Amazon *132-3*
Anglo American 135, 136
Angola 13, 88, 90, 174
Arab spring (2011) 1, 18, 46, 112, 113, 115, 188

Argentina 46, 72, 78, 82, 100, 101, 171, 176
    debt restructuring 177
    defaults 1, 11-12, 31, 34, 42, 98, 139, 175, 177, 191
    income inequalities 87-8
    nationalisations 18, 99, 100, 138, 139, 140
    Renault currency loss *128-9*
    "rogue policies" 96, *98-100*
Armenia 88
Arrow, Kenneth 5
Arthur Andersen 169, 182, 186
Asian countries 42, 52, 65, 102, 105, 121, 179
Asian Development Bank *see* ADB
Asian financial crisis (1990s) 1, 42, 43, 47, 61, 69, 169, 182, 186, 209
    housing bubble 51, 62, 152
    IMF and 171-2
    payments crisis (1997) 11, 25, 42, 61, 62, 70, 152, 173
asset bubbles 95, 233
Atlantic Charter 1941 7
Australia 6, 19, 28, 72-3, 97, 117
Austria 6, 55, 235
Azerbaijan 124

B

Bahamas 32
Bahrain 45, 73, 74

bail-outs 35, 61, 73, 171, 234
  banks 40, 41, 80, 142, 178, 235
  Cyprus 80, 89, 175, 178, 180
  Greece 80, 175, 178
  Ireland 80, 178, 180
  Jamaica 89
  Mexico (1994) 43, 171, 172
  Portugal 80, 178, 180, 235
  Russia 234
  Spain 80
balance-of-payments crises 10, 24, 84
Balkans 108
Baltic states 108
Bangladesh 82, 129
Bank of America 223-4
Bank of England 34, 63, 167, 173, 230
Bank for International Settlements
  see BIS
Bank of Japan 69, 81, 173
Bankia 142
banking crises 24, 40-1, 41, 53, 80, 94,
  229, 235
  2008-09 158, 197, 235
  early warnings 163
  euro zone 1, 36, 80
  Iceland 24, 40-1, 89, 197-8
  Nordic countries 45, 61
  and sovereign crises 193
  Turkey 1, 56
banking sector 13, 68, 89-95, 90,
  92-3, 114
  China 90, 91, 92-3
  EU 179
  risks 27, 30, 133
  US 95
banks 32, 40, 74, 95, 167, 191, 197
  bail-outs 40, 41, 60-1, 80, 142, 178,
  235
  collapses 27, 41-2, 42, 73
  lending 59, 182
  nationalisations 231
  see also Barings; JPMorgan
Barings 217

Basel accords 19, 92, 182, 183-5, 185,
  187, 238
  Basel I (1988) 10, 168, 183, 192
  Basel II (2004) 168, 183-4, 185
  Basel III 168, 170, 183, 184-5, 186
Basque conflict 116
Bechtel 223, 224, 225
Belarus 203-4
Belgium 235
Belize 14
BERI (Business Environment Risk
  Intelligence) 9-10
Berlin Wall, fall of (1989) 60, 171
Bernanke, Ben 47
Berne Union 9, 211, 213
Bernstein, Peter 3, 4, 29-30, 229
biases 161, 164
Big Bang financial reforms 168
big data 149
bilateral aid 58, 175
bilateral creditors 35, 174, 177
BIS (Bank for International
  Settlements) 41, 167, 169, 231, 232
black swan events 111, 149, 202, 232
Bolivia 87, 89, 99, 138, 138-9, 222
Bolshevik revolution 58, 110
bondholder committees 176
Botswana 191
Brady Plan 10, 78, 173
"brass-plate" incorporations 32
Brazil 11, 17, 46, 67, 72, 81, 93, 94, 105,
  153, 213
  capital controls 127
  currency problems 68, 69
  defaults 34
  IMF support 42, 171
  middle class 112
  one of "Fragile 5" 28, 69, 82
  politically allocated credit 91
  protest 112, 113, 114
breach of contract 19, 28, 126, 212,
  213, 214-15, 214
Bretton Woods institutions 9, 167, 173

Bretton Woods system 37, 167, 173
  breakdown of 35, 37, 40, 50, 152, 182, 200
BRIC countries 81, 105
budget deficits 27, 75, 84
budget surpluses 76–7
Buffet, Warren 215
Bulgaria 107
Bundesbank 60, 173
business cycles 48–50, 49, 53, 154–5
business environment 134–6, 205
Business Environment Risk
  Intelligence *see* BERI

C
Calverley, John 78
Calvo, Guillermo 65, 153
Cambodia 88, 227
Cameroon 14, 115
Canada 6, 72–3
capital controls 9, 11, 23, 37, 75, 95, 214, 231
  Argentina 99
  Brazil 69
  Cyprus 14
  Russia and 235
  selective 25, 127, 172
capital flows 10, 17, 23, 38–9, 42, 48, 54, 153, 229
  bonanzas and busts 41, 154, 154
  as crisis triggers 60–1
  emerging markets 28, 37
  global 12–13, 17, 18, 35–6, 36, 173, 180, 200
  liberalisation 25, 41, 42, 44, 138, 236
  private sector 177
  size 6, 12–13, 15, 39, 65, 96, 173, 179, 229
  volatility 64, 69, 236
capital markets 229, 235
Caribbean 71, 89
Carrefour 134–5
Catalonia 117

Cayman Islands 32
CDS (credit default swaps) 207, 215–17, 219
Central Asia 56, 142
Central Bank of India 237
central banks 62–3, 69, 163–4, 167, 173
  independence 15, 26, 39, 47, 160, 161, 198
  role 42–3, 61, 95, 234
  see also Bank of England; Bank of Japan; Bundesbank; Federal Reserve; PBoC
chaos theory 2, 5, 15, 149
Chavez, Hugo 139
Chiang Mai initiative 174
Chile 34, 98–9, 236
China 13, 43, 69, 70, 81, 90, 120, 122, 179, 237
  banking sector 90, 91, 94
  capital controls 127
  corruption 122–3
  domestic market 236
  during 2008–09 crisis 89
  exports to 86
  financial sector risks 2, 92–3
  foreign-currency reserves 39
  growth 93
  housing bubble 51
  and Japan 105
  liberalisation 92–3
  loans from 173, 222
  middle class 112
  modernisation 120, 121
  neocolonialism 96
  and North Korea 106
  opium wars 6–7
  and Philippines 104
  reforms 78, 91, 92–3
  rising power 17, 37, 81, 105, 173
  slowdown 44, 86, 222
  under Deng Xiaoping 124
  and US 14, 70, 72, 96, 120
  wages 135

Citibank 10
civil strife 28, *55*, 135, 218-19
civil wars 88, 110, 118, 124, 136
Claessens, Stijn 40, 230-1
climatic conditions 18, 72
co-financing 207, 218
co-operation, international 178
cold war, new 44, 109-10
collateral 209
Colombia 30, 34, 82, 109, 235
colonial era 6-7, 38, 50, 174
Commerzbank 10
commodities 54, 72, 91, 92
commodity prices 49-50, *49, 50-1,*
    72, 85, 86, 97, 98, 110, 163, 205
    booms 17, 109
    collapses 14, 35, 46, 50, *55*, 190
    cycles 27, 53, 134
    falling 135, 236
    rising 97, 98, 154
    vulnerability to shocks 204
confiscation 103, 213
conflicts 28, 38, 44, 89, 96, 220
    military 104, 105, 107-8
    over seabed rights 44, 105
    see also wars
contagion 15, 43-6, 65, 96, 148, 149,
    152, 200
    Cyprus and Greece 45, 89, 175
    transmission channels 44-6, 77,
        152-3
contagion risk 11, 33
contract renegotiation 205, 212
contractual disputes 18-19
corporate governance 182, 200
corruption 46, 83, 90, 122-3, 125-6,
    133, 137-8, 142, 143, 161
    China 122-3
    Philippines 209
    Ukraine 110
Costa Rica 34
counter-cyclical policies 233, 236
country limits 196-7, 197

country risk 1-15, 23, 31, 78, 147, 239
    assessment methodologies 148-51
    components 24-9, 30, 127
    defining 29-30, 238-9
    indicators 151-5, *154*
    limits 190-2, *193*
    modelling *see* models
    on a relative basis 150-1
    theory of 149-50
    see also country risk management;
        country risk mitigation
country risk appetite 189-90, *190*
country risk function 195-201, *195,*
    238
country risk management 29-30, 33,
    163, 180, 181-2, 192, 229, 238-9
    Basel accords and 182, 187
    management function 195-201,
        195, 197-8, 238
    multinationals 187-8
    non-financial organisations 188
    organisational structures for 29,
        189-95, *190, 193*
    outsourcing 199-201
    using models for 5-6, 29, 164-5
country risk mitigation 30, 238-9
    global level 166-80
    mitigants 6, 199, 203, 206-7, 226
    transaction level 202-22
country risk-rating model 5-6, 30,
    147, 151, 155-65
credit booms 47, 92, 93, 154, 233
credit bubbles 53-4, 77, 80, 154, 163,
    204, 233-4, 236
    Asia 42
    Iceland 197
    US 14, 47
credit cycles 48-9, 133, 154, 204
credit default swaps *see* CDS
credit growth 47, 163
Crédit Lyonnais 6, 58
credit parameters 204-5
creeping expropriation 97, 217

Crimea 105, 109, 110
cronyism 84–5, 91, 108, 121, 124, 137–8
Cuba 7, 8, 9, 58, 89
cultural factors 68, 114–15, 137
currencies 24, 41–2, 68–9, 77, 163, 227, 235
    floating 13–14, 43
    overvalued 71, 163
    undervalued 71
    volatility 129, 182
currency crises 12, 23–4, 41, 128, 129, 152, 163, 229
    1990s 59
    ERM 60
    Iceland 89
    sudden stops and 40, 41, 129
currency inconvertibility 212, 213–14, 221
currency pegging 59, 60, 61, 73, 98, 152
currency risks 159, 182, 210, 224
current-account balances 63, 67, 74–5, 75
current-account deficits 40–1, 66, 70–1, 74–5, 80, 83, 152, 158
    US 14, 233
current-account surpluses 70, 76–7, 85, 98, 99
cyclical factors 33, 53, 65, 156, 231
cyclical indicators 151, 154–5, 156
Cyprus 1, 14, 45, 94, 175, 191, 204
    bail-out 80, 89, 175, 178, 180

D
Dabhol power project (India) 16, 131, 141, 203, 222–5
data 12, 14, 25, 149, 234
data mining 15, 149
debt 13, 62, 67, 76, 77, 160
    restructuring 78, 88, 89, 107, 174–8, 175, 180
debt crises 40, 42, 46, 48, 83, 152, 183
    developing countries (1980s) 152, 171, 173, 207–8, 232

    see also sovereign debt crises
debt loads, developed countries 76
debt repayments 23, 71, 75, 76, 126–7, 209
debt-default cycle 234–5
debt-to-GDP ratios 74, 75–6, 175
decolonisation 7–8, 58, 114, 151, 180
default risk 108–11, 109–10
defaults 23, 24–5, 33, 38, 59, 80, 94, 232–4
    19th century 1, 6, 34, 58, 154, 176, 235
    1980s 6, 42, 59, 182, 233
    country risk analysis and 5, 15–16
    emerging markets 14
    excessive lending and 12
    and financial crises 78
    global financial centres and 153–4, 154
    housing cycles and 53
    interest rate increases and 11
    measuring probability 148–9
    serial defaulters 88
    wars and 28, 58, 108–11, 109–10
    waves of 16, 48
    see also under individual country names
Democratic Republic of the Congo 88, 140
demographic gift 52
demographics 37, 47, 52, 53, 68, 82, 133
    changes 36, 112
Depression (1930s) 6, 34, 37
deregulation 36, 61, 168
derivatives 36, 40, 43, 45, 125, 182, 207, 216–17
    market reforms 185
    vulnerable transactions 128
devaluation risks 9, 82, 214
devaluations 56, 62, 84, 93–4, 100, 129, 139–40
    higher costs due to 27, 219
developed countries
    debt loads 76

political institutions 116–18
  sovereign risk 62–4, 63
developed markets 12, 15, 159, 233
developing countries 68, 68–9, 170
  debt crises 171, 173, 207–8, 232
development 57, 58–9, 78, 112, 124,
  151–2, 159, 160
  institutions and 118–22, 119–21
  state-led 83, 122
direct investments 128–9
direct investors 218–19, 219–20
diversification 56, 85–7, 86–7, 94–5,
  115–16, 116, 119, 235–6
diversified developing economies,
  structural risk 79, 79, 81–3, 84–5
Dodd-Frank Act 2010 168–9, 170
Doing Business index 135, 161
domestic demand 31, 67, 70, 102, 130,
  131, 236
Dominican Republic 14, 177, 235
dotcom bubble 42, 50, 56, 133
dotcom crisis 50, 54, 56, 182
dual currency repayments 210
Dubai 45, 73, 74, 76, 91
Dubai Ports 143
Dynamics 142

E
early-warning function 15, 163
East and South China Seas 44, 105
East Timor 88
eastern Europe 11, 42, 63–4, 82,
  164
EBRD (European Bank for
  Reconstruction and Development)
  193, 217
ECB (European Central Bank) 63,
  117, 180
ECGD (Export Credits Guarantee
  Department) 9, 211
economic cycles 48
economic development 57, 151–2
  see also development

economic policies 12, 78–9, 83, 102,
  125, 157, 204
  risks 95–102, 98–100
  uncertainty 96, 113–14, 132–3
economic risk 24, 28–9, 219
economic structure 115–16, 116, 157
ECRM (European Crisis Resolution
  Mechanism) 178
Ecuador 34, 87, 109, 115, 138
EGSA (Empresa Electrica Guarachi)
  138, 139
Egypt 78, 82, 84–5, 90, 124, 175, 214, 221
  Baathist revolution 122
  fiscal crises 6, 84, 108
  overthrow of Mubarak 85, 107, 111,
    206, 214, 221
  privatisation 85, 123
  protests 46, 85, 113, 114
  strategic role 108
  Suez Canal crisis 8, 171
El Salvador 34
elections 47, 70, 91, 98, 100–1, 121,
  204, 224
elites 83, 108, 111–12, 114, 118, 122,
  123, 124
  Russia 120, 122
  Ukraine 110
emerging markets 1, 12, 13, 14, 17, 42,
  54, 81–2, 232
  flexible exchange rates 152
  foreign-currency borrowing 76
  growth 37–8, 50, 64, 81–2, 82, 153–4
  and international financial centres
    237
  investment in 130
  middle class 46, 112–13, 113, 113–14
  models for 15, 159
  ratings 14, 235
  slowdown 130
  sovereign wealth funds 36
  vulnerabilities 28, 93–5, 94
Empresa Electrica Guarachi see
  EGSA

energy prices 102, 110
energy sector 85, 98, 100, 110, 223
Enlightenment 3-4, 7, 229
Enron 131, 169, 182, 186, 223, 224, 224-5
environmental risks 188, 205
ERM (enterprise risk management) 19, 188
ERM (European exchange rate mechanism) 60, 102, 152
ESM (European Stability Mechanism) 174
ESMA (European Securities and Markets Authority) 169-70, 170
Ethiopia 30, 88
EU 47, 63, 96, 121, 133, 206, 227
    east European economies 82, 164
    emergency loans 63-4
    and Hungary 198
    monetary policies 37
    political risks 117
    and rating agencies 186
    sanctions 204
    sovereignty within 179-80
    Turkey and 56, 72
    UK membership 118
    and Ukraine 108, 109, 110
    see also euro zone
euro zone 42, 43, 62, 69, 80-1, 159, 174, 198
    crisis (2008-09) 36, 42, 44, 60, 72, 117, 172, 235
    southern 15, 30, 70, 164, 215
    sovereign debt crisis 15, 43, 62, 80, 124, 153, 185, 187, 221, 232-3, 235
    sovereign risk 185, 187
    sovereignty 179-80
European Bank for Reconstruction and Development see EBRD
European Central Bank see ECB
European Commission 117, 180, 198
European Crisis Resolution Mechanism see ECRM

European exchange rate mechanism see ERM
European Securities and Markets Authority see ESMA
European Stability Mechanism see ESM
Ex-im Bank (Export-Import Bank of the United States) 223-4, 225
exchange rates 35, 72, 88, 205, 236
    floating 4, 11, 39, 152
    real 71, 83
    volatility 204, 219
exchange-rate risk 24, 26-7, 28-9, 125, 128-9, 208
Export Credits Guarantee Department see ECGD
Export-Import Bank of the United States see Ex-im Bank
exposure limits 190-2, 193
expropriation 28, 95-6, 103, 138, 139-40, 211
    classic political risk 7-8, 58, 103, 181-2
    creeping 97, 217
    Cuba 9, 58
    mitigating risk of 213, 221, 222
    risk of 11, 18, 97, 188, 212
external factors 64-5, 71-3, 166
external push factors 12, 15-16, 52, 65, 151, 154, 155, 156, 159, 232
external shocks 23, 25, 28, 43, 65-6, 68-9, 77, 96, 131, 156
    cushioning against 13-14, 74-5, 75, 235-7
    vulnerability to 57, 74-7, 153, 155, 159
external vulnerabilities 156
extractive sector 140, 141, 205, 218-19, 219-20
extreme value theory 149

F
FATF (Financial Action Task Force) 170, 203

FDI (foreign direct investment) 6,
10–11, 37, 58, 97, 125–6, 168
by US 9, 37, 58
cushion against global shocks
74–5, 75
in Egypt 84
in India 225
in Russia 120, 121
Federal Reserve 50, 63, 68, 173, 230,
233, 237
interest rates 11, 47, 61, 62, 156, 158
monetary policy 1, 12–13, 36, 44
tapering 44–5, 65, 69, 153
Financial Action Task Force see FATF
financial centres, global 23, 34, 62,
153–4, 155, 232, 237
financial crises 12, 38–43, 40, 47, 78,
108–9, 173
19th century 34
1929 34–5, 167
1970s 39, 102, 152, 168
1994 39, 69
Asian see Asian financial crisis
(1990s)
booms preceding 154, 154
each one different 2, 11, 57, 150,
155, 233, 238
emerging markets 17, 42
Nordic (1990s) 45
predicting 147, 150
prevention 12, 18, 178
Turkey 54–6
see also defaults; global financial
crisis (2008–09)
financial instability hypothesis 48–9
financial instruments 2, 10–12, 13, 36,
40, 43, 200, 234
financial markets 42, 80, 95, 127, 158
liberalisation 39, 59, 61, 91, 158, 167,
168, 229
financial sector 66, 74, 82, 89, 90
integration 42, 45, 77, 127, 158
risks 27, 89–95, 90, 92–3, 94, 204

Financial Services Act see FSA
Financial Services Authority see FSA
Financial Stability Board see FSB
Financial Stability Oversight Council
see FSOC
Finland 51
first world war 7, 8, 34, 55, 111
fiscal deficits 66, 67, 70, 152
fiscal multipliers 172, 173
fiscal policy 13, 48, 96, 101, 131, 152,
234
Hungary 198
and monetary policy 15, 63, 95
US 81
fiscal surpluses 85, 98
flexibility 159, 179, 181, 189, 235, 238
foreign currency 24, 184, 208
foreign-currency risks 183
foreign-currency borrowing 76, 77, 82
foreign-currency reserves 30, 39, 76,
89, 153, 173, 235
foreign-debt-to-GDP ratio 158, 160
foreign direct investment see FDI
foreign investment, political
attitudes to 138, 138–9, 143
foreign payments imbalances 66,
70–3, 73–4
Foreign Terrorist Asset Tracking
Centre see FTAT
former Soviet Union 11, 107, 122, 171
former Yugoslav republics 107
"Fragile 5" countries 28, 69, 82
fragile states 88–9, 159, 162
fragmentation of global economy 18,
37, 38, 96, 170, 174, 179, 231
France 9, 35, 100, 107, 171, 175, 235
Friedmann, Milton 68, 172
frontier markets 13, 79, 79, 88
FSA (Financial Services Act) 168
FSA (Financial Services Authority)
187
FSB (Financial Stability Board) 161,
169, 182, 189, 231

FSOC (Financial Stability Oversight Council) 168–9
FTAT (Foreign Terrorist Asset Tracking Centre) 187–8
Fukushima Dai-ichi nuclear power plant (Japan) 232
future contracts 216
future-flow financing 208–9

G

G10 169, 233
G20 43, 169, 172, 173, 179, 182, 231, 233, 237
game theory 5
GATT (General Agreement on Tariffs and Trade, 1947) 9
GCC (Gulf Cooperation Council) 43, 73–4, 76
GDP growth 27, 158
GE 223, 224, 225
Gelderen, Jacob van 48
General Agreement on Tariffs and Trade) see GATT
geopolitical risk 17, 18, 28, 37–8, 103, 104–11, 105–7, 109–10, 115, 231, 232
  forecasting 147
Georgia 46, 88, 131–2
geostrategic risks 103, 180, 188
Germany 8, 55, 70, 109, 111, 175
  monetary policies 60, 102
Ghana 19, 82, 100
Glass-Steagall Act 1933 167, 168
global economy 2, 17, 33, 48, 237
  fragmentation 18, 37, 38, 70, 96, 174, 179, 231
global financial centres 23, 34, 62, 153–4, 155, 232, 237
global financial crisis (2008–09) 1, 26, 37, 43, 94, 127, 163–4, 170, 200, 215
  aftermath 5, 17, 42, 80, 182, 232
  capital export cycle and 40
  credit bubble and 42, 47

failure to predict 230
and globalisation 96
Gulf economies and 73, 77
lessons from 14–15, 148–9, 153–4, 158
and risk transfer 216–17
Russia and 119
Turkey and 56
vulnerabilities exposed 26, 95
global integration 17, 25, 26, 96, 108, 179, 181
global shocks 17, 65, 73, 89, 204
  cushioning against 235–7
globalisation 5, 10, 15, 38–9, 52–3, 96, 114, 127
  first era (19th century) 1, 6–7, 10, 34, 37, 38, 50, 167
  second era (late 20th century) 10, 34, 35, 37, 42
  third era 37, 38, 53
gold standard 34, 35, 38, 167
governance 26, 115, 122, 137–8, 152, 161, 188
  corporate 182, 200
governments 14–15, 33, 38, 70, 96, 127, 229
  bail-outs of banks 40, 41, 80
  interventions 25, 127
  and sovereignty 174
granularity 160, 161, 187
Great Depression (1930s) 6, 34, 37
Greece 30, 40–1, 62, 117, 172, 178, 186
  19th-century defaults 6, 235
  bail-outs 80, 175, 178
  and Cyprus 45, 89, 175, 204
  debt restructuring 175, 177, 180
Greenspan, Alan 230
growth 27, 59, 101, 102, 124, 130, 131, 154, 158, 205
  China 93
  euro zone 81
  volatility 125
guarantees 209, 226

Guatemala 34
Guinea 140, 142
Gulf Cooperation Council *see* GCC
Gulf states 44, 45, 56, 101, 122, 123
  support from 84, 85, 108, 174

H
Haglund, Dan 86–7, 86–7
Hahn, Frank 5
Halkbank 137
Haner, F.T. 10
Hawke, John D. Jr 185
high-profile projects 141–2
HIPC (heavily indebted poor
  countries) initiative 76, 175–6
historical perspective 33, 50, 57–65,
  151, 154–5, 229–31, 231–2, 234–5,
  238–9
home bias 36, 123
home-grown factors 12, 46, 65, 155,
  156
  payments crises 17, 28, 78–9
  vulnerabilities 15–16, 17, 23, 28–9
Honduras 34
Hong Kong 6–7, 51, 89, 221
housing bubbles 51, 233
housing cycles 53, 154
housing problem, London 101
Hungary 64, 68–9, 82, 174, 198
hyperinflation 82, 160

I
Iceland 24, 40–1, 89, 197–8
IFC (International Finance
  Corporation) 217, 226
IIF (Institute of International
  Finance) 12, 169
IMF (International Monetary Fund)
  9, 12, 35–6, 43, 96, 117, 169, 180,
  231
  and Argentina 99
  bail-outs 35, 54, 55, 56, 177, 234
  and Egypt 84

and Greece 175
and Hungary 198
loans from 42, 54, 55, 56, 58, 63–4
role 60–1, 171–4, 179, 233
SDRM 178
struggling 171, 179
and Ukraine 109, 110
and US 171, 173
Implats 219–20
incomes
  distribution 83, 112, 117, 161
  inequality 83, 87–8, 112, 124
India 17, 32, 37, 50, 81, 90–1, 105
  Dabhol power project 16, 131, 141,
    203, 222–5
  domestic market 236
  Licence Raj 137
  middle class 112
  Nestlé in 130
  one of "Fragile 5" 28, 69, 82
  protests 46, 112, 113, 114
indicators 62, 150, 151–9, 161, 163,
  163–4, 234
  cyclical 151, 154–5, 156
  of political instability 103–4
  of structural risk 79, 159
  of vulnerability 66
  see also country risk-rating model
Indonesia 11, 19, 26, 28, 69, 69, 81–2,
  86, 128
industrial sectors, sensitivity 134
industrialisation 59, 84, 102
inequalities 58, 59, 83, 87–8, 112, 124
inflation 13, 71, 128, 129, 131, 152, 158,
  160
  Argentina 88, 99, 100, 100
  fuelling 88, 100
  Nigeria 27
  targeting 95, 96
  Turkey 56
  Venezuela 138–40
inflationary pressures 101, 152
information 5, 40, 43, 149, 199

infrastructure 17–18, 26, 86, 135, 136, 136, 205, 220
infrastructure investment 6, 34, 38, 58, 81, 214
infrastructure projects 218, 222–7
innovation 48, 81, 116, 120, 121, 122, 234
Institute of International Finance *see* IIF
institutional development 61, 83, 115, 118–22, 137
institutional factors 68, 152, 155, 159
institutional investors 36, 75
institutional risk 122–3, 157, 159
institutions 8–9, 12, 78, 103, 121–2, 180, 234–5
  fragility 63, 83, 88
  lagging behind development 118–22, 119–21
  multilateral 9, 99, 137–8, 179, 193, 211, 217, 231, 233
  political 116–18
  and political risk 115–23, 116, 119–21
  strength 115–16, 116, 135, 225, 235
  too big to fail 95, 182, 184
  weakness 114, 117, 118, 122, 124, 137, 200
integration 77, 117
  financial markets 126, 127, 158
  global economy 17, 25, 26, 108, 179, 181, 200
  regional 46, 73–4, 108
interest rates 91, 93, 128, 161, 163–4, 205
  Federal Reserve 11, 47, 61, 62, 156, 158
  low 17, 76, 98, 100, 154
  rises 11, 27, 42, 50, 56, 59, 61, 61, 62, 69, 76, 100
  US 47
interest-rate risk 28–9, 128–9, 129
international bankruptcy code 178
International Finance Corporation *see* IFC

International Monetary Fund *see* IMF
international monetary systems 37, 53, 167–8
international regulation 167–71, 230, 238
investment booms 50–1
investment cycles 15–16, 154
Iran 8, 89, 104, 107, 111, 137, 162, 213
Iraq 104, 111, 115, 137, 177, 213
  interventions in 14, 84, 104, 105, 109, 109
Ireland 40–1, 80, 94, 178, 180, 186
Israel 104, 227
Italy 3, 9, 60, 62, 102, 117, 186, 213

J
Jamaica 89
Japan 37, 43, 47, 51, 62, 81, 232
  bubble (1980s–90s) 42, 51
  and China 105
  quantitative easing 69, 81
Jersey 32
Jordan 108, 175
JPMorgan 167, 200
jurisdiction risks 26, 29, 30, 125, 134–6, 159

K
Kazakhstan 13, 97, 124, 221
Kenya 82, 140–1, 209
Keynes, John Maynard 5, 12
Keynesian policies 48, 152
Kindleberger, Charles 35, 41–2, 233
Kirchner, Cristina 99, 100
Knight, Frank 5, 29
Kondratieff, Nikolai 48
Kose, Ayhan 40, 230–1
Kosovo 88
Kruger, Annie 178
Krugman, Paul 65, 152
Kuwait 45, 73, 74, 84, 213
Kuznets cycle 48, 51
Kyrgyzstan 46

L
labour conditions 135
Lagarde, Christine 69, 170
Lamfalussy, Alexandre 40, 237
Laos 227
Latin America 34, 59, 65, 87–8, 153
    19th-century defaults 6, 34, 58,
        109, 154
    1930s defaults 34, 167
    1980s defaults 1, 10, 42, 43, 75–6, 152
    expropriations 212
Leeson, Nick 217
Lehman Brothers 234
lending boom (1970s) 233
level of exposure 205–6
liberalisation 11, 55, 56, 61, 83, 93, 172
    capital flows 25, 41, 42, 44, 138, 236
    financial markets 39, 59, 61, 91, 158,
        167, 168, 229
    trade 132, 138, 167, 168
LIBOR interest rates 137, 156
Libya 111, 113, 123, 213
licence cancellation 9, 95–6, 138
Licence Raj 137
limit breaches 193, 194–5
liquidity 14, 40, 76, 153, 215
liquidity crises 23–4, 60, 76–7
Lloyd's of London 4, 212
local-currency debt 24–5
London, housing problem 101
London Club 10, 176
loss given default 135, 207
Luxembourg 32

M
MAC (material adverse change)
    clauses 206
macro-prudential policies 233, 234,
    236
macroeconomic imbalances 65–7
macroeconomic volatility 28–9, 125,
    130–1, 130, 135
Malaysia 11, 25, 93, 209, 236

management conflicts 196–7, 197–8
market sentiment 12, 14, 44, 68, 153
Marshall Islands 32
material adverse change *see* MAC
Mauritius 32
Mercosur 46, 72
Merkel, Angela 175
Mexico 59, 81–2, 109, 173, 183, 208–9
    bail-out (1994) 43, 171, 172
    defaults 34, 109, 235
    payments crisis (1994) 11, 42, 61,
        61–2, 69, 76, 152, 153, 182, 183
    and US 72, 207
middle classes 46, 51, 82, 85, 111
    rise of 37, 112–13, 113, 113–14
Middle East 50, 52, 88, 91, 107, 108,
    114, 212
middle ground convergence 236
MIGA (Multilateral Investment
    Guarantee Agency) 9, 11, 19, 211,
    212, 219
mining sector 50–1, 97, 134, 134, 135,
    136, 188
    taxes 19, 28, 117
Minsky, Hyman 48–9
models 5–6, 13, 29, 104, 147–51, 158–9,
    187, 199
    early-warning models 15
    limitations 11, 12, 15, 159, 231–2
    purposes 164–5
    see also country risk-rating model
monetary policy 39, 47, 64, 81, 102,
    173, 233–4, 236
    and domestic demand 131
    and fiscal policy 15, 63, 95
    spillover effects 96
    US 1, 12–13, 17, 36, 37, 39, 42, 44, 54,
        69, 82
Mongolia 13, 19, 44–5, 87, 97, 115
Moody's 6, 115, 158, 173
moral hazard 7, 12, 92, 174, 182
    IMF loans and 35, 60–1, 172, 173, 177
Morales, Evo 139, 222

Mozambique 13, 88, 136, 140–1
Mubarak regime 46, 84, 85, 107, 111,
    206, 214, 221
multilateral finance 99, 168, 175
multilateral institutions 9, 99, 137–8,
    179, 193, 211, 217, 231, 233
Multilateral Investment Guarantee
    Agency see MIGA
multilateral participation 58, 217–18
multinationals 8, 9, 14, 45–6, 76, 143,
    236
    FDI 10, 58
    risk management 181–2, 187–8, 189
    subsidiaries 31–2, 76
    supply chains 35, 37, 45–6
Myanmar 88, 209

N
Nasser, Gamal Abdel 8, 84, 124
national fragmentation 114–15
national policies 231
nationalisation 7–8, 9, 28, 58, 95–6,
    103, 114, 139–40, 142, 181–2
    banks 231
    becoming rarer 18, 97, 188, 212
    Bolivia 139
    Egypt 84
    Latin America 138, 138–9, 139–40,
        212, 222
natural catastrophes 18, 105, 232
NDF (non-deliverable forwards) 216,
    217
Nestlé 8, 130
the Netherlands 4, 6, 226, 235
network maps 45
network theory 149
Neumann, John von 5
Nicaragua 34
Nigeria 26–8, 82, 83, 105
non-deliverable forwards see NDF
non-transfer risk 212, 213–14
Nordic countries 45, 61
North Africa 28, 91, 108

North Korea 104, 105–7
Northern Ireland 116
Norway 51, 72–3

O
obsolescing bargain mechanism 141
OECD 163, 169, 183, 185, 232
off-balance-sheet accounting 40, 43,
    167, 184, 234
Office of Financial Research see OFR
Office of Foreign Assets Control 203–4
Office of the Quartet 227
offshore accounts 208, 222
offshore financial centres 79, 89
OFR (Office of Financial Research)
    168–9
oil 72, 105
oil crises (1970s) 46, 171
oil prices 44, 104, 121, 224
    falls 11, 27, 73, 85
    rises 46, 55, 59, 224
oil producers 59, 61, 84, 107, 108, 123,
    124, 164
oil revenues 26, 27, 73, 111, 139–40
Oman 74
OPEC 10, 46, 55, 59, 85
operational risk 10, 26, 27, 118, 128–9
    mitigation 207, 218–19, 219–20
OPIC (Overseas Private Investment
    Corporation) 211, 223–4, 224, 225
opium wars (19th century) 6–7
Orascom Telecom 143
organisational structures 181, 189–95,
    190, 193
originate-and-distribute model 170,
    205–6
Ottoman empire 6, 7, 54, 55, 107
over-borrowing 34, 76, 88, 153, 157,
    230, 235
over-lending 12, 28–9, 33, 34, 35, 52,
    153–4, 155, 229–30, 232
Overseas Private Investment
    Corporation see OPIC

P
P&O 143
Pakistan 175, 177
Palestine 104, 203, 225–6, 227
Paraguay 46
Paris Club 9, 100, 174, 175–6
Parmalat 169
patronage 55, 114, 121, 122, 133, 137, 138, 142
payments crises 1, 2, 15, 76–7, 166, 229, 232–4
  global financial centres and 153–4
  home-grown 17, 28, 78–9
  income inequality and 83
  political risk and 124
  risks of 23, 159
  see also defaults
PBoC (People's Bank of China) 92, 93
pension funds 4, 99, 198, 236
PEPs (politically exposed persons) 142, 204
permanent income hypothesis 68
Peru 34, 88
Philippines 30, 51, 82, 104, 209
Poland 68–9, 107, 109, 117
policy uncertainty 96, 113–14, 132–3
political contagion 46
political crises 23, 89, 99, 131
political instability 46, 85, 103–4, 112, 115, 124, 161
political institutions 116–18
political risk 9, 11, 24, 27, 29, 56, 103–4, 125, 157
  avoiding implicit value judgments 123–4
  and defaults 28, 111
  demographics and 52
  developed countries 124, 143
  financial losses due to 140
  forecasting 147, 232
  increasing 37, 123
  indicators 159, 161
  institutions and 115–23, 116, 119–21

  labour conditions and 135
  nationalisation and expropriation as 7–8, 9, 31, 58, 138, 138–9, 181–2, 212
  new forms 18, 188, 231
  and payments crises 124
  strategic countries 107–8
political risk insurance *see* PRI
political trends 28, 111–15, 113–14
political violence 27, 52, 212, 221
politically exposed persons *see* PEPs
portfolio flows 6–7, 10–11, 23, 74–5, 125, 127, 128
Portugal 6, 80, 118, 178, 180, 186, 235
poverty 87–8
PRI (political risk insurance) 206, 207, 210–15, 211, 213, 214, 216–17, 218, 219, 220, 222, 226
primary exports 72–3, 86
principal components analysis 148
private credit/GDP ratio 90, 93, 94, 94
private sector 121, 174, 228
private-sector borrowing 67, 76, 80
private-sector capital flows 173, 177
privatisation 55, 59, 83, 85, 93, 97, 99, 123, 168
pro-cyclicality 162–3, 184, 194, 200, 210, 237
probability 3–4, 5, 25, 29, 147
property bubbles 62, 73, 76, 77, 80, 142, 197, 221
property prices 163, 190
protectionism 11, 14–15, 37, 38, 96, 102, 117, 127, 231
  Egypt 84
  post-1929 34–5, 167
protests 18, 46, 52, 84, 101, 116, 123, 139–40
  Egypt 46, 85, 113, 114
  middle class 46, 112–13, 113–14
  Russia 101, 112
public debt *see* sovereign debt

public debt crises *see* sovereign debt crises
public sector 121, 137
public-private funding 226-7
Puerto Rico 7
pull factors 155
push factors 35-6
    external 12, 15-16, 52, 65, 154, 155, 156, 159, 232
put options 210
Putin government 120, 121, 122

Q
Qatar 13
QE (quantitative easing) 15, 39, 68, 69, 81, 95, 236
Qtel 226, 227
qualitative approach 148, 150
qualitative indicators 161, 164
quantitative easing *see* QE
quantitative methods 148-9, 231-2

R
railways 6, 38, 50, 55, 133, 167
rating agencies 10, 63, 115, 123, 127, 153, 162-3
    criticisms 15, 235
    regulation of 169-70, 186-7
rating models 25, 150-1, 200-1, 202, 231
    see also country risk-rating model
ratings 10, 117, 157, 186, 187, 188, 191, 235
    blended 221-2
    see also sovereign ratings
real economy 47, 73, 95
recessions 14-15, 18, 46, 54, 55, 56, 73, 178, 198, 232
recovery ratio 135
regime change 107, 109, 110, 113, 132, 188, 209, 221
regional groupings 174, 179, 180
regional integration 46, 73-4, 108

regional linkages 45, 77
regression 148, 158
regression to the mean 4, 150
regulation 25, 37, 95, 166, 182, 200, 231, 237-8
    of banking sector 56, 61, 93
    changes 19, 213
    complexity 18, 83, 170, 178-9, 186
    and internal organisation of country risk 183-7, 186-7
    international 167-71, 230, 238
    of multinationals 187-8
    of rating agencies 186-7
    and risk management 19, 181
    of sovereign risk 185
    weak 89
    see also Basel accords
regulators 47, 142, 186
regulatory bodies 135, 169-70, 179
regulatory risks 26, 27, 95, 97, 133, 178-9
regulatory uncertainty 125, 131-2, 223
Reinhart, Carmen 41, 45, 230, 234-5
religious factors 68, 107, 114, 116
remittances 10, 71, 84, 126-7
Renault 128-9
repatriation 10, 23, 99, 209, 236
repression 106-7, 115, 123
Repsol 99, 100, 139, 140
reputational risk 137, 142, 188, 203-4, 205
reregulation 167, 168, 186
resource curse 86-7, 86-7, 88
resource nationalism 18, 97, 140-2
resource-based economies 79, 79, 85-8, 86-7, 116, 122
resources 87, 88, 95, 98, 105
Rio Tinto 136, 140
risk 2-4, 5, 29, 35, 40, 215
risk appetite 44, 60, 62, 189, 189-90, 198, 215
risk management 3, 8-9, 19, 43, 181, 182, 187

risk management function 29, 182, 195–201, 195, 197–8, 202
risk transfer instruments 210–17, 211, 213, 214, 219
risk-weighted assets *see* RWA
Rogoff, Kenneth 45, 230, 234–5
Roshan telecoms project 16, 203, 225, 226, 227–8
Rostow, Walt 48, 151
rule of law 26, 30, 83, 114, 122, 123, 135, 137
rules-based system 18, 178–9, 231
Rurelec 138, 138–9
Russia 13, 17, 42, 56, 58, 81, 87, 105, 227
  annexation of Crimea 105, 109, 110
  country risk 30
  defaults 1, 11, 24, 42, 72, 110, 111, 177, 182, 234, 237
  and EU 109–10
  and former Soviet states 107
  fragile institutions 111
  investment-grade rating 235
  loans from 174
  modernisation 87, 119–21
  protests 101, 112
  sanctions on 2, 104, 121
  tax investigations 133
  and Ukraine 108, 109–10, 115, 121
  and US 109–10, 119
  utility price freeze 132
RWA (risk-weighted assets) 183, 184, 185
Rwanda 88

S
S5 (systemically important economies) 43
sanctions 2, 88, 104, 105, 121, 137, 162, 204
Sarbanes-Oxley Act 2002 182, 187
Sarkozy, Nicholas 175
Saudi Arabia 85, 104, 105, 107, 115

savings 66–8, 66, 67, 75, 83, 91
scenario analysis 162, 199
Schumpeter, Joseph 48
Scotland 117
seabed rights 44, 105
SEC (Securities and Exchange Commission) 10, 182, 186
sector-specific risks 125, 133–4, 134
securitisation 170–1, 184, 206–7, 230, 234
security risks 27–8, 135, 227
separatist pressure 18, 116, 117
Serbia-Montenegro 177
shadow banking sector 51, 91, 92, 93, 95, 185, 207, 230
short-termism 101
Sierra Leone 88
Singapore 13, 80, 236
Sinosure 211, 222
Skidelsky, Robert 167–8
Slovenia 30
small-island economies 79, 89
social change 28, 37, 56, 118, 137
social trends 28, 111–15, 113–14
Solow, Robert 5
Soros, George 60
South Africa 19, 81–2, 93, 105, 135, 140–1, 219–20
  one of "Fragile 5" 28, 69, 82
South Korea 11, 51, 76, 80, 83, 93, 124, 173
  and Japan 106
  middle class 112
  and North Korea 105–6, 107
South Sudan 87, 88, 209
South-East Asia 46, 72
southern euro zone 15, 30, 70, 164, 215
southern Europe 118, 238
sovereign bonds 44–5, 232
sovereign debt 15, 24, 30, 76, 80, 82, 158, 186
  EU 63

Nigeria 27
sovereign debt crises 40, 41, 94, 158,
192, 229–30
euro zone 1, 43, 124
see also debt crises
sovereign default risk 150–1, 159, *184*
sovereign defaults 23, 41, *41*, 115, 117,
148–9, 182, 191
preceded by IMF programmes 173
sovereign effectiveness 157
sovereign ratings 6, 10, 25, 30, 81, 184,
192–3, 235
downgrades 80, 81, 117
sovereign risk 24, 24–5, 26, 27, 29, 30,
185–7, 191
developed countries 62–4, *63*, 185
sovereign wealth funds 27, 36, 85
sovereignty 7–9, 18, 174, 178–80, 230
Soviet Union 11, 72, 107, 122, 171
Spain 51, 80, 94, 142, 186, 221
defaults 6, 7, 235
and ERM 60, 102
separatist movements 116, 117
spillover effects 96, 148, 169, 215
Standard Bank 225–6, *226*
standards 169, 230, 231
Starbucks 132–3
state 11, 121, 122
state sector 122–3
state-dominated banking sector
90–1, *90*, 92–3, 216
stockmarket crash (1929) 34, 233
strategic countries 107–8, 175
strikes 18, 99, 100, 161, 220
structural reforms 59, 78, 83, 172
structural risk 79–89, *79*, *81*, *84–5*,
86–7, 159
structural weaknesses 70, 95, 155
structuring 206–7
sub-Saharan Africa 76, 90, 176, 209
subprime mortgage-backed products
15, 42, 43, 132, 133, *186*
subsidiaries 31–2, 76

Sudan 87
sudden-stop crises 12, 17, 23, 40, 41,
60–1, 129, 153
vulnerability to 56, 61–2, 66, 68, 76,
93–4, 204
sudden-stop models 153–4, *154*
Suez Canal crisis (1956) 8, 171
supply chains 45–6, 82–3, 139
Sweden 45, 51
Switzerland 8, 32, 212
Syria 1, 109, 115, 122
system-integrator firms 35, 37, 45–6

T
T&C (transfer and convertibility)
risks 19, 24, 25–6, *26*, 29, 30, 95, 125,
126–7, 183, 192
mitigation 208, 210
Taiwan 11
take-off model 151–2
Tanzania 140–1
tapering 36, 44–5, 65, 69, 153, 236
tariffs 9, 35, 59, 102, 132
taxation 132–3, 140–1
taxes 19, 28, 97, 99, 117, 143, 198
Telasi 131–2
Telmex 208–9
tenor 193–4, *193*, 210, 222
terms-of-trade shocks 46, 72
terrorism 28, 89, 103, 116, 135, 161
Tesco 134–5
Thailand 11, 46, 51, 62, 81–2, 93,
111–12, 113, 115
Thatcher, Margaret 118
"this time is different" 230–1
thresholds, setting 160
time horizons 162, 193–4, *193*, 197, 210
too-big-to-fail entities 95, 182, 184
trade 37, 45–6, 71–3, 82, 132
liberalisation 9, 132, 138, 167, 168
trade blocs 82, 179
trade deficits 70
trade finance 37, 58, 125, 125–6

trading desks 196–7, 197–8, 198
transfer and convertibility risks *see*
T&C
transition economies 11, 171, 175
transition periods 17, 37–8, 52–3
transparency 26, 83, 137, 177, 199, 236
weak 13, 90, 122, 123, 133, 234
transport 36, 87, 205
Tullow Oil 142
Tunisia 71, 82, 111, 113, 113, 114, 193
Turkey 67, 68, 81–2, 93, 97, 105, 118,
137
crises 1, 42, 54–6, 102
and EU 56, 72
and IMF 173, 174
income inequalities 111–12, 113
one of "Fragile 5" 28, 69, 82
protests 46, 112, 113, 114
tax investigations 133
Turkmenistan 123

U
UAE (United Arab Emirates) 74, 77
UK 34, 40–1, 43, 50, 62, 107, 111, 176,
209, 221
2008–09 crisis 109, 197–8
bail-outs 80, 171
bank collapses 42, 178
banking regulations 133
deregulation 168
and ERM 60, 102
EU membership 118
and gold standard 35
housing problem 101
and Iran 8
and mining companies 97
monetary policy 60
overseas investment 6, 95
privatisations 168
property bubble (1990s) 51
social trends 111
tax-avoidance furore 132–3
Thatcher government 118

utility prices 97
see also ECGD; Northern Ireland
Ukraine 17, 46, 82, 174
2014 crisis 2, 23, 44, 108, 109–10,
121, 188, 232
protests 46, 112, 113, 113, 114
and Russia 108, 109–10, 115, 121
UN 7, 88, 179, 227
uncertainty 2, 4–5, 15, 29, 101, 125, 147,
154–5, 179
unemployment 60, 73, 81, 85, 117,
134, 161
unrest 84, 100, 107, 116
urbanisation 37, 51, 68, 82, 85, 112,
133
Uruguay 46, 177
US 1, 8, 34, 43, 121, 176, 213, 227
and Afghanistan 14, 105, 107–8,
109, 109
assistance for Jordan 108
bank collapses 42, 178
banking crises 40–1, 197–8
banking sector 95, 133
and Basel accords 185
and China 70, 96, 120
corruption regulators 142
credit bubble 14, 42, 47
crises 50, 61, 234
current-account deficit 14, 233
deregulation 168
dotcom bubble 42, 50, 56, 133
economic recovery 50
FDI 9
financial crisis (2008) 234
fiscal policy 81
housing 45, 51
and IMF 171, 173
income distribution 117
insurers 211, 212
interest rates 42, 47, 50, 69
and Iran 104
and Iraq 14, 84, 104, 105, 109, 109
and Mexico 72

monetary policy 1, 12–13, 17, 36, 37,
39, 42, 44, 54, 69, 82
and North Korea 106
and rating agencies 186
rating downgrade 117
regulation 132, 168–9, 182
Russia and 109–10, 119
"savings glut" 47
sensitivity to foreign investment
143
shadow banking sector 95
shale gas 72
tapering 36, 44–5, 65, 69, 153
and TPP (Trans-Pacific Partnership)
179
and TTIP (Transatlantic Trade and
Investment Partnership) 179
and Ukraine 109
wage stagnation 80
see also Federal Reserve; subprime
mortgage-backed products
US dollar 35, 37, 50, 61, 71, 227
utility tariffs 97, 98
Uzbekistan 122

V
value judgments 123–4
Vedanta 135
Venezuela 25, 46, 82, 100, 112, 127
defaults 34, 115, 235
income inequality policies 87–8
nationalisations 138, 139–40, 212
Vietnam 82, 122, 213
volatility 28–9, 44, 76, 93, 101, 125,
173, 200
capital flows 180, 236

currencies 129, 182
economic policy 204
exchange rates 204, 219
vulnerability factors 66

W
wars 28, 37, 38, 80, 89, 107–8, 109, 174
Afghanistan 14, 105, 107–8, 109
civil 88, 110, 118, 124, 136
and defaults 58, 108–11, 109–10
Iraq 14, 84, 104, 105, 109, 109
Wataniya telecoms project 16, 203,
225–6, 227
watch lists 193, 194, 197
weighting 157, 158, 159, 160
willingness to pay 115, 155, 184
World Bank 9, 38, 49, 91, 139, 193, 211,
217, 224
Doing Business index 135, 161
HIPC initiative 76
World Trade Organisation 120, 179
WorldCom 169, 182

Y
YPF 18, 99, 100
Yugoslavia 176

Z
Zaire (now DRC) 75, 176
Zambia 19, 135
Zimbabwe 89, 218–19, 219–20
Zimplats 218–19, 219–20

PublicAffairs is a publishing house founded in 1997. It is a tribute to the standards, values, and flair of three persons who have served as mentors to countless reporters, writers, editors, and book people of all kinds, including me.

I. F. STONE, proprietor of *I. F. Stone's Weekly*, combined a commitment to the First Amendment with entrepreneurial zeal and reporting skill and became one of the great independent journalists in American history. At the age of eighty, Izzy published *The Trial of Socrates*, which was a national bestseller. He wrote the book after he taught himself ancient Greek.

BENJAMIN C. BRADLEE was for nearly thirty years the charismatic editorial leader of *The Washington Post*. It was Ben who gave the *Post* the range and courage to pursue such historic issues as Watergate. He supported his reporters with a tenacity that made them fearless and it is no accident that so many became authors of influential, best-selling books.

ROBERT L. BERNSTEIN, the chief executive of Random House for more than a quarter century, guided one of the nation's premier publishing houses. Bob was personally responsible for many books of political dissent and argument that challenged tyranny around the globe. He is also the founder and longtime chair of Human Rights Watch, one of the most respected human rights organizations in the world.

•   •   •

For fifty years, the banner of Public Affairs Press was carried by its owner Morris B. Schnapper, who published Gandhi, Nasser, Toynbee, Truman, and about 1,500 other authors. In 1983, Schnapper was described by *The Washington Post* as "a redoubtable gadfly." His legacy will endure in the books to come.

Peter Osnos, *Founder and Editor-at-Large*